UNBROKEN
WHOLENESS

"This book will change many lives. It is the result of a life deeply and courageously lived. It offers powerful stories and practices that will help readers move more and more toward healing and unlocking their inherent wholeness and power. These teachings will take us closer to realizing the Beloved Community we all yearn for."

—KAIRA JEWEL, author of *We Were Made for These Times: Ten Lessons on Moving through Change, Loss, and Disruption*

"Wow. With a holistic vision breathtaking in scope, John Bell shares his own heart and path. He enables each of us to see ourselves experiencing personal power and healing, all while contributing to transformation of life on Earth. Beautiful and powerful! Soothing yet strong!"

—FRANCES MOORE LAPPÉ, author of *Diet for a Small Planet* and (coauthored with Adam Eichen) *Daring Democracy: Igniting Power, Meaning, and Connection for the America We Want*

"We live in urgent times, facing multiple and overlapping crisis of climate change, racial and political polarization, economic inequities, gun violence, and much more. We can lose sight of the beauty and fragility of this human life and the world around us. We can forget the powerful legacies and inspirational voices like Thich Nhat Hanh and Rev. Dr. Martin Luther King, Jr. In *Unbroken Wholeness*, Dharma teacher John Bell illuminates the wisdom of Nhat Hanh's and King's vision of Beloved Community and his own transformational life, weaving together a rich tapestry and a call to action grounded in the vulnerability of his lived experience and teachings on nonviolent social action and more. This is a must-read for anyone seeking to do good, protect the planet, and transform racial and social injustice."

—VALERIE BROWN, coauthor of *Healing Our Way Home: Black Buddhist Teachings on Ancestors, Joy, and Liberation* and author of *Hope Leans Forward: Braving Your Way toward Simplicity, Awakening, and Peace*

"True vision is building a bridge across the abyss in order to provide a pathway for others to find safe passage. John Bell is the embodiment of a visionary and a bridge-builder, offering us the courage and the practical ways to come home to ourselves and to life. Paradoxically, by delving deep into his own pain and suffering as well as the pain and suffering of the world, John has discovered profound joy and compassion. From this place, he offers us hope that the Beloved Community has the potential to be a dream come true."

—JO CONFINO, cohost of the podcast *The Way Out Is In*

"How can we nurture and realize the Beloved Community that Martin Luther King Jr. dreamed of? We need good guides such as John Bell, and good guidebooks such as this one."

> —DAVID LOY, author of *Ecodharma: Buddhist Teachings for the Ecological Crisis*

"John Bell's roadmap to the Beloved Community is articulate, eloquent, comprehensive, heartfelt, and grounded in deep experience. It's the best invitation to the Buddhism of the future I've ever read, weaving together profound insight, trauma-informed practice, and social action. A well-thumbed copy should be in every dharma center library and act as the guide to many Sangha discussion groups. Six stars out of five!"

> —JOHN H. NEGRU, author of *Bodhisattva 4.0: A Primer for Engaged Buddhists*

Integrating Social Justice, Emotional
Healing, and Spiritual Practice

UNBROKEN WHOLENESS

SIX PATHWAYS TO THE BELOVED COMMUNITY

JOHN BELL

PARALLAX PRESS
BERKELEY, CALIFORNIA

Parallax Press
2236 B Sixth Street
Berkeley, California 94710
parallax.org

Parallax Press is the publishing division of Plum Village Community
of Engaged Buddhism

Cover photograph © by Ian Teh
Cover design by Katie Eberle
Text design by Maureen Forys, Happenstance Type-O-Rama
Illustrations by Richard Shepherd
Author photo © John Bell

Printed in the United States of America

Library of Congress Cataloging-in-Publication Data
Names: Bell, John, 1961- author.
Title: Unbroken wholeness : six pathways to healing, inclusion, and
social
   justice / John Bell.
Description: Berkeley : Parallax Press, 2024. | Includes bibliographical
   references.
Identifiers: LCCN 2023030650 (print) | LCCN 2023030651 (ebook) |
ISBN
   9781952692710 (trade paperback) | ISBN 9781952692727 (ebook)
Subjects: LCSH: Religious life--Buddhism | Happiness--Religious
   aspects--Zen Buddhism. | Mindfulness (Psychology)
Classification: LCC BQ9286.2 .B45 2024 (print) | LCC BQ9286.2
(ebook) |
   DDC 294.3/444--dc23/eng/20231025
LC record available at https://lccn.loc.gov/2023030650
LC ebook record available at https://lccn.loc.gov/202303065

1 2 3 4 5 VERSA   28 27 26 25 24

CONTENTS

1

BELOVED COMMUNITY: THE REALITY AND THE NOBLE ASPIRATION

Reality, Aspiration, and Framework

Now in my late seventies, I am keenly aware there are many fewer days ahead than behind me to be in this body on Earth. I love life so deeply and long for the end of unnecessary suffering. The sense of my limited time, my mortality, makes me feel the need to try to express the fullness of what lies deep in my heart about healing our beloved world. I have nothing to lose, and a hurting Mother Earth is calling.

I am immensely grateful and deeply content with the life I am blessed to live. I actively feel the gift of having a body and a mind. I look around and see enormous human kindness and caring, courage and resilience, individual and collective determination to fight the good fight for truth, justice, freedom, and joy.

At the same time, I am heartbroken about the vast suffering in the world that begs to be healed. I have wept buckets of tears and raged to the heavens about human cruelty. I have felt powerless to change things. I regularly have bouts of despair about our struggling ecosystem, continued racial injustice, extreme economic inequality, and deepening divisions among people. I see hurt in all directions.

I imagine that you too have your moments of gratitude and heartbreak that weave through your life. For me, living in that gap between the wounded world and my heart's desire is both excruciatingly painful and ultimately motivating.

The Aspiration for a Beloved Community

The world is laced through and through with jaw-dropping beauty and heart-numbing horrors. We humans are born into this life to navigate these joys and woes as best we can. I hold in my heart a deep aspiration—for a world unified, just, peaceful, and harmonious, that supports the full flowering of individuals and all species. I long to live happily in the Beloved Community. I am not alone in this longing—I've met hundreds of people who have expressed a similar aspiration. Many of us carry an intuitive idea of what a safe, healing, loving world in balance might be. Words like *sacred, divine, the Kingdom of God on Earth, the Pure Land, Gaia, living happily in the present moment, sustainable ecosystem, fair economy,* and *a happy planet* point to this heartfelt notion. Some might say this is a very human aspiration, a wish for a better world. Others might say it goes deeper than a wish; it taps into an inherent "knowing" that we bring into human form from the mysterious depths of creation. Whatever the truth, a line from the iconic US labor and Black Civil Rights Movement's song, "We Shall Overcome," expresses it well: "Deep in our hearts, we do believe, that we shall all be free someday."[1]

We are not just wanting to transform racism. We are not just wanting to change our economy to one of sharing. We are not just wanting to end war and violence. We are not just wanting to heal our emotional wounds. We are not just wanting to save the planet. We want all these and more, on the way to living in a Beloved Community.

The term "Beloved Community" is often associated with Dr. Martin Luther King Jr. He put a strong public spotlight on an idea that has been held deep in the hearts of humans for millennia. People across centuries and cultures have yearned to live in a peaceful, harmonious, and sustainable world. Many indigenous peoples, as best they could, have lived according to this idea. Utopian thinkers through the ages have created versions of this very human aspiration. Enlightened spiritual teachers have pointed the way. Dr. King's uplifting of this aspiration was a great gift to humanity.

However, many people mistakenly think that Beloved Community is made up of folks like us, our kind, our people, our kindred spirits, our special group. This is much too narrow a definition. Dr. King, Zen Master Thich Nhat Hanh, and many others who have contributed to the idea of the Beloved Community, grounded in their respective spiritual traditions, envisioned it as a manifestation of the way love or God or the divine shows up in the material world.[2] For Christian leaders, the Beloved Community might be the Kingdom of God on Earth. In Buddhism, it might be considered the Pure Land—a realm considered suitable for a noble rebirth. Spiritual leaders seem to imply that the Beloved Community already exists as the bedrock of reality. Thich Nhat Hanh might say it is alive and whole in the ultimate dimension—the deeper truth of our interconnectedness. And, of course, the Beloved Community doesn't just apply to human beings but includes all species and the Earth itself.

In this historical dimension where we live and breathe, the Beloved Community is an aspiration, and our task is to realize its fullness. It is imagined as the community that is based in love and compassion, that lives in harmony, that excludes no one, where everyone belongs, where conflicts are minimal and are resolved peacefully, where oppression is a relic of history, where hurt and mistreatment are quickly healed, where there is a shared commitment to the common good and the well-being of all, where the sacred and vast unknown are honored. As an aspiration, it is "the more beautiful world our hearts know is possible," to use the lovely title of a book by Charles Eisenstein.[3]

The painful gap we often feel between that vision and where we are is a measure of our deep conditioning to feel separate. We're so conditioned that it's not uncommon to feel separation within ourselves—our minds and bodies—evidenced by our myriad of conflicted feelings and the stubborn divide between our actions and our deepest values and aspirations. But we humans are not and cannot be separate from the rest of the natural world or ourselves. We are part of unbroken wholeness. Unfortunately, this primal ground of our being is often obscured by hurtful experiences, wrong perceptions, miseducation, oppression, and more. We mostly forget our essential connectedness and wind up divided and disunited, cut off from ourselves, each other, and nature, and we hurt others and the Earth as a result.

The challenge is clear. How do we do the inner and outer work necessary to come back to ourselves in order to include everyone and all species in a peaceful, harmonious, creative, caring, relational, global community? This might be a more fruitful question than whether Republicans or Democrats will win the next election, or who's to blame for the spread of misinformation, or how we safeguard democracy, or how we save the gray wolf. All these are important, but they fall short of a unifying purpose.

What if we ask questions like: What makes us happy? How much do we need? What helps all of us be safe? What kind of a community do we want to live in? How do we want to be treated by others? How do we want to contribute to the collective good? What is fair? How do we share Earth's limited resources? How do we cultivate reverence for all life? What is the balance between individual freedom and collective well-being? How do we restore, renew, reconnect, reweave our relationships with ourselves, one another, other species, the natural world, and the cosmos? What does a world look like that reflects our sacred nature? And then, how do we get there?

Six Pathways[4]

This book explores interrelated components that are necessary to move us toward a seismic shift in human imagination from "me" or "us" to "all"—the Beloved Community. These components integrate social justice, emotional healing, and spiritual practice. They are not complete or sufficient, but together they begin to form a holistic, mindfulness-based approach toward making the Beloved Community real. These six interrelated pathways are:

1. **Cultivating wise view:** Grounding our actions in spiritual depth.

2. **Healing hurt and trauma:** Releasing grief, despair, fear, and powerlessness so that we may think, act, and love more deeply.

3. **Transforming racial and social oppression:** Linking climate justice with racial justice and economic justice to break habits of exploitation and foster human unity.

4. **Building deep local community:** Creating dependable space to recover, refresh, and renew ourselves in the face of environmental and social suffering, and to deepen solidarity.

5. **Living ethically:** Practicing reverence for life, deep listening, kind speech, and mindful consuming so that we nurture our compassion to counteract hatred, blame, and "othering."

6. **Engaging in mindful social action:** Individually and collectively taking action that is nonviolent in methods, transformational in vision, and aimed toward realizing the Beloved Community.

Each section of this book is devoted to one of these components. Each includes frameworks of understanding or practice that have proven invaluable to me, and stories from my life related to that component. Sprinkled throughout the book are short practical applications called "Practice suggestions" or "Reflection questions." Certain concepts are revisited in different sections because those practices or views apply to more than one of the six pathways.

I imagine these components as intersecting circles, each impacting the others:

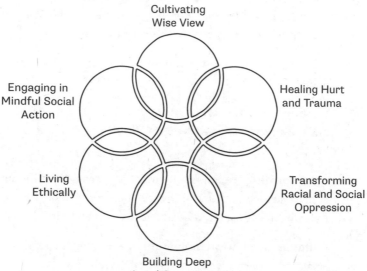

Foundational Views

It is important for me at the outset to share a set of viewpoints that guide my thinking. I cannot claim these as my own, since I culled them from many thinkers, spiritual ancestors, and social justice movements, to whom I offer a deep bow of gratitude. This list has been refined in my conversations with climate justice activists over the past several years. You, dear reader, have your own set of guiding principles, whether explicit or not. As you review this list, you might reflect on what you resonate with or diverge from, and why.

Grounding Action in Love

○ **I bow in humility and awe before the miracle of creation.** I acknowledge that I am a manifestation of this great mysterious energy called Life, and that humans are among the youngest species and have much to learn about living harmoniously embedded in nature.

○ **I offer deep gratitude to all our ancestors.** I extend my thanks to all species in all dimensions through all of cosmic evolution. I am because they were. Gratitude keeps me pointed toward love, generosity, compassion, and nonviolence as guides to action.

○ **I am guided by love.** I am motivated first and foremost by a revolutionary love that seeks transformation at the base of our consciousness and our society, and seeks a mending of our broken relations with other humans and species; a love that sees no permanent enemies and believes justice is a manifestation of love; a love that is infinitely grateful.

○ **I carry a deep aspiration for liberation.** Deep in my heart, I hold a hope for collective healing and liberation from suffering of people, animals, plants, and minerals.

○ **I believe there is sacred nature in all.** Every person has an inherent Buddha nature, or Christ nature, or God nature, or Source Energy, which is whole and unbroken. I am inextricably bound up and embedded in the natural world, out of which I cannot fall. Our existence absolutely depends on an infinite web of causes and conditions.

Recognizing Suffering and the Roots of Suffering

○ **Suffering obscures our nature.** Awareness of our true nature can become buried by bad experiences that make us shrink into a smaller self. This suffering is both individual and collective, personal and institutionalized, pervasive and deep.

○ **Separation is a deep wound.** I believe most humans carry the wound of separation: separation from our true nature;

separation from our own bodies; separation from each other and from people who seem different from us; separation from our country and other countries, from the natural world and other species, and from the cosmos itself. This fairly universal conditioning gives rise to division, dualism, "us versus them" thinking, domination and oppression in all its ugly forms. This, not other people, is the enemy that needs healing and transformation.

○ **Greed, hatred, and delusion are institutionalized.** Long ago, the Buddha identified what he called the three poisons at the root of all suffering: greed, ill will, and ignorance of our interconnected existence. These have become institutionalized and mutually reinforcing. Our brutal economic system has institutionalized greed, which promotes consumerism, profit-making, competition, individualism, and a growth mentality, since enough is never enough. Ill will is institutionalized by militarism (the United States has over eight hundred military bases in eighty-five countries), mainly to protect corporate interests and resources; by the mass incarceration, racism, and killing of Black, Indigenous, and People of Color (BIPOC) folks; and by white supremacy and nationalism. The delusion of a separate existence is institutionalized by policies that discriminate against certain groups, value individual achievement over collective cooperation, undermine community cohesion, and promote nationalism (for example, "America is number 1!").

○ **Humans have caused widespread destruction and eco-system collapse.** In the past two hundred years, since the beginning of the industrial revolution—a mere blink in the 4.5 billion years the Earth has been around—we humans have had an outsized impact on our planet's ecosystems. Through a combination of ignorance, unintended consequences, and unbridled greed, we have extracted, mined, drilled, clear-cut, polluted, poisoned, overfished, overgrazed, overfertilized, overdeveloped, and overpopulated our beloved planet to the point of a grim eco-crisis. Despite our good efforts and intentions, climate scientists say we might be past tipping points; we could be headed over a cliff of environmental catastrophe leading to failed societies, the rapid extinction of hundreds of thousands of species, and the possible elimination of humans.

o **Capitalism needs transformation.** Our current economic system exploits, disrespects, and oppresses the majority of the population, and concentrates wealth and power in the hands of relatively few individuals. This is an overarching structural cause of much suffering. Until we create a caring, fair, cooperative, and democratic economy, the Beloved Community will not be attainable.

Recognizing Well-Being and the Path to Well-Being

Transformation of systems of domination and the realization of the Beloved Community are possible. There is a way out of the suffering caused by our illusions of separation.

o **Wise view is key.** I understand that the views I hold make a big difference in how I think, feel, and act. Therefore, I am committed to cultivating views that point toward inclusion, cooperation, and wholeness; that generate caring, connection, compassion, and kindness; and that are rooted in the truths that everything changes and everything is interconnected. In practice, I choose to view the intersecting social crises as a door to awakening to a higher human consciousness.

o **Reality is vaster than our notions about reality.** I acknowledge that there is the seen world and the unseen and unknown world. Most of what troubles us, occupies our attention, and confuses us is in the seen world, the material plane. But this dimension is embedded in a vast unseen reality about which we know very little. Any predictions about the future must be tempered with "Who knows?"

○ **I am rooted in mindfulness.** I ground myself in universal spiritual teachings, and I am committed to bringing mindfulness, compassion, healing, and nonviolence to protecting myself, all beings, and the Earth. I aspire to live an ethical life by practicing reverence and respect in all directions, as well as generosity, kind speech and deep listening, sexual responsibility, and wise consumption.

○ **Racial, social, and climate justice are inseparable.** I understand that mending our relations with the Earth requires mending our racial relations. For this reason, I choose to focus much of my energy and action at this nexus.

○ **Social justice, emotional healing, and spiritual practice are intertwined.** Each takes as its aim the enhancement of human life. However, the three are often separated into mutually exclusive spheres. The people involved in social justice often underestimate or dismiss the role of emotional distress in political work or rarely take time to do "personal work." Without a way of managing their emotional hurts, activists fall prey to reactive thinking or discouragement, burn out, or use painful emotions like anger as organizing tools. People primarily involved with therapy or the healing arts can overlook the societal oppression that gives rise to personal unhappiness—and if they don't address these social ills, the hurts keep piling in. Likewise, spiritual practitioners often detach from the world of politics to leave such concerns "in God's hands" or until consciousness evolves to a higher level. I think that these three areas need to be practiced together. Each one is insufficient without the other two.

○ **Inner transformation and systems change must accompany each other.** If I only busy myself with trying to relieve external signs of suffering, I will inevitably feel frustrated, hopeless, and powerless. Certainly, I must respond to others' immediate suffering with action. But I also need to do the inner work of healing my own suffering.

○ **Healing feelings of powerlessness is central.** I am sometimes assailed by the feeling that this is all too overwhelming. It feels hopeless. Like most of us, when I was young I saw or experienced things that were wrong, but I was too little and powerless to stop them. Healing these internalized childhood sources about feelings of powerlessness is vitally important. Without healing, these feelings can severely hamper my capacity to act on behalf of liberation.

○ **I am called to act.** I am called to do all I can to avert the worst, protect what I can, and promote transformation of our ignorance. I try to act without attachment to outcomes. Without knowing the impact of my actions, nonetheless I act and do my best.

○ **I am grounded in Kingian nonviolence.** I am firmly rooted in a nonviolence approach that emphasizes deep personal transformation, community building and service, a willingness to endure suffering, and mindful action toward creating the Beloved Community.

○ **Community is essential to liberation.** Obviously, I cannot realize the Beloved Community or transform our society alone. Neither can I attain personal liberation alone. Indeed, humans cannot exist alone. We need each other. We need to be devoted to cultivating closeness and intimacy in community. Community is where we can rest, learn, lead, love, and serve. At various times it can be a refuge, a refueling station, a safe oasis, and a sacred space for love and creativity.

At other times, the communities we build are essential to achieving power through unity. No movement succeeds without building a cohesive internal community.

My Journey to Understanding the Beloved Community

Each of us is a unique, miraculous being, never having existed before and never to come again. Each of us is shaped by an infinite number of causes and conditions, as Buddhism teaches. Among these, we are shaped by our social conditioning around dimensions like gender, race, ethnicity, class, religion, geography, and age. Unless we are aware of this reality and name the historical coordinates from which we view the world, we are likely to unconsciously accept and reinforce the status quo. And the status quo is a long distance from the Beloved Community. Therefore, I want to acknowledge the "social locations" that shape my perspectives.

I am a cisgender heterosexual White man, raised working-class but now solidly middle-class, highly educated, older, married with adult children, raised Catholic and religious, now a Buddhist Dharma teacher. I have spent my working life in the fields of education, youth leadership development, racial healing, peacemaking, counseling and trauma work, and environmental justice. (Throughout this book, I have intentionally capitalized adjectives describing people's race or ethnicity—Black, Brown, Latinx, Asian, White, and Indigenous people—so as to reduce polarization and an implied hierarchy of importance. I have not capitalized terms like *white supremacy* or *white racism*, which refer to concepts or structures, not people.)

My background has given me both wounding (from my working-poor roots, as a young person, and as a Catholic boy), and unearned privilege (by being White, educated, heterosexual, and now financially secure). This awareness helps me keep my privilege in check, even though imperfectly, and helps make room in my heart for the hardships suffered by others. Trying to recover right relations with each other and end racism and other forms of oppression is messy work. Owning and stating our social locations without defensiveness or judgment can help lay a foundation for compassionate dialogue aimed at diminishing divisions among us.

But I didn't know all this as I was growing up. It took a long time to understand.

O

"Unbroken wholeness in flowing movement."[5] This is how quantum physicist David Bohm described reality in *Wholeness and the Implicate Order.* Ever since I read this statement years ago, I have held it as a precious touchstone, a beautiful expression of a large truth.

From early on, I lived with a dual awareness. One awareness was of how broken things were. Growing up, I had a kind of knowing, a sensing that things were out of whack, in violation of right relationship. Here are a few examples.

I was born during World War II. My father was in the US Army, and my mother, as a military spouse, had to work to make ends meet. So, she sent me away to live with her parents for six months during my first year of life. A crucial early bonding was lost for her and for me. My father's childhood as the son of an itinerant worker also left him with many scars, which eventually led him to a long struggle with alcoholism, and this caused great suffering in our family.

In my childhood, we lived in a working-class neighborhood with kids from unhappy homes, and their parents drank heavily. For fun, the boys would chop down trees or step on ladybugs. I felt crushed myself, but I caved. I couldn't stop them or even say anything. We lived in the beautiful Pacific Northwest, in Washington state. We'd drive up into the mountains and suddenly I would see wide swaths of clear-cut forest land, with stumps and burned slash leavings where a great forest had been. They were big unnatural scars on the land, and they made me sad.

We lived across the Puget Sound from Seattle. There were Indigenous people all around, the Suquamish and the S'Klallam tribes. They lived on reservations a few miles from me but I didn't know anything about them. I lived in Kitsap County. Kitsap was a Suquamish warrior, but I didn't know anything about that then. I never asked what "Kitsap" meant. Seattle was the chief of the Suquamish people, but I didn't know that either. Only much later, maybe in college, did I hear the famous letter attributed to Chief Seattle that speaks of the White settlers' disconnect from the land.

During the 1950s, there was a growing fear of nuclear war. We had air raid drills. As kids in school, we had to get under our desks until the sirens stopped. We watched scary movies of gigantic mushroom clouds from atomic bomb explosions. In the 1960s, as a teenager and young adult, I watched Black people in the civil rights struggle being attacked by dogs and water cannons or beaten senseless by police. I was horrified and angry. Then there was the Vietnam War. I was in my early twenties. Day after day, my young friends and I watched heartbreaking images on TV—the endless stream of bombs dropping from the open bomb bays of B-52s, the fiery explosions on the radiant green below, the screaming children running toward the cameras, the scorched villages—and the burning monk. These images are still with me, not completely healed. But I knew then that the war was deeply wrong.

These are just a few of the ways I became aware that something wasn't right in the way people treated each other and the natural world. Probably each of us has such a list. Most of us carry with us some sense of not being in right relationship. This means we also carry with us a keen sense of what right relationship is. So, the other part of my dual awareness is the experience of wholeness.

For example, when my parents were drinking or fighting in the house, I found refuge at the top of the weeping willow tree in the front yard and looked out at the Olympic Mountains. Their beauty and peacefulness reconnected me to something infinite. When I was a little older, we lived in a tiny house right on Puget Sound.

Long walks on the stony beach, and time floating in a kayak I built when I was thirteen, helped me feel at home.

As a boy, I was deeply Catholic. Jesus felt like a close companion. I loved the silence of the sanctuary, the uplift of the Gregorian chants, the gorgeous vestments of the priests that brushed my arm when I served mass as an altar boy. The lives of the saints inclined my heart toward service and sacrifice for the well-being of others. I even considered becoming a priest.

So, in my formative years I experienced both wholeness and brokenness. Much of my life since has been the effort to reconcile these two aspects of reality. I studied philosophy in college. I became a political activist and tried to help heal racial and class wounds. My dozen or so hallucinogenic drug trips blew open "the doors of perception," as Aldous Huxley called our conditioned consciousness.[6] This led me to become involved with Hindu meditation and then Buddhist practice. I also had the good fortune, in my late twenties, to begin an ongoing and deeply liberating process of transforming my personal suffering through decades of peer counseling. A huge blessing has been my fifty-year-plus marriage to Dorothy Stoneman, with whom I share work, politics, and family. We met in the context of the social justice movement, in church the Sunday after Dr. Martin Luther King Jr. was killed.

Along the way, my spiritual teachers pointed to the inherent wholeness of life. Jesus taught me that "what you do to the least of these, you do to me." Saint Catherine of Siena reminded me that "all the way to Heaven is heaven."[7] I remember reading that Gandhi had a practice of sitting on a park bench in Delhi, watching people flow by while he said to himself, "Here comes God. Here comes God." Mother Teresa said, "I must be willing to give whatever it takes not to harm other people and, in fact, to do good to them. This requires that I be willing to give until it hurts."[8] Martin Luther King Jr. insisted, "All life is interrelated. We are all caught in an inescapable network of mutuality, tied into a single garment of destiny. Whatever affects one directly affects all indirectly. We are made to live together because of the interrelated structure of reality."[9] Thich Nhat Hanh instilled in me that our purpose in life is to wake up from the delusion of separateness.

I probably first heard the term *"Beloved Community"* from Dr. King during the 1960s, when I was a young man protesting the Vietnam War and marching for civil rights for Black people. The idea of people living together in peace, caring for one another, being rooted in love and compassion, in a world where discrimination and oppression were a distant memory immediately resonated with me. That was the world I longed for, the ideal that all the activism was aimed toward. My life since has been devoted to realizing the Beloved Community.

Because I am part of the Plum Village Community of Engaged Buddhism founded by the late Venerable Thich Nhat Hanh, Buddhist concepts and sensibilities are generously sprinkled throughout this text. I hope they are offered without dogmatism, maybe even adding new and interesting dimensions for readers from other spiritual traditions.

I attempt to apply a mindfulness lens to a wide spectrum of private and public life in ways that might be understandable and accessible to the reader. For me, applying a mindfulness lens means trying to be awake to what is happening in the present moment as best I can; trying to see the impermanent and interconnected nature of reality; questioning common dualistic thinking of "us" and "them;" aspiring to look at all beings with eyes of compassion; seeing the universality of suffering and the irrepressible human aspiration for happiness; connecting the links between individual and collective struggle and liberation; always looking for root causes that underlie present conditions; grounding myself in the fact that everything changes; and striving to offer perspectives and projects that nourish the flourishing, well-being, peace, and joy of all beings and the Earth.

Lastly, I approach the idea of the Beloved Community with humility and a certain trepidation because I have no idea if and how a collective Beloved Community might emerge in human consciousness. I have faith that it can and eventually will pierce our species' awareness, and that we'll see how in reality, humans already exist in community with one another and without separation, part of the unbroken wholeness reaching into every corner of the cosmos. This knowing, this certainty, this *love* has the power to inform and transform every relationship and every action. Yet the collective insight doesn't happen in a straight line, or predictably, or without backsliding. It is not in anyone's control. It is not without disappointment, doubt, and despair. Perhaps the Beloved Community will not come in my lifetime. Nonetheless, I hold fast to the aspiration.

I need to admit that I have no idea why we are here and what it's all about—life, or creation. Why does anything exist? It is a mystery. We don't really know, though we seem driven to keep trying to know. Zen teacher Robert Aitken Roshi said, "Our practice is not to clear up the mystery but to make the mystery clear."[10] Reality is inherently uncontrollable, unpredictable, and unreliable. Most humans don't like to live with this uncertainty, so we make up stories to explain the mystery. We need stories to guide and comfort ourselves in the face of the unfathomable. But they are just stories.

Any plans, frameworks, proposals, and views put forth in this book are woefully inadequate and incomplete. Over time, many ideas explored in this book will be superseded by more developed ideas from others. I contribute temporary notions to the many voices and forces, known and unknown, past, present, and future, working toward realizing the Beloved Community. Maybe my version is a false version, analogous to thinking that the world is flat. I am reminded of the adage that if you want to make God laugh, tell God your plans. These perspectives are offered humbly with the hope that they are a modest contribution to our noble collective efforts to relieve suffering and promote a happy, harmonious Earth community.

O

Before exploring the six pathways toward a Beloved Community, let's step back into the larger context of our current historical period.

Moving toward Breakthrough

A perfect storm of immense suffering is gathering quickly, on the horizon for some and already here for others. The long list is heartbreaking when we pay attention. There are many external signs of trouble—a toxic mix of brutal capitalism, an extractive economy, the increasing wealth gap, rampant and persistent racism, assaults on democracy, the degradation of the natural environment, the loss of biodiversity, the suffering of our nonhuman neighbors, disruptive pandemics, and continuing use of violence and warfare in international relationships.

Much personal suffering results from and interacts with these social ills, including world hunger, increasing forced human migration, global childhood trauma, depression, divorce, substance abuse, suicide, mounting personal debt, and widespread insecurity. Perhaps most human beings live with general unhappiness and discontent, settling for a half-life of getting by, making do, and distracting ourselves with short-lived pleasures. This causes many of us to look around for someone to blame for our unhappiness, reinforcing existing social divisions.

What creates this situation? Is there something that gives rise to all these challenges? What might they have in common? And can they be transformed?

More than fifty years ago, Dr. King named racism, poverty, and war as the "triple evils" preventing us from living peacefully. More recently, the Poor People's Campaign, led by Rev. William Barber and Rev. Liz Theoharis, has adopted King's trio and added environmental destruction to racism, economic injustice, and militarism.

These leaders are building a grassroots movement unified across race, class, and gender lines to address these huge structural issues.

Twenty-six hundred years ago, the Buddha was raised with material wealth and privilege but nonetheless became discontent. He was so driven by the question of why people suffer that he left his wife and newborn son to devote his life to finding the solution. And he found it. He named the three poisons at the root of human suffering as greed, hatred, and the delusion of a separate, individual existence, cut off from wholeness.

The external social structures and the internal personal suffering are intimately related, and both need transformation at the base. I have heard debates between those who say we must replace capitalism and transform politics, and those who say we need a spiritual enlightenment for real change to be possible. This debate is pointless because realistically, neither is going to happen in the short term. And yet, doing nothing is unacceptable because suffering is deepening, and those who are even partly aware cannot stand by while things get worse.

Bhikkhu Bodhi, an American Buddhist monk, scholar, and activist, put it clearly:

> Humanity is unlikely to undergo a dramatic spiritual rebirth in the short time left to us, while ever more nations seek to embark on the path of economic development by burning fossil fuels. Transformations in our social and economic system are likely to occur gradually and to require a long stretch of time for their impact to be felt. However, we face a situation of utmost urgency: Urgent because of what is at stake: mass extinctions; famines, droughts, floods, and epidemics; traumatic ethnic, religious, and cross-border strife; the loss of human civilization. Urgent because the window of opportunity is closing: we have *at best* only twenty or thirty years left to reduce carbon emissions by 80 percent; even better to arrive at 100 percent reduction by 2040. And we are moving in that direction far too slowly, if at all. We've got to get real. Spiritual

people and progressives in particular have got to be practical and realistic. So, what can we do that is simple, practical, and realistic—though by no means easy?[11]

Many of us carry an aspiration for the Beloved Community, whether we call it that or not. Even as we survey the social and ecological suffering, we can see that side by side with cruelty, greed, warring, and discrimination are human capacities for love, cooperation, sharing, and harmony. Everyone wants to be happy, to be free. No one wants to suffer. It really is that clear. What we need are ways out of suffering.

I've heard people say the next twenty-five to fifty years is a breakdown or breakthrough period, a stage that will kill us or cure us. It is a time that calls upon us to successfully address at least the following interrelated challenges for a breakthrough. We need to:

Reverse the damage to the planet's life-support systems before the ecosystems, soil fertility, forests, fisheries, and water supplies are too far depleted to sustain life. It is imperative to stop burning fossil fuels and to slow global warming before it melts the polar ice caps, floods coastlines worldwide, and changes wind, weather, and agricultural patterns.

Eliminate racism and poverty and make the basics of a decent life available to all people before we are engulfed by violent popular uprisings or numbing social collapse—both of which could flow from the existing gross inequities.

Reduce world population growth before sheer numbers push the carrying capacity of the Earth beyond repair. When I was born in 1944, there were fewer than two billion people on the planet. Today we are eight billion—a fourfold increase in my lifetime. Each new person needs food, water, energy, housing, clothing, and other necessities, all coming from Mother Earth.

Stop the spread of infectious diseases like HIV/AIDS and lethal viruses like COVID-19 before they overwhelm our capacity to create antibodies and provide medical care.

Systematically dismantle the culture of violence and cultivate collective ways of peace before current and coming stressors explode into violence, war, and possibly nuclear disaster.

Imagine and create a fair economic system that aims for the well-being of all rather than vast wealth for a few; that distributes resources, opportunities, power, and profits in a way that does not perpetuate extreme inequality and that creates a just society with cooperation as the dominant mode of relationship.

Heal worldwide trauma, which stems from a multitude of modern and historical causes and stunts the lives of billions of people, and which causes insecurity, reactivity, violence, and depression. We need effective and accessible methods for both personal and collective healing.

Two Key Obstacles: The Oppressive Economy and Collective Trauma

We have created a society in which the rich become richer and the poor become poorer, and in which we are so caught up in our own immediate problems that we cannot afford to be aware of what is going on with the rest of the human family or our planet Earth. In my mind I see a group of chickens in a cage disputing over a few seeds of grain, unaware that in a few hours they will all be killed.

—Thich Nhat Hanh, *The World We Have: A Buddhist Approach to Peace and Ecology*

Two of the challenges mentioned in the previous section deserve elaboration because they are the overarching obstacles to realizing the Beloved Community—namely that we live in an oppressive global economy, and we are soaked with collective trauma.

The Oppressive Economy

We live in a global economy that exploits, mistreats, disrespects, divides, and oppresses most people, where the wealth, power, and political control are concentrated in the hands of relatively few individuals. Until we transform our fundamentally unjust economy into a sharing, caring, cooperative, democratic economy, the suffering we work so hard to address will continue to pile on, and transformation at the base of society will be unattainable. Naming and building awareness about the economy as the primary external structural generator of massive suffering can help us orient our social change efforts around an overarching goal of transforming this economy.

Understanding even a little of the history of our economic system can provide context for our change-making efforts. About ten thousand years ago, humankind transitioned from nomadic hunter-gatherer groups to settled farming and herding communities. Since then, humans have been living in class-based societies where a few individuals control most of the wealth created by the majority. The ruling groups of any class society throughout human history have used and continue to use all means at their disposal to maintain control and power—including persuasion, promise of protection from invaders, and meager forms of economic security on the one hand, combined with force, violence, threats, skewed distribution of resources, political control, propaganda, and oppression on the other. Owning classes have evolved whole economic systems that lasted for centuries.

Slavery was practiced by many early societies in which humans were owned by the wealthy or the conquering powers. Next came feudalism, where the landowner did not own the laborers outright but owned the bulk of what they produced on the land, allowing the hardworking serfs to keep a pittance for survival. Capitalism is a current economic form in which owners extract the labor of working people for as little as they can get away with, resulting in an upward flow of wealth to the top 1 percent of the population.

Wealthy classes have devised a variety of oppressive systems, including classism, racism, sexism, anti-Semitism, heterosexism, ageism, adultism, and others. These forms of oppression not only foster widespread mistreatment but also keep people pitted against each other. We are deliberately divided, fighting among ourselves, prone to blame and shame, suffering from internalized oppression, made to feel powerless, and therefore settling for scraps of well-being offered by the system. We are too weak to mount a collective challenge to the powers that be. When we realize this, it becomes crystal clear why it has been nearly impossible—except in rare moments of political uprising—for people to join together as an unstoppable force to transform class society and unfair economic systems.

Collective Trauma

Trauma is the other huge obstacle to realizing the Beloved Community, and it is intimately connected to the oppressive economy. In a certain sense, we all come from traumatized backgrounds. What our ancestors have been through for thousands of years is lodged in the cells of our bodies even now. Almost without exception, no matter our lineage, we come from histories full of trauma, whether from tyranny, poverty, enslavement, plagues, wars, genocide, colonization, or another variety of systemic oppression. Most of our ancestors did not have it easy. Nor did most of them have the means, know-how, or safety to heal their personal wounds or transform their life-limiting social structures. They endured hardships and survived as best they could, and internalized the wounding such that it was passed on to the next generation through their messaging and modeling. Recent studies also indicate that trauma can be passed down through the morphing of DNA through the impact of the environment on genes, called epigenetics.[12]

Who can say where all the trauma began? There is no one and no single group to blame. Slavery was practiced in many early human societies, well before modern racism existed. The caste system in India is thousands of years old. Patriarchy has ruled for even longer. Natural disasters and unstoppable plagues wiped out whole populations forever. All these and more add up to a recipe for vast inherited unhappiness. Traumatized people create social structures of trauma that continue to traumatize future generations. Even though today's disease is a stew of old individual and collective traumas, we hardly notice the blend of causes and conditions. We think instead, "That's just the way things are." The fact that we don't see the reality of inherited trauma is itself a mark of our traumatization and collective numbness.

To be sure, all along the way, many individuals have grown through hardship and served as courageous beacons of light. In a collective sense, the human spirit has reached for inclusion, cooperation, and justice, with occasional revolutions or transformations that ushered in greater peace and well-being. Humans have made amazing strides in well-being and life-enhancing technologies. But overall, the ten-thousand-year history of a class-based society has been a rough road filled with suffering and surviving.

To heal, personal trauma must be viewed in the context of collective trauma; personal healing must go hand in hand with collective healing. The two are inseparable. Further, most of the threats to humankind's well-being converge where frozen institutions meet collective trauma in a gnarled knot. The social ills are interrelated crises, and their resolutions are intertwined.

It is time we stop blaming each other and come to recognize that we are all victimized by a trauma-riddled system. All people are not victimized in the same way nor to the same degree, but the humanity of most everyone has been diminished, dishonored, and disrespected by systems born from a trauma-steeped, oppressive economy. We need each other's help to end oppressive systems. Women cannot end patriarchy without the active cooperation of a large segment of men. People of Color cannot end white supremacy without White accomplices. The Beloved Community cannot be achieved if anyone or any group is left out. A fractured humankind must be rewoven into a whole community. This is the true and radical work of liberation.

Inner and Outer Transformation

All harmful societal challenges share two features: (1) they are interrelated, so working on one impacts the others, and (2) they are perpetuated by both external structural and personal inner elements that need changing.

For example, Hop Hopkins, the director of transformational culture at the Sierra Club, connects the dots around climate change and racism when he says, "You can't have climate change without sacrifice zones, and you can't have sacrifice zones without disposable people, and you can't have disposable people without racism."[13] Eliminating racism requires stopping racist behavior, changing racist laws and policies, redressing past injustices, undoing conscious and unconscious biases, and healing the personal internal damage done by racism. Furthermore, since racism was created in colonial America to support early capitalism, capitalism needs to be replaced by a sharing, caring economy. Similarly, the various challenges and forms of oppression that make up our current crisis have an intersecting nature.

Rising to meet these challenges can be daunting and exhilarating because it can call forth the best from us and move us closer to realizing the Beloved Community. The six pathways help us prepare for the challenge.

2

CULTIVATING WISE VIEW

Our Viewpoint Matters

The way we see the world shapes the way we treat it. If a mountain is a deity, not a pile of ore; if the forest is a sacred grove, not timber; if other species are biological kin, not resources; or if the planet is our mother, not an opportunity, then we will treat each other with greater respect. This is the challenge, to look at the world from a different perspective.

—David Suzuki

During the battle of Sarajevo in 1992, a cellist named Vedran Smailović went to the public plaza while the fighting was going on and began playing his cello amid the rubble. He did this every day for twenty two days. The soldiers asked him, "Why are you playing where we're bombing?" He asked back, "Why are you bombing where I'm playing?"[1]

I love this story because it says that our viewpoint matters. Do we focus on the violence or the beauty? Our view shapes how we feel, think, and act. Regarding the climate situation, racism, economic injustice, or other social ills, what is our view? What is the narrative we are telling ourselves? How is that narrative affecting our feeling, thinking, and acting? What might be a wise view that leads to more wholesome outcomes? Wise view is a first crucial step on the path to deepening our consciousness because it sets the direction. If we hold wise view, no matter how long the journey is, we're heading in the right direction. Without wise view, we can get stuck or wander in the wrong direction for a long time.

In relation to climate change, for example, many narratives are of the gloom-and-doom variety. They say things are bad and getting worse, or that we have passed the tipping points, or that we should buckle up for worse hurricanes, floods, wildfires, and seawater rise. These narratives are based in science, but they are also interpreted and shared by thought leaders who may be caught in a mind-set of threat or worry, and publicized through a news media that makes money by breaking news based in drama or fear. The negative stories can be counterproductive by making people feel overwhelmed to the point of giving up. It is vital to nurture empowering narratives that encourage people, corporations, and governments to see possibilities for a global renewal rather than collapse.

The Four Noble Truths of Ecological Suffering

One framework for cultivating wise view is from the Buddha, who proposed the Four Noble Truths: there is suffering, there are causes of suffering, there is well-being, and there is a path to well-being. The solution is to awaken from the delusion of separateness and realize our inherent goodness and our interconnectedness with everything. With this realization we will abide in peace, joy, understanding, and love. This was his promise: that awakening is possible. He, and Buddhist teachers since, have provided us with many practices to generate healing and awakening. Pretty sweet.

In relation to the climate situation, to take just one of the intersecting crises facing humankind, it might go something like this.

First Truth: Ecological Suffering Exists

The Earth and its beings are hurting. The ice is melting; seas are rising; fires, floods, and storms are intensifying; species are dying out. Things are likely to get worse: crop failures, food and water shortages, cities and coastlines flooding, huge species die-offs, mass human migration, regional conflicts, tyranny, and failed states. And in a grave injustice, it is low-income communities, poorer nations, and communities of color that are suffering and will suffer the most harm even though they have contributed the least to climate change. It's not a pretty picture. But we are asked to look deeply at this suffering, instead of turning away—not to scare ourselves into despair but to know better how to respond.

Second Truth: There Are Causes of Ecological Suffering

In short, the cause is us humans. Yet there are many external causes. For example, our population has quadrupled in my lifetime to eight billion people, and each person requires lots of stuff. In addition, many have been taught to consume more than they actually need, and this is draining the Earth's resources. Down through human history, people have wanted life to be less difficult and more comfortable. So we used fire, then coal, then oil. We didn't know that depending on fossil fuels would result in global warming and climate disruption. Two hundred years ago, no one woke up one morning and decided that they were going to make any species go extinct. Mostly it is the result of unintended consequences—there's no one to blame. But of course, we also have developed a global economic system that values profit over people and inculcates a culture of consumerism. Racism, patriarchy, and oppression support this system, which exploits and degrades people and the Earth.

Ecological suffering also has roots in our inner consciousness. The Buddha identified what he called the three poisons at the root of suffering—desire or wanting, hatred or ill will, and the delusion of separateness. In relation to climate change, we are ignorant about or in denial of our complete dependency on the natural world and have been conditioned to feel cut off and separate. Being out of right relationship with nature generates what I think of as widely unacknowledged existential loneliness, grief, and insecurity. These, in turn, have created vast individual and collective suffering as well as systems that are the driving forces of climate change. By recognizing this, we can begin to transform.

Third Truth: Renewed Planetary Well-Being Is Possible

An empowering narrative is that it is possible to overcome the negative effects of craving, aversion, and ignorance. Related to the eco-crisis, this narrative assumes that humans can shift our collective consciousness and our behavior enough to avert the worst outcomes, reverse global warming, and create a sustainable balance for life and the planet. It assumes that the Beloved Community has a strong likelihood of emerging if we embrace climate science and follow a path of compassion, healing, restoration, and love.

Fourth Truth: There Is a Path to Curb Ecological Suffering and Sustain Human Civilization and Earth Balance

This book unpacks many pieces of the way forward: cultivating wise view; healing grief, despair, fear, and feelings of hopelessness; healing and transforming social oppression; building strong, deep, local community; living an ethical life; and engaging in mindfulness-based Earth justice work.

Current Crises Are Doors to Beloved Community

I have found it useful to ask questions about my views. Which views are based in ignorance, hurt, or oppression? Which perceptions lead toward peacefulness, appropriate action, and well-being? In the absence of certainty, which narrative or view leads in the most life-affirming direction, as far as I can tell?

First, I need to keep reminding myself that all views, including mine, are wrong or incomplete because all views are partial. No one has the whole picture. Climate science points to a bleak future. Media outlets are feeding us daily doses of bad news about the world. All of this hooks our unhealed and often unrecognized reservoirs of despair and fear, feelings from childhood and generational trauma, which were there long before we knew anything about climate change or extractive capitalism or fake news. We are prone to project those old feelings onto today's predicaments and say they are too big to change. But how might this be different if we had healed those old hurts? In truth, we do not know how this climate story ends.

Trying to hold my view with a certain humility, here is the story I am currently telling myself. I am deeply grateful to be alive at this moment in human history because the better angels of our nature are being called forth. Life is offering us an opportunity to ask fundamental questions about who we are. We might think of it as a *collective* hero's journey that is asking us to unflinchingly face the truth of our predicament, overcome our demons and dragons, and call on the forces of love and courage to help bring us through this perilous time. It's obvious that we need a collective awakening for civilization to continue, and that we need to evolve as human beings. So, I find it helpful to cultivate the view that curbing climate change and securing racial justice and ending poverty are doors of awakening, and steps toward realizing the Beloved Community.

What does that look like in action? What would it mean if each of us took full responsibility, self-defined, for the well-being of the Earth and its creatures? It looks like this: we do everything in our power. Do no harm. Deepen inner peace for outward action. Act as loving change agents. Practice compassion, inclusion, and forgiveness.

What are we called to do that is currently covered by feelings of confusion, despair, grief, and anger? What if we make the healing of those feelings paramount, in order to transform our timidity and confusion, in order to unlock our fuller collective power? What if we vow to do our best to choose love over fear in each situation? Might we begin to see a flourishing of compassion, a deepening knowing of our interdependence, a beginning anew in mending our ruptured racial relationships, a developing economy of sharing, enhanced collective power toward stopping the degradation of nature, growing harmony among nations, an increasing wisdom about living lightly on Earth, and an enlivening ability to enjoy the present moment? And, oh yes, the end of bombing while cellos are playing?

No guarantees, but the effort is surely worthy of our noble nature.

Reflection Question

What is the story you are telling yourself about the climate crisis? How is that story helping or hindering you?

Impermanence and Interbeing

Impermanence

Another piece of cultivating wise view is to contemplate impermanence, the truth that all things change. In the arena of climate change, for example, the greatest ecological crisis happened 2.3 billion years ago, when a species quickly spread across the planet, filling every niche, giving off a noxious gas that killed most life forms. The species was bacteria. The gas was oxygen. This "catastrophe" paved the way for oxygen-breathing life forms, eventually leading to you and me. Planetary change is in continuous transition. We cannot hold it still. This is also true for our bodies, our work, our families, our government, our civilization, the ecosystems—all are in flux. Indeed, most of the species that have ever existed on Earth are now extinct. Earth and all its creations are but a moment in the mysterious cosmic flow.

We are understandably attached to our particular species on our particular planet. Letting go of the idea that we humans are not the center of the universe is challenging. When we resist change, we suffer. Wise view asks us to learn to look deeply at the reality of change and not cling to our views or preferences. This can help us find freedom in the midst of inevitable change—and freedom helps us respond more appropriately to the changes.

This doesn't mean we give in to climate change, racial injustice, or social collapse, or that we have no responsibility or duty to act. It does mean we can loosen our grip on having things turn out the way *we* want them to. We can listen more carefully to others. We can pay more attention to people outside our circles and to beings that are not human. Acting in this manner can help us develop compassion and lessen suffering, and renew our relationship with the natural world.

Interbeing: Our Connection with All of Nature

Another crucial element of wise view is that nothing exists as a separate entity; everything is connected to everything else. In Eastern teachings, there is a beautiful image of Indra's Net—an infinite web with a faceted jewel at every node, reflecting every other jewel.

Interbeing is the awareness that we are not separate from the Earth, but rather we *are* the Earth. When we are open and still, we can know without a doubt that we carry the Earth in every cell of our bodies. This awareness can awaken a deep desire to care for the Earth, as we want to care for ourselves. What we do to Earth we do to ourselves and each other. And how we are with each other, collectively, is how we are with the Earth.

When John Seed, a rain forest activist, was asked how he avoids despair, he said: "I try to remember that it's not me, John Seed, trying to protect the rain forest. Rather, I am part of the rain forest protecting itself. I am that part of the rain forest recently emerged into human thinking."[2]

Another aspect of interbeing is the recognition that each of us shares a basic human nature with every other human being: with the Maldives islanders who are losing their islands to rising sea levels, and also with the oil barons and climate crisis deniers. The people who stormed the US Capitol on January 6, 2021, are my human siblings, part of the Beloved Community. We all want to be happy and safe, and we all are highly conditioned to be attached to our points of view. To the extent that we can effectively deal with our judgmental and polarizing minds, we have a better chance to overcome these feelings of separation, and to see all beings with eyes of compassion, even as we try to stop destructive activity.

Still another aspect of interbeing relevant to building the Beloved Community is that since all is interconnected, we can begin anywhere in our healing, preserving, and protecting work and know that it reverberates across the fabric of the whole universe. We don't need to argue, for example, about whether we should work to dismantle racism first or stop climate change first. They are intimately intertwined. One caution: understanding interbeing does not mean we do not need to act. As Thich Nhat Hanh frequently reminded us, seeing and acting go together. Understanding interbeing means that if we start where we are, with what we love, and look deeply, we will eventually see how our area of focus is related to the whole fabric of the eco-catastrophe.

Despite my feelings of separateness, my actual relatedness is infinite. Thich Nhat Hanh had a wonderful way of helping us understand the *impossibility* of being an independent, separate self-entity. At many retreats I attended, he would hold up a piece of paper and ask if we could see the cloud in the paper. Without the cloud, there would be no rain to water the tree from which the paper came. Can you see the sun that gives energy to the tree, and the soil organisms that nourish the roots? Can you see the logger who cut the tree, and the chainsaw, and the person who made the chainsaw, and the oatmeal the logger had for breakfast, and the farmer who grew the oats? And can you see the tires on the logger's truck and the rubber tree in Indonesia, and on and on? If we take away any of these elements, the paper will not exist. After offering this deep way of looking, Thay always explained that the paper was made up entirely of nonpaper elements.

Likewise, I am made up entirely of non-John elements. As an exercise sometime, you might like to write down as many elements as possible that make you who you are. If you are specific and keep listing, you will never reach the end! Take away any of the elements—say, your ancestors, or the food that has nourished you, or the language you use to communicate, or the simple fact that you turned left one day instead of right—you would not be who you are.

A short poem by Rumi sums it up:

> If God said, "Rumi, pay homage to everything that helped you enter my arms," there is not one experience in my life, not one thought, not one feeling, not any one action I would not bow to.[3]

Here's another view:

> You are comprised of eighty-four minerals, twenty-three elements, and eight gallons of water spread across thirty-eight trillion cells. You have been built up from the spare parts of the Earth you have consumed, according to a set of instructions hidden in a double helix and small enough to be carried by a sperm. You are recycled butterflies, plants, rocks, streams, firewood, wolf fur, and shark teeth, broken down to their smallest parts and rebuilt into our planet's most complex living being.[4]

Here's an example from my own process of connecting the dots. I was finishing lunch on the third day of a five-day mindfulness retreat with Thich Nhat Hanh in the 1990s. I had slowed down enough to be more present to what I was eating. The only food left on my plate was one green grape. I punctured the skin with a fork and noticed the juice oozing out. My mind went on a reverie something like this: *Hmmm. It's fall. This grape most likely comes from California. I know there is a drought in California, and water is piped in from as far north as Washington, where I grew up. I know that most of the fresh water is stored in the glaciers of the Cascade Mountains. I also know that the prevailing winds blow in from the west, probably all the way across the Pacific from China. I know that China had thousands of coal-fired power plants whose particulates went up into the atmosphere, to be picked up by the prevailing winds, which dropped rain and snow on the Cascades, which then melted down into rivers and were channeled into irrigation pipes heading for grape fields in California, where the water came up through the grape stem, into the grape that is about to go into my mouth. Oh, it's so clear why I need to care about burning coal in China.*

I had a direct experience of interbeing!

Looking Deeply at Our Hand: Touching Interbeing

To glimpse interbeing, dear reader, you might like to try looking at your hand. Bring curiosity to this part of the body that people mostly take for granted. Slowly, notice the colors, the shapes of the fingers, the shapes of the nails (no judgment about them being too dirty or too long!), veins on the back of the hand, bones, lines across the palm. Bend your fingers and notice the skin on the knuckles tightening and loosening. Take it slow.

Now, while continuing to look, think on things your hand enables you to do: touch your face, turn a door handle, wash dishes, caress your loved one, write a note or a song or a love letter, hold a weapon, play a musical instrument, throw a ball, offer food to a hungry person.

Next, shift your attention to the awareness that every cell of this hand contains the DNA of your birth mother and father and all your ancestors. When you move your hand, all those ancestors enable you. You also carry some of your ancestors' triumphs and struggles in your hand.

While cradling your hand, realize that this hand is a gift of 3.8 billion years of biological evolution. Fins, wings, claws, talons, hoofs, paws, and finally, opposable thumbs, which accelerated human brain development. This very hand is brought to you by your ancestors across species, by biological and creative forces well beyond your knowing. And yet, here is your hand.

One last noticing. When the left hand gets hurt, the right hand immediately comes to help. It doesn't blame the left hand, scold the left hand, or leave the left hand to hurt. It knows the left hand is part of the body and embraces it right away. If the left hand hurts, the right hand will be impacted. Caring for the left hand is also caring for the right hand. No discrimination. Similarly, each of us is a cell in the body of Earth. When a part of the Earth is damaged or is hurting, we suffer too. Taking care of any part of the Earth is taking care of ourselves.

The Paths of Personal and Social Transformation Are Not Separate

It is delusion to think I can be genuinely happy when the world is messed up. Put another way, the source of most personal suffering is that each of us is embedded in a worldwide web of suffering from which we cannot escape even if we deny it, look away, distract ourselves, or muffle ourselves in a safe individual cocoon. Happiness is not possible when the world is drowning in a sea of suffering. Since we inter-are, what hurts you hurts me. During the long struggle to end apartheid, the South Africans recognized the social nature of hurt when they chanted, "An injury to one is an injury to all. An injury to one is an injury to all."[5]

This is not to say we can't carve out a zone of well-being for ourselves. But if this isolates us from the suffering of the world or reinforces our feeling of overwhelm—if we believe the world's problems are just too big and there's not much we can do—then we need to deepen our approach so we understand that we are transforming our "personal" suffering to better assist others to transform their suffering, which in turn releases more energy for relieving collective suffering.

To a large extent, the world reflects our collective consciousness. If the world is hurting, we must be hurting. If the world is polarized into us and them, the good and the bad, we must somehow be divided inside ourselves. So, transforming ourselves is the starting place. Many wise teachers, including Albert Einstein, Martin Luther King Jr., Thich Nhat Hanh, and Brené Brown, have expressed that all lasting and meaningful change begins on the inside. If we are to use the climate crisis as a door of awakening, our *personal* goal needs to be to transform our greed into generosity, ill will into compassion, and delusion into wisdom. Likewise, our collective goals need to be to transform an ever-expanding, for-profit economy into one of sharing and sustainability; transform militarism into peaceful, nonviolent, and kind relations; and transform the underlying story of Western civilization from one of separation and competition into one of interwoven interdependence.

In *The Art of Power*, Thich Nhat Hanh puts it this way: "If we continue abusing the Earth this way, there is no doubt that our civilization will be destroyed. This turnaround takes enlightenment, awakening. The Buddha attained individual awakening. Now we need a collective enlightenment to stop this course of destruction."[6]

A wonderful quote that stands the conventional modern view of human hegemony on its head is from Robin Wall Kimmerer, a Potawatomi Indigenous woman and university botanist. In her book, *Braiding Sweetgrass: Indigenous Wisdom, Scientific Knowledge, and the Teachings of Plants*, she says:

> In the Western tradition there is a recognized hierarchy of beings, with, of course, the human being on top—the pinnacle of evolution, the darling of Creation—and plants at the bottom. But in Native ways of knowing, human beings are often referred to as "the younger brothers [and sisters] of Creation." We say that humans have the least experience with how to live and thus the most to learn—we must look to our teachers among the other species for guidance. Their wisdom is apparent in the way they live. They teach us by example. They've been on earth far longer than we have been and have had time to figure things out.[7]

Below is an exercise to help connect us more intimately to a piece of the natural world.

Caring for a Specific Life Form: A Two-Week Earth Meditation Practice

Love is what most deeply connects us to each other, other living beings, and the cosmos. Love is both a natural way we feel about others when there are no obstacles to our love, and also a quality that can be deliberately cultivated.

The Earth is suffering a lot right now from lack of enough love from human beings collectively. Renewing our love for our Mother Earth and its beings is a necessary first step in renewing a wise relationship with our environment.

We usually come to love what we attend to and care for. As a mindfulness practice for the next two weeks, choose one thing in the natural world to focus on—a tree, a creature, a rock, a small body of water, a flower, a patch of moss, an indoor plant—something in your immediate environment that you don't usually pay much attention to.

Spend some time each day observing it closely as an object of meditation. Offer it exquisite attention. Observe its color, dimensions, texture, and shape. Look at it from different angles. Touch it gently, if possible. Become curious about it, read about it, study it, learn its reason for being there, maybe its history or evolution. Let it into your awareness and into your heart. Offer it loving kindness. Offer it care and respect. Find ways of connecting to it. Investigate its relationships to its surroundings. Appreciate it as a wonder of creation. Maybe create a love poem or song about it. Enjoy it.

You might like to journal about your exploration. For example: Why did you choose this thing as your focus? How does your relationship to it change over the two weeks? What are you learning about it and about yourself? How does attending to it influence your feelings about it over time? Do your mind and heart experience attraction or aversion to it, and why? What implications does this practice have on your life?

As with all forms of meditation, there is no expected goal or outcome. Your experience will be unique. Mindfulness is bringing nonjudgmental awareness to whatever is present before us—seeing things as they are, not how we want them to be. This is an invitation to practice lending your mindful attention to a specific part of your natural environment and letting the relationship unfold.

The Climate Crisis

As an example of wise view, I'd like to end this chapter with a comprehensive and succinct view about the climate emergency, written by Buddhist monk, scholar, and activist Venerable Bhikkhu Bodhi based in upstate New York. It is a deep understanding of our predicament that links the external structural and internal personal dimensions. It also offers a road map for action.

A Buddhist Diagnosis of the Climate Crisis[8]

By Venerable Bhikkhu Bodhi

I. Ecological Truth of Suffering: Future Perils, Creeping Crisis

A. The four **incipient catastrophes** (our fate if effective action is not taken)

1. Unbearable heat waves, large tracts of the Earth become uninhabitable, massive die-offs

2. Floods, violent hurricanes, whole communities destroyed

3. Rising ocean levels (3–6 feet): ice sheets melt, island nations and cities lost

4. Social chaos: nations collapse, anarchy reigns

B. The four **vanishing foundations** of human civilization

1. **Land:** soil erosion, droughts, desertification, creeping sea encroachment

2. **Water shortages:** exhausted aquifers, vanishing glaciers, longer dry spells, water pollution

3. **Food:** crop failures, lower grain yields, loss of fisheries, degradation of land by monocrops

4. **Social stability:** regional wars, ethnic-religious conflicts, migration, tyranny, failed states

II. Ecological Truth of the Origin of Suffering: Roots of the Crisis

    A. The four **pervasive global threats** that cause I.B

       1. Population growth

       2. Poverty

       3. Global warming

       4. Destruction of natural ecosystems and biodiversity loss

    B. The four **sustaining causes** of II.A

       1. Dependency on **fossil fuels** for electricity, agriculture, transport, construction, heat, etc.

       2. **Free-market economic system** that exalts short-term profit and other quick returns above long-term economic stability and allows corporate domination of political system and mass media—the Triumvirate of Domination

       3. Model of **industrial agriculture:** land clearance, high carbon emissions, consumption of meat

       4. A reckless **consumerist culture** driven by debt

    C. The **four inner roots** of II.B, "mind is the cause of good and bad"

       1. **Greed:** of corporations, financial institutions, politicians

       2. **Fear and anxiety** in the general population over jobs, terrorism, economic security, surveillance

       3. **Arrogance:** national, racial, cultural, social, "American Exceptionalism," "Manifest Destiny," natural entitlement, scorn for peoples, values, cultures of the traditional world

       4. **Ignorance:** "obfuscation and distraction" leading to apathy, skepticism, denial, e.g. members in Congress who refuse to admit climate change is real

D. The **deep meta-program** (source code) behind II.C, an ideological cancer

1. The **metaphysic** of personal atomism, objectification of others and of nature

2. The **ethics:** rational behavior means seeking to maximize one's own private self-interest; commodification of nature and other people

3. The **application** of the program: quest for exponentially increasing returns on investment

4. The **consequences:** pursuit of infinite growth; colonization of all other domains of value by market value

III. Ecological Truth of the Cessation of Suffering: Saving the Earth and Redeeming Human Civilization

A. To avoid I.A and B, we must promptly and seriously address II.A, B, C, and D

IV. Ecological Eightfold Path: The Way to Save the Earth and Redeem Human Civilization

A. **Four prerequisites** to a solution = right view, right intention, right speech

1. **Clearly discerning**, understanding, and explaining the dangers of escalating carbon emissions

2. **Understanding and explaining** the benefits of a transformed economy, social order, and culture—especially adoption of green technology, which encourages enlightened self-interest

3. **Awakening** a sense of global justice: the impact of climate change on communities around the world, especially in the Global South

4. **Inspiring solidarity** based on universal love and compassion: enlightened altruism

B. **Eliminate obstructions** = right action and right effort

1. Break the grip of corporations on politicians by limiting the role of lobbying and election contributions; reject trade agreements that allow corporations to abrogate laws and regulations adopted by sovereign governments to protect health, social well-being, and the natural environment.

2. Break the grip of corporations over the media: stricter regulation; end media empires.

3. Reform the political system: support publicly financed elections; give real opportunities to independents and third-party candidates.

4. Establish greater power balance in international bodies such as the UN: give traditionalist countries more power in decision-making.

C. **Four pragmatic solutions** = right action, right livelihood, right effort

1. **Mitigation:** clean energy technologies, especially solar and wind power, with transfers to the traditional world; better energy efficiency such as retrofits, LED lights, electric cars; sustainable agriculture via agroecology

2. **Adaptation:** rectify environmental damage—flood control, firefighting, rescue missions

3. **Resilience:** prepare people to face change and loss; poverty alleviation, food security, health care, family planning and birth control, education especially of girls

4. **Change:** from growth economy to steady-state economy; principles of sufficiency and contentment over infinite growth and endless consumption

D. **Cultivating spiritual mindfulness** = right mindfulness and right concentration

1. **Respecting natural value:** reverence for the earth, honoring nature and other species; restoring a sense of sacredness

2. **Restoring human value:** affirmation of human dignity, celebration of human unity and equality; new models of governance rooted in solidarity

3. **Rediscovering aesthetic and intellectual value:** more leisure, less work, paid vacations

4. **Seeking ultimate value:** cultivating higher consciousness beyond greed and fear

V. **Actualizing the Goal**

Realization of peace, happiness, and prosperity on Earth.

3

HEALING HURT AND TRAUMA

Why Healing?

Inner healing, social transformation.
You can't have one without the other.

This quote was the tagline on the back of every issue of *Tikkun* magazine for many years. *Tikkun olam* is a Hebrew phrase that means "repair of the world." For me, the quote succinctly points to the truth that the Beloved Community is not possible without deep repair of the individual and collective hurt that has created such trouble in our world.

Wherever we go, we bring our personal baggage with us. Our fears, insecurities, and negative emotions infect every aspect of our lives. It is crucial that we have a way of understanding and healing these wounded parts of ourselves for our own well-being and collective well-being.

Furthermore, as we contemplate the profound environmental changes ahead, we come face-to-face with deep feelings. Despair, depression, and sadness are normal responses to the possibility of extinction, the continuing ravages of white supremacy, and the destruction of the environment. How do we find ways of allowing ourselves to let our hearts break open at both the present suffering and the suffering that is predicted? Our feelings need to be embraced as passing states to be healed, not as reasons to give up or remain passive. Life is still miraculous; even when suffering deepens, there is still so much to love and protect. But without healing practices, hurts and fears accumulate, and we are prone to respond unskillfully, perhaps numbing out, acting with urgency, denying feelings, burning out, getting depressed, or giving up. We need effective ways of healing our personal and collective suffering.

This chapter shines a light on various aspects and stories of healing in the hope that you find encouragement and practical ways to heal. I focus on three pathways of healing and personal change that I have practiced: peer counseling, mindfulness, and compassion.

Part I.
Peer Counseling as a Pathway to Healing

Every problem, every conflict, every illness, every chronic disorder, every social injustice, every way that one feels bad about oneself has a history. That history can be long in development, sometimes over millennia, and can be the result of an infinite number of causes and conditions, often invisible or untraceable. The view we hold about human nature shapes our attempts at understanding the root causes of suffering and its healing.

I wandered through my first three decades without the clarity I have now about human nature, hurt, and healing. I'll illustrate the first pathway to healing by sharing about my personal journey to understanding.

In the late 1960s and early 1970s, I used hallucinogenic drugs. I had a total of about a dozen LSD and mescaline trips. They were life-changing experiences for two reasons. One was the extended glimpses they gave me of a larger world that was more alive, colorful, vivid, and present than I normally lived. A typical trip lasted ten to twelve hours, and I was lucky because I never had what people termed "a bad trip." On my first trip, I basically laughed for twelve hours! Everything touched my funny bone. It felt like my unfiltered natural response to life was joy! The altered brain state either created or revealed—it's not clear which—an imaginative, interconnected, ever-changing, awesome world. And I responded with wide-eyed wonder, open-heartedness, and acceptance of whatever came without clinging to the moment. It felt truly liberating. This part of my drug trips eventually led me to explore altered states of consciousness, chanting, meditation, quantum physics, psychic healing, and paranormal phenomena.

The other life-changing aspect of my drug trips was that as the high wore off over four to five hours, that amazingly alive world closed down. I was not normally given to crying, but I found myself crying and crying as I felt the openness, fearlessness, vividness, and love of that high state slipping away. I realized that my "normal" life was much smaller, scared, conforming, and squeezed fairly dry of authentic living. On the tail end of each trip, I would cry harder than I had ever cried, even as an infant or a child. The crying opened huge vats of grief for all the years I had spent sleepwalking through my life, for all the gray tones that colored my days instead of the vibrant colors I experienced while high. I knew this greater aliveness must be covered with emotional hurts I could only begin to name. I knew much emotional work lay ahead of me if I had a chance of reclaiming the joy and freedom that my highs uncovered.

In the working-class community where I grew up, therapy was not something people did. Drinking themselves into numbness was how they dealt with pain. Even though by 1971 I was the first in my family's line to graduate from college and become a middle-class professional (a teacher), I still had little access to my feelings and no experience with therapy. But in addition to the emotional openings that came through the drug trips, the other big clue that I needed emotional help was that I kept getting stuck in hurtful repetitive patterns with my primary partner, whom I loved deeply and who eventually became my wife. These emotional knots became so destructive that we were in danger of splitting up.

As the saying goes, when the student is ready, the teacher will appear. My teacher for emotional healing appeared in the form of

Re-evaluation Counseling (RC). I began practicing RC along with meditation in 1971 as a direct result of my drug trips.

Re-evaluation Counseling appealed to me because it was a peer counseling approach, the theory was completely in the hands of the practitioners, and the goal was human liberation from all irrationality and oppression. The founder and chief theoretician, Harvey Jackins, was a Marxist and former labor union organizer and political activist. RC fit snugly into my own politics.

Since I began the practice of Re-evaluation Counseling, I've done thousands of hours of emotional release on my own "stuff" through talking, crying, trembling, feeling anger, and laughing. I have taught classes, led workshops, fostered leadership, authored articles and manuals, raised my children, nurtured my marriage, and helped develop organizations inspired by the principles and practices of RC. As a result, I've explored the territory deep inside, scouring out lots of my pain (with plenty left to heal) and releasing much of my inherent love, vision, good thinking, creativity, and power (with plenty left to release).

Because Harvey Jackins was a political activist and broad thinker, the RC process of healing naturally led to a systematic and profound uncovering of the internalized effects of oppression on individuals. Within the RC community, there are workshops and journals for all kinds of constituencies and social identities, detailing the internal effects of all the forms of oppression. As a facilitator of RC classes and workshops, I've helped myself and others heal and release our internalized oppression, prejudices, and oppressor patterns, as well as envision ourselves free from these hurts. I have watched people move through their feelings of powerlessness to a place of confidence and effective leadership; from deep self-hate to pride in their cultural backgrounds; from being isolated, scared individuals to being powerful and well-loved organizers of groups. I've witnessed the miraculous unfolding of human potential as people heal from notions of a small self to an understanding of their unlimited, interconnected potentiality in relation to others. As a community of RC practitioners, we have learned how to build unity across oppressed groups, release feelings that arise from prejudices and stereotypes, understand how the oppression of one is related to the oppression of all, reclaim appropriate pride in our backgrounds but think beyond identity-group politics, and develop sound leadership among diverse practitioners around the world.

Sustaining All Life

Sustaining All Life, the climate justice initiative of Re-evaluation Counseling, assumes that everyone is naturally intelligent, cooperative, and caring, but that accumulated hurts block these qualities. Young people, if allowed, would recover from hurtful experiences through a natural healing process, by crying, trembling, raging, laughing. When we share our painful experiences fully, not holding back emotions, hurtful feelings begin to dissipate. We are freed from the behavior and from feeling left by the hurt. We can regain the natural ability to heal from hurt by being listened to with caring interest by someone who understands this process and who will remain relaxed in the face of our difficulties. Without this personal work it will be difficult to effectively address and resolve the climate crisis.

RC is now practiced in seventy-eight countries. It is not widely known because nobody is making money from it. It is not advertised. It is not in the marketplace. It is a practice spread entirely through interpersonal sharing among people who learn about it directly from a friend or acquaintance. Practitioners, or co-counselors, exchange time, not money, listening to each other after they have learned the fundamentals of the theory and practice in a class that costs very little. RC teachers are certified within the RC community, not through costly, college-based, professional certifications.

Through the RC approach, I experienced emotional healing as a key for human liberation. Through my own counseling and through counseling others, I came to understand firsthand how human irrationality is at the root of much personal unhappiness and worldwide injustice and violence. RC provided a straightforward process for healing hurts and irrationality: take turns listening to one another in co-counseling, discharge the hurts through emotional release, and hold out a view of human beings at their highest potential. The practice of RC is so natural to me now that what most people experience as a breakthrough when they finally have a good cry or other emotional release, I experience as a routine everyday thing. RC is not the only form of healing, nor is healing the only way to work on liberation. But I am convinced that liberation cannot happen without healing, and that RC is the most direct and effective method I've come across in my life.

RC Co-Counseling: Theory and Practice

The theory is straightforward. By nature, humans are beautiful, loving, and wholesome. But this nature gets obscured by the accumulation of distress experiences—and our hurts cause us to develop rigid ways of acting and feeling. We recover our true nature by learning how to intentionally use our innate ability to heal through a process of emotional discharge. This helps us dislodge the pain and take the emotional charge off hurtful memories so that, little by little, present-moment experiences no longer trigger irrational reactions rooted in the past. The RC methodology teaches people how to create conditions of safety, and exchange respectful attention and effective listening, to help each other do the emotional releasing necessary to free us from reactive responses. In doing so, we recover our full intelligence and power.

Let's unpack this in more detail.

Human Nature

Human beings arise from unbroken wholeness, from the vast mystery of existence. *By nature*, every person is inherently valuable, enormously intelligent, deeply caring, immensely powerful, infinitely creative, naturally cooperative, and innately joyful!

I can hear some of you thinking, *This guy is from another planet if he thinks people are like that! Sure, maybe a few highly evolved spiritual beings are like that, but most of us don't show up like this in our lives.* However, if I hold the belief that people's true nature is like I described, the next question I need to answer is: How come people do *not* look and act like that? What happens to make people look and act different from their true nature? Let me repeat, I believe:

> By nature, all human beings are
>
> Inherently valuable
>
> Enormously intelligent
>
> Deeply caring
>
> Immensely powerful
>
> Infinitely creative
>
> Naturally cooperative
>
> Innately joyful

Hurtful Experiences

The simple answer is, we get hurt. We get hurt by mistreatment, misinformation, and mistaken views. We can get hurt through illness, accidents, and natural disasters. We get hurt by social oppressions and generational trauma passed down through families. Going a little deeper, the Buddha taught that the cause of this hurt is ignorance of reality—not being able to see the interdependent nature of all things, not understanding that everything is impermanent and trying to hold on to what must inevitably change.

Wrapped around the giant wound of feeling separate and apart from reality, for any individual there are the scars of untold layers of hurtful experiences—things that happen to us because we are born into a world full of suffering and delusion. Unwholesome conditions exist, like being unloved, scorned, rejected, not valued, humiliated, abused, disrespected, miseducated, oppressed, ignored, not welcomed, lied to, mistreated, made to feel powerless, misled, physically hurt, pampered into numbness, not accepted, insulted, demeaned, or made to be afraid. Who has not suffered some subset of these hurts? Who has recovered completely?

Diminished Capacity and Poor Self-Image

When people are under stress or are in a state of emotional upset, they usually can observe that they are not functioning up to their normal capacity. This is apparent in things people commonly say: "After my mother died, I walked around in a fog for weeks," or "I was so nervous about the test that I forgot everything," or "I was so mad I couldn't see straight!" So, the first immediate result of hurt is that our thinking power temporarily diminishes. And if we get hurt repeatedly in a similar way, that area of our intelligence is subjected to chronic interference.

The second result of being hurt is that we begin to feel bad about ourselves. Most of us were not being loved, respected, or cared about while we were being hurt. We got the message that something was wrong with us; we were not good enough, smart enough, capable enough, deserving enough, and so on. We are left with bad feelings about ourselves in the area of repeated hurt.

Rigid Patterns

To deal with the effects of being hurt, people develop ways of coping and surviving called "patterns." These are rigid, repetitive ways of being that once helped us get through a difficult time but are now obsolete and don't fit the present, yet they still hang on. There are two kinds of patterns that are useful to know about: occasional patterns and chronic patterns.

Occasional or intermittent patterns are behaviors or reactions we have when certain conditions are present. For example, if you have stage fright, what happens to you? You might sweat, get nervous, forget your words, or go blank—even if this doesn't happen in normal conversation. Therefore, it's likely that you had a negative, hurtful experience in a group situation to cause these abnormal reactions. If you ask someone who has stage fright to describe the first time they felt this way, they almost always say it is rooted in a specific experience that happened when they were younger. Fear of dogs is rooted in a bad experience with a specific dog. Fear of heights is rooted in a specific experience of falling or fear of falling.

A person with such a phobia will predictably experience the same reaction to the same kind of situation. Most of us are aware of many of our occasional patterns. We think of them as our little hang-ups. Mostly, we don't think of them as too serious. But they tie down a portion of our emotional energy and our effectiveness. And sometimes they severely limit our actions. For example, in an RC class I taught, one of the students was a tenant organizer, but she said she could never go to the top floor of any building. This not only seemed irrational but also made her a less effective organizer, since she had to exclude people who lived on the top floor. On a hunch, in the safety of a co-counseling group, I asked her what had happened to her on the top floor of a building. Haltingly and with tears in her eyes, she said that she had been raped, and the assault had happened on a top floor. This began a long process of her healing from that horrendous experience. Eventually, her fear of top floors faded.

The second kind of pattern consists of chronic behaviors and feelings that are always present in a person. These are heavier patterns that result from repeated hurtful experiences. People often identify with their chronic patterns, saying, "That's just who I am." You can recognize a person in the grip of a chronic pattern because that person is almost *always* that way, whether the circumstances warrant it or not. For example, someone is chronically shy, or is always critical and predictably tears down any good idea or initiative, or always feels depressed or complains, or always needs to be the center of attention.

No matter what pattern a person is exhibiting, they are showing you something about *how* they got hurt. For example, if someone is constantly critical, you can be fairly sure they were roundly and frequently criticized as a young person. If someone is chronically shy, you can bet they got a heavy dose of rejection or neglect. If someone is always needing to be the center of attention, you can guess they did not get the kind of attention they needed when they were young.

Seeing these patterns gives clues about how to help or manage such patterned behavior. For example, a person caught up in a pattern of criticism needs appreciation—the direct opposite of the pattern. Unfortunately, because of being so critical, this person rarely gets appreciated, and in fact often gets criticized. Appreciating a person with a chronic critical pattern might give them space to soften a little in the moment, even though deeper healing is needed.

Another kind of chronic pattern comes from having been systematically mistreated or disrespected because of being part of a particular group in society. People play the role of either victim or oppressor. According to the assumption about our inherent wholesomeness, neither role is our real human nature. We get conditioned into accepting these roles. And most of us flip back and forth between the two. For example, a man who was the victim of abusive beatings as a boy is often likely to grow up to beat the women and children in his life. White people, mistreated as children or called "white trash" for being poor or working-class, often turn those feelings of being disrespected toward People of Color. A young Black mother, under the emotional strain of being oppressed as an African American, as a woman, and as a young person, can end up abusing or mistreating her own children.

Many of the ways people feel bad about themselves come from having been raised in certain groups. People who have been so mistreated that they cannot think outside of the victim role often feel unworthy, powerless, and deserving of mistreatment. They can also feel negatively toward others in their same group. This is internalized oppression.

For other people, it is too painful to experience the feelings of being a victim of abuse or oppression, so at the first chance, if possible, they flip to the other end of the oppressive relationship. To put it crudely, it feels more comfortable to do the beating than to receive the beating. However, someone who is acting abusively or oppressively toward someone else has been abused or oppressed themselves. Flipping from one end of an oppressive relationship to the other is a dynamic that helps hold the "isms" in place.

How Healing Happens

The good news is that we have a built-in capacity for healing, and there are many ways of healing emotional pain. Healing is complex, but most healing processes include several common threads. One of these threads is to feel listened to and understood. Another is the outward signs of emotional release of pain: crying to release grief and loss, shaking and shivering with fear, getting angry to release frustration or a sense of injustice, laughing about light fears and embarrassments, animated talking that comes with a fresh telling of an upset. Yawning is also associated with the healing of physical hurts and illness. This emotional discharge is the outward sign that inner wounds are healing.

Much healing happens naturally. You can see it most clearly in infants and young children. When a toddler falls and hurts their knee, or gets lost in the supermarket, or is frustrated trying to tie their shoe, what is the first thing they usually do? Cry. You don't have to teach a child to cry. It is a natural response. It is their way of getting someone to pay attention to the fact that they are hurting. If a child can get someone to pay attention long enough and welcome their crying or other release, then they release the emotional part of the pain, get it out of their system, and return to being their regular self, not sulking, not holding the pain in, not shutting down.

But what often happens? Typically, a parent, a teacher, an older sibling, or another older person interferes with this process. Many people are uncomfortable with crying and think the child will feel better if they stop crying. Crying is mistaken as a sign of the hurt rather than the healing of the hurt. People use various methods to shut down tears, and the young person gets the repeated message that it is not good to cry. For example:

- invalidating the hurt: "There, there, everything is all right. No need for crying."

- physically stopping the crying: "Here's your pacifier (or ice cream cone, or lollipop)."

- distracting the child: "Look at the pretty bird!"

- adding fear and threat to an already painful experience: "Shut up or I'll really give you something to cry about!"

What happens when the hurt can't be expressed in a natural way? The child must store it, repress it, keep it inside. This happened to most of us to one degree or another. Our built-in capacity to heal was interfered with. As we grew, so grew our load of unreleased pain. Most of us are walking around carrying a truckload of past grief, fear, and anger.

Sharing our responses to the reflection questions would be quite touching. Sometimes the memory is still fresh, and tears or other feelings might come with the retelling.

> **Reflection Questions**
>
> When was a time you cried or felt like crying? A time you shivered in fear or felt a cold sweat? A time you felt angry? Laughed in embarrassment?

How to Create Safety

If we have a built-in way of healing our hurts, and if we know that the release of feelings can help us unlock the fullness of our nature, the question becomes: How do we create conditions and places where this level of healing can happen? What makes you feel comfortable enough to share personal things? Most people include many of the following:

Conditions That Help Create Safety

- feeling respected and cared about
- being really listened to
- having eye contact
- seeing body language that communicates interest and patience
- receiving undivided attention
- having no judgment coming from the listener
- feeling heard and understood
- feeling liked and appreciated
- being assured of confidentiality

The quality of attention makes all the difference. Humans care deeply about what is happening to us, to those around us, to our world. Each of us is continually assessing how safe it is to show we care. But many of us have been hurt when we showed our caring, so we learned to hide it, to look bored or indifferent, or to put on a fake front. As a result, many of us need to be encouraged to *practice* giving quality attention. It's as if we are learning a new skill or relearning a forgotten one. One thing is clear from the literature on therapeutic methods: the critical factor for success is the quality of the therapist's attention. When the conditions for safety are right, a person spontaneously and naturally begins to cry, or laugh, or feel fear, or feel anger, or speak with fresh anima- tion, and so releases the hurt. Such release brings understanding and insight: "Oh, that's why I've always acted that way!"

Results of Releasing Painful Feelings

There are short-term and long-term benefits to releasing our feel- ings. How do you usually feel after you have a good cry? Usually, people feel lighter, like a burden has been lifted. It doesn't nec- essarily make the problem or source of the hurt go away, but it clears the mind to better manage the situation. Crying hard over the death of a loved one doesn't change the fact that they are gone, but it gives us more mental space to deal with the relatives, the arrangements, the necessities of reality. The short-term result is that we feel better and think more clearly.

The long-range effect of looking deeply into the causes of our suffering, and of being listened to sufficiently that we discharge the pain, is that our troublesome patterns and old habits gradually dissipate and eventually disappear.

Release Plus New Behaviors

Healing from chronic patterns is a two-part process. The first part is discharging the distress, aided by the loving attention of a co-counselor. The second part happens as you lead your life by deciding to act differently from how your patterns have condi- tioned you to act. For example, let's say I have struggled all my life with being shy. First, in the safety of the co-counseling relationship, I would tell my listening partner my early experiences of being neglected, rejected, and ignored, or whatever led to the development of shyness as a coping mechanism. I would release the emotions through crying, trembling with fear, feeling anger, and even laughing at light fears and embarrassments.

But most of my life is not spent in these safe listening partnerships. So, outside the listening session, I would decide to adopt an attitude and actions that are in the direction of how I want to be. If I have a pattern of shyness, I might decide to walk into a group with the attitude and posture wherein I expect people to like me, to act friendly and outgoing—the opposite of being a wallflower. What happens when I take a new direction like this? At least two things. First, if I act confident rather than shy, it can prompt different feelings and responses in other people, such as more interest and less discomfort. It also can bring up the painful feelings that the habit of shyness was designed to keep down. Breaking this habit would be excruciating at first, and I would likely feel like a fake. I could take those feelings into the safety of a co-counseling session and discharge them. Over time, discharge plus holding a positive direction change both negative feelings and behavior.

Returning to Our Real Nature

To summarize, this framework for healing says we have a wholesome human nature that gets obscured by hurt and mistreatment, which makes us feel bad and think less clearly. This results in unwholesome patterns of behavior rooted in distress. Yet we also have a built-in ability to heal from past hurts by telling warm, attentive listeners about our experiences and releasing painful feelings through the external signs of crying, shaking, laughing, feeling angry, talking animatedly, and yawning. We can learn how to deliberately express our feelings in the safety of a co-counseling partnership. If we do this repeatedly, it helps us feel better and function better, and it gradually eliminates deeply ingrained patterns. Releasing feelings and trying on new pattern-breaking directions eventually brings us back to knowing our real nature.

Freeing ourselves from irrationality and old distresses, person by person, can directly contribute to realizing the Beloved Community.

The Mafia Hit Man Transforms

Here is a story about dramatic change that resulted from a co-counseling process. For years in the 1970s, at my home in Harlem, I taught ongoing Re-evaluation Counseling classes in which people learned to exchange warm, respectful attention as part of healing old distress. A woman I will call Ellen had been in one of these classes for about a year.[1] The class was a multiracial group of sixteen people from different economic classes. In the mix were a nuclear engineer, three working-class mothers from a community school in East Harlem where I worked, a therapist, several radical political activists, a Harvard-trained economist, a minister, and a couple of artists. Ellen was a very humble, Irish working-class, salt-of-the-earth woman, married to an Italian man. They lived in East Harlem with their two young sons. She loved the counseling. Each week she co-counseled with someone in the class and participated in the group class. She was making great strides in her life, opening to her own power and capabilities, undoing layers of internalized women's oppression and working-class oppression. She was getting more confident. Her leadership skills were emerging.

During the class and her sessions, she often talked about her husband, Rocco. She loved him, she told us in these confidential settings, but she was disturbed by his job—he was a hit man for the mafia. He was the guy who would pull up alongside a targeted car, roll the window down, and shoot the other guy with his shotgun. Rocco would drop Ellen off at class and pick her up at the end. He had a stereotypical mean look—short, stocky, with a strong, thick neck, and thick speech. Needless to say, I was very respectful whenever I met him.

After about a year in the class, Ellen came to me one night and said that Rocco wanted to join. "Join what?" I asked. "Join the class," she said. I was stunned for a moment. I asked why. It seemed that she had been going home and telling him about the class and what was happening for her in the counseling sessions. He could see she was changing in positive ways. He was curious. I took a deep breath and said, "Okay, bring him next week."

Rocco came to class the next week. The group sat in a circle of chairs. There was one large, comfortable wing chair with deep red plush upholstery. Rocco claimed that chair, and no one objected. He pushed the chair way, way back into the corner of the room, far out of the circle, and sat with his arms crossed over his chest. He sat there, not saying a thing . . . week after week . . . after week! Other members of the class came up to me during the breaks and whispered things like, "What is going on with Rocco? It's weird." I said, "I don't know, but I do know one thing. He keeps coming back."

Rocco was watching and listening carefully, checking me out, checking out the other members of the class. Like each one of us, he needed to know how safe it was to talk about what was deep in his heart. Each of us has our own timeline, our own conditions necessary to feel safe. One evening, after several months of watching, Rocco said, "I wanna talk."

He scooted his chair up into the circle and told us his story, which went something like this: "I grew up in East Harlem, which then was mostly an Italian neighborhood. When I was ten years old, I got polio. I wore braces on my legs and was gimpy. The neighborhood boys made fun of me and beat the shit out of me. The only way I could survive was to get tough as nails. The older guys saw something in me and said, 'Hey, we got a job for you.' They protected me and gave me respect. As I got older, they had me doing some terrible things. I've done a lot of bad things in my life." Everyone in the class knew what he was talking about. He lowered his eyes and his voice, paused, and then said quietly, "I don't want to do it no more."

There was rapt attention. Half the group was in tears. Suddenly, this thug, this hit man, this menacing presence, became a real person whose struggles were understandable and whose pain drew out our compassion. Rocco began counseling with others in the group on a regular basis. He let himself laugh and show his sweetness. He edged up to his stored fear and found anger waiting there. Little by little he began to trust us more. We proved that we could listen without judging him, not shrink when he talked about "terrible things," and handle his fear and anger without flinching. We showered him with genuine appreciation, which made him giggle. By the end of the first cycle of classes, Rocco was actually hugging people, if a little stiffly, even the guys. He became a beloved member of the group. He had never been listened to and loved and accepted like that before. It was a marvel to him.

As time went by, Ellen increasingly came into her own. She eventually left Rocco. For his part, he ultimately moved out of East Harlem and cut his ties to the mafia. I lost contact with him, but last I heard, he was doing fine.

I am forever grateful for the lessons of this experience: Listen well. Don't judge a book by its cover. People take their own time to show themselves. The conditions for safety are different for each of us. Never give up because transformation is possible for anyone. Hold fast to the inherent worth of every human being. With time and the right conditions, every person moves spontaneously toward their true nature.

My Co-Counseling

Regular Deep Co-Counseling Sessions

For the past thirty-five years, I have maintained a weekly co-counseling session with a friend. We alternate going to each other's homes. We split ninety minutes. I listen to him for forty-five minutes, then he listens to me, or vice versa. We offer no advice, no comments, no judgments. We offer each other undivided attention, compassion, and a sacred space to look into whatever needs healing. These weekly deep listening sessions have helped me explore and release my early childhood hurts and increasingly uncover my innate capacity to care, to think clearly, and to act more fearlessly, which has allowed me to be more effective in my personal relationships and my social justice work.

Specifically, when it is my turn to be listened to, in the safety of his loving attention, my mind naturally moves to what is upsetting me. No matter what it is, I have learned how to allow the feelings to surface and to release them. I might cry over loss, endings, and disappointments. Or I might shake with fear about nightmares or scary events from my past that I never had a chance to heal, or fear about mistreatment in the present, or worry about the future. I might feel anger about past, present, or future things. There are times when I focus on the goodness of my life or the miraculous nature of Life itself. Sometimes I use my friend's attention to envision what I most want. Sometimes I use a phrase like, "Now that I am free from fear (or whatever is the obstacle to my aspiration), what I will do now is . . . (complete the sentence)." I repeat this as many times as needed.

Elements of Deep Listening

When it is my turn to be a listener, I hold the other person in high regard and assume their inherent goodness, no matter what they may be exhibiting on the outside. I think of the person as separate from their distress patterns and treat them with complete respect. I try to be present and available. I assume the person knows best how to lead their own life and doesn't need my advice or direction. I communicate acceptance and lack of judgment as best I can and offer them my undivided attention, focused concentration, and awareness. I encourage feelings; I am inwardly happy when

they are crying or expressing other emotions, because I understand that the release is a key component of healing. And I honor
confidentiality.

Holding a Direction

As I wrote earlier, most of my time is not spent in a co-counseling session with deep discharge of painful emotions. For me, an
essential practice has been to maintain a daily affirmation process that deliberately contradicts my old negative feelings. For
example, for years I struggled with feelings of isolation and didn't
feel at home in groups or with myself. It helped to participate in
weekly co-counseling sessions discharging the early childhood
roots of that patterned feeling. But I needed to guard my mind
and heart from those old feelings taking over. So, I created a
short paragraph that I repeated as often as needed: "I used to
feel isolated and separate, but now I belong right in the center
of things and feel safe and welcomed in the world." Saying this
to myself keeps me pointed toward my inherent goodness and
wholeness.

Complete Self-Appreciation

Extending this direction-holding further, I have learned that
any ways I feel bad about myself or put myself down are rooted
in early distress, or maybe inherited distress recordings that I
received from my ancestors. Therefore, it has proven helpful to
appreciate myself in both general ways ("I am a good human
being") and in ways that specifically counteract distress that I
have internalized ("I am a generous and loving man"). This is
not just the power of positive thinking or "fake it till you make
it." Rather, these self-appreciations guard the mind from old,
untrue messages, and this—along with discharge of the hurt
that accompanied the messages—eventually leads to freedom
from those negative self-images. When that freedom is attained,

I no longer need to keep repeating the affirmations. I know they are true.

Practice Suggestion

Try writing down things you like about yourself. Be specific. Keep going. Enjoy it.

To take it a step farther, read your list out loud to a trusted friend.

A Few Cautions

Usually, people can discern their own limits and don't go beyond what they are ready to explore emotionally. But occasionally someone's deep trauma might be triggered. Should that happen, it could be beneficial for that person to talk with someone skilled in handling strong emotions soon after the co-counseling session.

This healing process is natural and happens at a different pace for each person. It should never be forced or rushed. There are real reasons why people don't trust, open up, or show their feelings. Most of us have had little opportunity or safety to do our healing work. Each person needs to be in charge of what they explore and how quickly. The listener provides safety, encouragement, and attention but does not direct or advise the person being listened to.

In the other direction, sometimes a person can remain stuck in old habit energy or a patterned way of thinking and acting, and is not able to shift the narrative or deepen their inquiry into their suffering. In this case, the person in the listening role might offer some encouragement or perspective, without any coercion. Co-counseling classes teach skills for assisting, so over time, people gradually become more skillful at helping each other without intruding, judging, or advising.

Part II.
Mindfulness as a Pathway to Healing

Mindfulness meditation and mindful living are the second healing path that I have practiced over the past fifty years. In this section, I will explore what mindfulness is and describe practices that are relevant for healing our personal suffering, transforming powerlessness, and engaging in social action—all necessary parts of realizing the Beloved Community.

Mindfulness is a vast field of teachings and practices, well beyond the scope of this chapter. Some key concepts related to mindfulness have made their way into mainstream Western societies: cultivating nonjudgmental awareness of what is happening in the present moment, being aware of the truth that everything is connected to everything else, understanding that nothing lasts and everything changes, nurturing compassion for all beings, letting go of notions that cause us and others to suffer.

Most people come to mindfulness practices because they are suffering in some way. Maybe they lost a loved one and feel bereft. Maybe they had a life-altering illness or accident. Maybe they have been chronically unhappy or depressed and feel lost. Maybe they are distressed about the state of the world. Maybe they are restless, searching for peace.

My Journey to Mindfulness Practice

For me, the path to mindfulness began with feeling deeply troubled by the immense and unnecessary suffering in the world, coupled with a vague dissatisfaction with my own life. I was introduced to formal meditation practice in 1971. My wife and I were living in Santa Cruz, California, on a yearlong break from teaching in East Harlem. For nine months, I spent my days in a community bookshop, reading books on mystical experiences, altered states of consciousness, creativity, and Eastern religious thought. I also experimented with medical healing at a distance, used psychedelic drugs, and went to an intensive marathon therapy weekend. I thought of myself as a curious seeker, which was true, but I was also discontent. During that year, I became friends with a woman who observed my various searches and said to me, "John, you are like someone trying to find water by digging a lot of shallow holes. It's down there. Just pick one method and go deep." That had the ring of truth. Since I trusted her, and she was practicing Transcendental Meditation (TM), I chose to be initiated into that mantra practice.

After sitting for twenty minutes and silently repeating the sacred secret mantra, I would feel relaxed and peaceful. Interestingly, in the early weeks of this mantra practice, I would often realize that I had drifted away from the mantra and was saying, "Hail Mary, full of grace, the Lord is with you. Blessed is the fruit of thy womb, Jesus." I had snapped back to my Catholic childhood rosary practice, which I then realized was my first meditation practice.

After exploring Eastern practices with TM, Ecknath Easwaran, Swami Muktananda, Ram Dass, and Chögyam Trungpa Rinpoche, I met Zen Master Thich Nhat Hanh. I first encountered him in person in 1982, when I helped organize a peace conference called Reverence for Life, which took place the day before an unprecedented million-person march against nuclear weapons that Thich Nhat Hanh helped lead. At the conference, he offered one of the keynotes. His message and presence touched me deeply. I began reading his books and going to see him whenever he came to the United States. He was clear about the need to transform suffering, both personal and collective.

Throughout the next several decades, I learned many healing methods from Thich Nhat Hanh. To understand those practices, it is important to know some of the basic Buddhist teachings that ground them. Buddhist teachings are vast, so what follows are the bare bones, for readers who are not very familiar with Buddhism.[2]

The Four Noble Truths

Thich Nhat Hanh often presented the Four Noble Truths in a different order than the standard sequence. He organized them as follows: Well-being and freedom exist (the Third Noble Truth). There is a path to well-being and freedom (the Fourth Noble Truth, or the Eightfold Path). Alongside well-being, there are also ill-being, suffering (the First Noble Truth), and understanding the roots of suffering (the Second Noble Truth). I like this rendering because it puts the emphasis on well-being, freedom, and the capacity to live an awakened life right up front.

Two Dimensions of Reality

Reality is a whole cloth, or as quantum physicist David Bohm put it, "unbroken wholeness in flowing movement."[3] In Buddhist thought, there are two aspects of this wholeness. One is called the *ultimate dimension* of reality, where there is no separation, no oppression, no suffering. This is our true home. In the ultimate dimension, we already live in the Beloved Community, which is simply a name for our essential, unbroken connectedness. As we touch this, we are free, relaxed, happy. At the same time, we live in a *historical dimension* of reality, which contains linear time, suffering, war and oppression, a physical body that experiences ten thousand joys and ten thousand sorrows, ages, gets sick, dies. One metaphor for the inseparable relationship between the ultimate and historical dimensions is the relationship between the ocean (the ultimate) and the waves (the historical). As the teaching says, when the wave knows it is the ocean, it is free from suffering caused by the notion of a separate existence.

This teaching is helpful because it reminds me that while I am engaged in action to heal and protect the Earth, to end racism and all oppression, to stop war and violence, and to help midwife a new era of Earth harmony and sustainability, at the same time, I am already home, whole, unhurt, a radiant manifestation of the great ultimate dimension. Therefore, I can work with patience, compassion, and nonviolence, perceiving no enemies, only opportunities to love and grow.

Our Inherent Buddha-Nature

Buddhism holds that all beings, human and nonhuman, have an essence that is noble, whole, and inherently valuable. (This is similar to the view of human nature held by Re-evaluation Counseling, described earlier.) This true nature gets obscured by powerful social conditioning to feel separate from our true nature and to feel unworthy or inadequate or lonely. Mindfulness meditation, practiced with diligence and persistence, can eventually penetrate these veils and once again put a person in touch with freedom and equanimity. Attending to feelings and looking at suffering becomes easier as we learn to quiet our minds and accept things as they arise.

Impermanence

Mentioned earlier in this book, impermanence means that everything changes. This is the nature of reality. Nothing lasts—not our bodies, not our lives, not our civilization, not our ecosystems, not our species. When we try to stop inevitable change, we suffer. The spiritual practice is letting go, relaxing our grip, loosening our need to control, surrendering to the ever-changing flows of life. It won't always turn out the way I would like. But at the same time, what I don't like won't last forever.

Interbeing

Another foundational teaching, also mentioned earlier, is that nothing exists as a separate entity, that everything is connected to everything else. One aspect of interbeing related to healing is that what I think of as "my" suffering is not my suffering alone, and that it has roots in the larger society and historical period. "My" suffering has an infinite number of causes and conditions. Take any of these away and my suffering doesn't exist, or it changes.

Liberation from Suffering

No human being escapes suffering. Some experience significantly more suffering than others. Suffering is both individual and collective. When we were born, we didn't ask to be subject to abuse and trauma, or to be damaged by systems of oppression, or to be conditioned to feel separate, or to endure hunger or violence, or any of the infinite ways that humans suffer. But here we are. If unhealed, suffering can cloud our thinking, make us reactive, turn us against each other and ourselves, and generate even more suffering at all levels. True freedom requires us to acknowledge, accept, heal, and transform our suffering. Liberation is possible at both the individual and collective levels. This healing is absolutely necessary to realize Beloved Community.

The Practice of Ethical Behavior

For me, my Buddhist practice has three primary components: mindfulness, concentration, and ethics. Together they can lead to insight and awakening. In brief, mindfulness is lending evenhanded awareness to everything that arises in the mind. Concentration is narrowing the focus to one thing to develop stillness of mind. However, mindfulness and concentration will become agitated and unsettled if our actions do not align with reality. Therefore, how I live ethically every day is where mindfulness practice shows up in action, in my speech, in my thoughts. See Chapter 6 for more on ethics.

Mindfulness Practices for Healing

I have learned life-changing mindfulness practices for healing from Thich Nhat Hanh, who offered many different approaches. Below are a few.[4]

Noting

While quieting our minds through attending to our breath or in silent contemplation, we can observe feelings coming and going. Sometimes called recognizing, the practice is to simply notice and name the kind of thought or feeling that is present, such as "thinking" or "planning." Rather than follow a thought, we just name the category. With practice, it can become clear that thoughts fall into a limited number of categories—for example, remembering, fantasizing, planning, analyzing. With feelings, we simply notice what is present and say, "feeling sad" (or angry, jealous, fearful, and so on), or "this feeling too" to whatever comes. We note the feeling or thought and let it go. One method is to imagine sitting on the bank of a river, watching our thoughts or feelings as if they were leaves and logs floating by, then going over a waterfall. This practice can provide a solid anchor as we allow different feelings and thoughts to arise and fall away like waves on the sand, to use another helpful image.

Changing the Peg

When we sense that the thought or feeling that is arising is too much for us to hold at the moment, it is wise to move our attention off suffering and onto something positive or interesting, or at least neutral. In older methods of carpentry, pieces of wood were joined with a peg. Sometimes a rotten peg had to be replaced by pounding a new one into the same hole. Thich Nhat Hanh used this metaphor to point to the many tools at our disposal for watering positive seeds—that is, nurturing what is wholesome and beautiful. When a negative feeling seems to dominate our awareness without resolving, we can deliberately choose to get our attention off our troubles by reading a poem, listening to music, taking a walk, reciting a sutra, caring for another person.

Taking the Hand of Suffering

When suffering arises and we are grounded enough, this practice encourages us to embrace and befriend the feeling, and not to treat our sadness or unhappiness as an enemy. Thich Nhat Hanh suggested that we imagine holding our anger or sadness in our arms tenderly, like a mother holds her crying baby. "Dear anger, I recognize you. Come, stay with me. I know you are suffering. I know how to care for you." The practice is to just be with the feeling, not getting overwhelmed or swept away, and not running away. "So, this is what sadness feels like. Hmm. Very interesting." Kind and gentle.

Loving Our Wounded Inner Child

When we find ourselves suffering, another practice Thich Nhat Hanh suggested is to think of ourselves as a five-year-old child and send love and compassion to our young self, telling the five-year-old (or ten- or fifteen-year-old) what they need to hear, listening to the suffering of that inner child with compassion. A helpful variation is to imagine someone that we are having a difficult time with as a five-year-old child, and to consider what might have happened to them that gave rise to their troublesome behavior.

Beginning Anew

This is an elegant process for renewing tattered relationships or keeping a relationship fresh. It is usually done in pairs, although it can also be used in small-group settings. Each person in the relationship takes turns doing the following: (a) appreciating the other person, called "watering their flowers"; (b) apologizing for ways they may have hurt or offended the other person, called "expressing beneficial regrets"; (c) sharing how they are suffering because of something the other person may have done; (d) explaining how the other person might help to relieve that suffering or resolve the situation.[5]

Look Deeply at the Roots of Suffering

When persistent feelings seem to have a deep hold on us and won't go away, we can practice exploring the roots of distress. In my experience, the roots are either in repeated experiences of hurt beginning early in our lives, or in a severe incident of trauma or hurt at any vulnerable moment along the way. Mindful, deep looking into our feelings can help us understand their origins. What is helpful is to have a friend listen warmly and attentively while we explore the past. Typically, tears and fears and laughter and anger accompany the release of deep and long-lasting hurts. The emotional release allows understanding to arise. We realize, "Oh, that's why I have always felt like that!" We receive insight. This is consistent with the practice of co-counseling, described earlier.

Remembering Our Blue-Sky Nature

The blue sky is a metaphor for the vast container that holds all states of mind. All kinds of weather go through the blue sky, but the blue sky is unaffected by the weather. Likewise, our true wholeness and inherent goodness are always there, even when various mind states cause us to forget our nature. The practice here is to remember, to re-touch our connection to that blue sky. To describe it, we use words like *spacious*, *free*, *happy*, *connected*, *oneness*, *well-being*, *no separation*, *no separate self*. Each of us has experienced our blue-sky nature many times—perhaps while walking in a silent forest, or gazing at our beloved, or suddenly feeling alive, or opening our heart to a piece of music or a poem. These blue-sky moments are often spontaneous and unplanned, as if we were surprised by joy.

You might enjoy exploring your own blue-sky moments as outlined in the practice below, either by yourself or with a friend.

A Note on Trauma-Informed Practice

Although these practices offer broad and deep support, mindfulness is not a one-size-fits-all approach. For some people, quieting the mind, attending to the breath in meditation, or opening up to the hurt in their life might trigger trauma responses that can be harmful to a healing process. This also applies to RC co-counseling. Research shows that trauma has diverse sources and a wide range of damaging impacts. It can show up as individual dysregulation and trauma-perpetuating systems such as institutionalized racism. Understanding something about trauma can motivate us to learn to recognize triggers, learn ways to calm ourselves, regulate our reactions, and regain a rational, composed state of functioning.

The practices outlined in this section can help regulate our nervous systems and bring us back into what might be called the zone of mindfulness.[6]

Practice Suggestion: Blue Sky Practice

In meditation retreats focused on mindfulness and emotional healing, I often ask folks to begin with a practice for touching the ultimate dimension. I open by inviting people to sing a happy old popular song called "Blue Skies" by Irving Berlin.

> Blue skies smiling at me
> Nothing but blue skies do I see
> Bluebirds singing a song
> Nothing but bluebirds from now on

In this practice, the blue sky is a metaphor for the larger reality that holds everything. Feelings and other mind states are like weather passing through the blue sky. If we identify with the weather, we can easily forget that the blue sky is always there and holds all weather, and that weather is temporary. Finding ways of touching where we live, our ultimate nature, our blue skies, is a deep and useful practice. The Blue Sky Practice explores this.

The practice is done in partners. Each person takes an uninterrupted five- to ten-minute turn to tell their partner about times they experienced blue sky.

After breathing in silence, the speaker might remember a time they felt whole, connected, completely loved, one with everything. They might recall feeling unlimited compassion or other aspects of the ultimate dimension.

Or they might look around and touch the blue sky in the present.

The listener is asked to assume the attitude of Buddha. How would Buddha look at the speaker? How would Buddha listen? What attitude would Buddha have toward the speaker? For those of us who have notions of how our Buddha-nature would be and act, this is a reminder to let our posture and attitude reflect these ideas of Buddha. And of course, what Buddha would be seeing is the awakened nature of the speaker.

In sharing about the experience afterward, practitioners predictably report delight in being able to bring memories of blue-sky times into present awareness, or simply to look, listen, or feel the blue sky-ness of the moment. Some people's tears flow surprisingly quickly when they turn their attention toward the ultimate reality. Basking in the warm attention of the listener seems to help the process.

One Story of Emotional Healing

Healing from emotional distress and hurt happens in many ways. There is no single formula that applies to everyone, in different cultures, in different historical periods. I am only sharing about three pathways that have proven effective for me. To make this more concrete, here is one story of healing from my life that combines co-counseling, mindfulness, and compassion.

I was several days into a weeklong solo mindfulness retreat. I kept noticing that my habit of being in what I call my "planning mind" was fairly compulsive. I would be sitting in meditation, thinking about my to-do list. I'd be trying to eat a meal mindfully, and I'd find myself imagining a phone conversation with my partner. Thich Nhat Hanh has said that when we eat, we are often not chewing our food; we are chewing our thoughts! My planning mind was like a default mind space. I began to laugh each time I noticed it. I tried to be friendly and accepting: "Oh, you again, dear planning mind."

When it happened halfway through a period of walking meditation, I stopped and said, "John, it's okay. You're safe. You don't need to run to your projects. It's safe to be in this body, in this moment, right here." Then, like a thunderclap, I remembered what I'd heard Thich Nhat Hanh say many times: If in meditation you find yourself running to the future or running to the past, it means you don't feel safe in the present.

Why didn't I feel safe in the present? Suddenly, I thought of my parents. When I was growing up, my mother and father were unhappy people. They suffered. They drank alcohol to numb themselves. There was an ocean of sadness in the home. Alcohol abuse, financial insecurity, and working-class oppression were a slow-drip version of trauma that affected me deeply. I did not want to drown in that sadness. So, I got busy. I built model airplanes and model cars. I painted them meticulously with tiny brushes. I arranged the models in displays and made up stories with them. I created my own little world where I was in control, and it was orderly, beautiful, creative, and safe. It was how I survived.

That early strategy was the best thing I could figure out to survive my family's distress. It developed into useful lifelong skills of being an excellent project manager, being well organized, being able to create organizations and get things done. It served me well. But it also became a prison of sorts because it was compulsive and kept me running to the future and less able to be happy in the moment.

That was an important insight: I got busy making plans and projects to survive family suffering. It was not safe to be myself as a child, to be in the moment. The home atmosphere was volatile and unpredictable. My parents, though they tried their best, were suffering too much to provide me with consistently safe, kind, and interested attention.

Their suffering was embedded in collective suffering. They came of age during the Great Depression and internalized feelings of financial insecurity. My father's father was an itinerant salesperson who dragged the family from city to city, causing my father to feel unrooted. When my mother was two years old, her mother died as a result of the great influenza pandemic in 1918 and 1919, which killed millions worldwide. For my mother, that crucial maternal bonding was cut, leaving a huge scar. Both my parents were conditioned by class oppression to feel inadequate, insufficient, and unworthy compared to the standards of success held up to them.

As I was still doing walking meditation, thinking about all this, I felt an uprush of compassion for my mother and father. I started talking to them out loud and crying. I wanted them to be happy. I asked them to do walking meditation with me. With one of them on either side, we walked, holding hands. I kept talking to them through my tears, saying, "Maybe I can heal your unhappiness."

It was a beautiful experience, but I had more healing to do. In many deep listening sessions with my co-counselor, I continued to explore these childhood experiences about times I didn't feel safe, and about my parents' suffering. I cried huge vats of tears from the loss of years when I felt I couldn't be myself in my family. The grief of that reality, plus my boyhood sadness about my parents' sadness, was immense.

During sitting and walking meditation, I used an anchoring phrase, like "Safe" or "I belong here." Just breathing in and out reconnected me to the body and the present moment. Thich Nhat Hanh offered many short phrases, called *gathas*, as reminders. I often used this one: "I have arrived. I am home."

One last piece helped. Since I'm not on the meditation cushion or in a co-counseling session all the time, I created a kind of North Star that pointed me in a wholesome direction. As I became aware of the tug of planning mind or old feelings of isolation, I told myself things like: "I'm safe right here." "John, it's okay to be right here." "Be beautiful. Be yourself." "Be here now." "What if you stay right here? What if you don't run to your projects?"

This was, and still is, an iterative process. Meditating on safety. Releasing the feeling of being unsafe. Repeating gathas or directions about being safe. Feeling compassion for my parents. Deciding to relax into the present moment more. And repeat.

The result has been increasing freedom from that compulsive planning mind, a growing ability to enjoy the present, and a deeper knowing that it is safe.

Transforming Powerlessness

Consider this question. If you were not afraid, what would you do for the healing of the world? Not a different you, not a superhero, but as you are. If you were not afraid of losing the respect and affection of people? If you were not afraid of making mistakes? If you were not afraid of loving as much as you love? If you were not afraid of speaking your deepest truths? If you were not afraid of risking your job, or your health, or your wealth, or your comfort, or your life? Then what would you do for the healing of the world?

Practice Suggestion

Close your eyes for a moment and contemplate these questions.

The Warrior

In *Zen and the Art of Saving the Planet*, Thich Nhat Hanh says that we have in us a meditator, an artist, and a warrior. I'd like to talk to the warrior part of you. He says:

> The warrior brings a determination to go ahead. You refuse to give up. You want to win. And, as a practitioner, you have

to allow this fighter in you to be active. . . . We should not be afraid of obstacles on our path. . . . Obstacles are not really obstacles. They are an accelerator of wisdom, of aspiration.[7]

The idea of a warrior typically calls up images of soldiers, violent conflict, and military strategy. This is not what Thich Nhat Hanh is referring to. He is calling forth a set of qualities truly needed to face the challenges before us. Spiritual warriors are fighting for liberation from suffering. Excellent warriors train together for years, and they value discipline, precision, fearlessness, and compassion. They cultivate calmness, develop enormous trust in themselves and one another, and act with confidence and efficient effort. True warriors are willing to be vulnerable to express softness as well as fierceness; to be tender, open, unarmored while also being direct, alert, and firm. Spiritual warriors have no doubt about their inherent worthiness. They are always practicing to be present; they are not lax or lazy. This training allows them to stand together and not shrink in the face of their opponent or suffering. They can look squarely at fear and powerlessness.

At many Buddhist temples in Southeast Asia, there are two statues guarding the gate. One is Avalokiteshvara, the representation of infinite compassion. The other is a wrathful and frightening-looking statue meant to communicate to those who enter that ill will, greed, and delusion have no place here. The images represent the physical force of a community that protects cherished values and stands against corruption and impurity. This is also the spirit of the warrior. This is our potential. We have a warrior in us. However, I hasten to add that most of us, myself included, do not usually show up as warriors. Why not?

Pervasive Conditioning to Feel Powerless

Feelings of powerlessness are often an unnamed obstacle to being a warrior. Powerlessness interferes with our individual and collective willingness to act on our aspiration for a better world with boldness, fearlessness, and love.

Old Feelings of Despair and Powerlessness

When we face the enormity of suffering on Earth, we can often feel overwhelmed, despairing, scared, and powerless. For most of us, those feelings were present in us long before we knew anything about climate change, racism, or poverty. When we were children, we experienced so much that was wrong, and things were beyond our power to change. We were small and powerless. So, we internalized those feelings of being too small to make a difference. Unhealed, we have carried these feelings with us into adulthood, and we project them onto the big social issues of the day.

Powerlessness is a huge barrier to humans mobilizing to limit harm and to cultivate the world we want to live in. While it is true that many people are engaged in social justice work from a place of fierce compassion, solidarity, and service, it is also true that there is a more pervasive societal denial, distraction, and paralysis about the situation that needs addressing. Bill McKibben of 350.org puts it this way: "The crisis seems so big, and we seem so small, that it's hard to imagine that we can make a difference."[8]

How We Learned to Feel Powerless

In my own life, a few things stand out. Perhaps you have noticed similar events in your life.

An early and deep lesson in powerlessness happened when I was a toddler. I have a clear memory of this. I wanted to be close to my mother. I was crying for her. My mother, a generally loving person, placed me in a crib in a room by myself to cry it out. She believed some of the child-rearing experts of the day, who advised parents to let babies cry by themselves because it strengthened their lungs! So, there I was, standing up in my crib, crying, the late afternoon sun slanting through the venetian blinds, making striking line patterns on the wood floor. I cried and cried. I used all my baby strength to try to scoot the crib nearer to the door. I cried louder and louder. She never came. Finally, I gave up. Defeated.

Powerless. I could not get what I needed, despite my best efforts. And I don't think my lungs got stronger as a result.

As I grew, I witnessed so many things that I knew were wrong but couldn't stop them because I was too small. I couldn't stop my father from drinking or heal the hurt that made him drink. I couldn't stop the parents next door from beating their kids. I couldn't stop the bigger neighborhood boys from pulling the legs off insects. I couldn't stop the Catholic nuns in my grade school from making us children feel full of sin. I couldn't say how scared and confused I was when we had to get under our desks to practice for an air raid attack. As a new student in the high school locker room, I couldn't stop the bullies from picking on the weaker boys. In my later teen years, I watched the TV news and felt helpless about Black people being beaten by police, and numb to the raw footage of violence in Vietnam. And on and on.

Universal Experience

You have your own examples of painful early memories. I think seeing things that we knew were wrong and not being able to stop them because we were little is a fairly universal human experience. The truth is that every human baby—innocent, pure, beautiful, sacred—is born into a traumatized world full of suffering and oppression, even in the best of situations. Parents and caregivers do the best they can but are often under the pressure of their own hurts. Then twelve years of schooling, at least in Western countries, ranks us and tells most of us that we are a "C" person, just average. What is an "average" miraculous human being? And then, pile on racism, sexism, classism, and adultism, which tell most of us that we are not good enough, smart enough, or worthy enough, and for some who are most targeted, we are in danger. Whew! As we grow, the full range of our humanness gets whittled away, or criticized, or stomped out, as we learn how to fit into our family's and society's expectations. It's no wonder many of us feel powerless. Hardly anyone survives childhood and adolescence with their full self-confidence, power, and fearlessness intact.

In Truth, We Are Not Powerless

Let's be clear. We might *feel* powerless, but we are *not* powerless. Of course, there are forces, policies, laws, structures, culture, and state powers that reinforce feelings of powerlessness. But the reality is that people have tremendous power when acting in community. If factory workers walked off the job, if students refused to go to school, if information workers blocked electronic communication, if consumers boycotted products, if truckers stopped hauling freight, if bank clerks stopped processing money exchanges, then the whole social system would come to a halt. The people have tremendous collective power.

Feelings of Powerlessness Limit Our Warrior Nature

The conditioning to feel powerless is pervasive. It keeps most of us feeling small, staying quiet, going along to get along, not questioning authority, accepting injustice, and settling for comfort, entertainment, and distraction. Or conversely, the powerlessness finds us complaining, blaming, criticizing others, and otherwise acting out our discontent. This is not the way of a warrior.

It is essential to transform our feelings of powerlessness to release our greater agency, confidence, and ability to join with others in making a difference. The perfect storm of social issues—a deepening environmental catastrophe, persistent systemic racism, an exploitative and unfair economic system, democracy under attack, and widespread psychological and personal suffering—this immense set of challenges is asking us to recover from feelings of inadequacy and apply our true power to loving and restoring our beloved world. This is key to individual and collective liberation. How might we do this?

Practices to Transform Feelings of Powerlessness

Here are some of my favorite practices proven to heal my feelings of powerlessness.

Start with Wise View

I try to remember that despite outward appearances, inside each of us is a miraculous, unbroken, beautiful being. Any other way we show up is the result of unwholesome messages or experiences that came our way. This is especially true of me, and it is especially true of you!

Commit to Transform Powerlessness

We can make a conscious commitment not to *believe* our feelings of powerlessness and to do what it takes to heal and recover our full warrior capacities. We need to summon courage to examine and feel the old feelings in order to transform them.

Recognize Feelings of Powerlessness

Recognizing suffering is a key practice. Try to recognize and question each thought or feeling that says, "I can't do it," or "It's too much for me," or "I'm not smart enough (or strong, or brave, or powerful enough)." Challenge self-limiting thoughts with a countering thought: "I *can* do it," or "This is *not* too much for me to handle," or "Let me at it!" Sometimes I've used this image to counteract fear: "Where does a nine-hundred-pound grizzly bear sleep? In a hollow log? In a cave? . . . Anywhere she wants!"

Use Phrases of Connection

Many of us have been thoroughly drenched in messages about being separate. Notions of being a small, isolated self reinforce feelings of powerlessness and cause us to develop what I call habits of separation. In my experience, if I'm feeling better than, inferior to, critical of, disdainful of, hateful toward, threatened by, scared by, or powerless in relation to another person or a group of people, I can be sure that I'm caught in old habits of separation. This is not my fault. The conditioning is relentless. These habits of separation tend to keep us divided from each other and weaken our efforts to mobilize solidarity in challenging injustice.

We can use phrases of connection to counter narratives of separation. For example, we can say to ourselves: "I am intimately connected with everything and everyone," or "I vow to wake up from the delusion of separateness." One time I was in Newark International Airport, waiting between flights. I found myself making up stories about other passengers, and they were not flattering stories. I said to myself, "John, what are you doing? You know nothing about these people. Please stop!" I devised a phrase that I've used many times since, when I am in a public space like an airport, a supermarket, or a subway. I look around and say: "This is my home, and these are my people." When I do this, immediately my attitude shifts. Judgment gives way to curiosity and tenderness toward them.

Stop Complaining and Criticizing

Complaining, blaming, and criticizing are expressions of powerlessness, rooted in a feeling of not being able to change the situation. To help ourselves out of that trap, we can choose to act from compassion, optimism, and openness. For example, we can offer solutions rather than complain. If we don't agree with someone's view, we can ask them what brought them to their view, and listen mindfully to deepen our understanding. We can refrain from demonizing anyone or any group. We can assume others suffer and wish to be happy, just like us, and that we have more in common than in conflict. These efforts go a long way toward counteracting feelings of powerlessness.

Explore the Roots

To loosen the grip of powerlessness, we can explore the roots of our feelings in safe settings, perhaps with a therapist or a friend in co-counseling or deep listening sessions. We can recall early messages and incidents that made us feel powerless, and maybe replay the incident with an ally so we don't feel alone in facing the feelings. It helps to give ourselves time and space to cry, to tremble with fear, to feel anger arise, and to laugh.

Practice Deep Listening with a Partner

Decades of weekly co-counseling sessions in which my partner and I listened deeply to each other for equal lengths of time, along with meditation, have helped me explore and release early childhood hurts, including experiences that lay in feelings of powerlessness. Gradually, recovering more fearlessness has allowed me to be ever more effective in social justice work. I encourage you to develop a deep listening partnership for yourself.

Imagine

Feelings of powerlessness lie like a wet blanket over our capacity to think, love, and act boldly to bring about the personal and social transformation we want. Multiply this by eight billion people, and you can sense the enormity of this collective obstacle. Imagine instead an alternative wherein you work in harmony with others to actively manifest a powerful upwelling of social solidarity, creative action, and loving relations. Imagine being a member of a community that is released from conditioned feelings of powerlessness. What couldn't you do together?

Make a Pledge

I invite us all to make a vow to undo and heal our internalized feelings of powerlessness in order to assume our full warrior nature on behalf of healing the world, each in our own way. Here's a lighthearted approach that I learned from an early teacher of mine. Bring to mind a difficulty you are facing, and say aloud, preferably with a big smile: "I am obviously completely incompetent and totally inadequate to handle the challenges that reality places before me. However, fortunately or unfortunately, I am the best person available for the job."

Part III.
Compassion as a Pathway for Healing

Broadway Bicycle Boy

It was summer in New York City. I was walking along Broadway near 112th Street when a boy about eight years old came riding up from behind me on his bicycle and crashed a few yards in front of me. He was wearing shorts, and I could see he had skinned his knee. He was hunched over, grabbing his knee, squinching his face in pain, but holding it in and not emitting a sound. I approached him, knelt down, pointed to his knee, and said, "That must hurt." "*Yes!* It really hurts." He screamed and burst into tears. As he finished his round of crying, he looked up to see who this stranger was. I smiled, pointed to his knee again, and said, "That must still hurt." "*Yes!* It still hurts." And he was off again, sobbing and pointing to his knee.

I made a simple decision not to rush on. I stayed and paid attention to his hurt. After a few more rounds of crying about his knee, he looked up to see if I was still there. Do you know what he did next? For fifteen or twenty minutes, he pointed to scars on various parts of his body and told me how this one happened, and that one happened, and this one over here happened. It was as if he'd never had a chance to tell someone completely how much it hurt or how scared he was. He had quite a few stories. After a while, his tone became happy and confident. Then he got on his bike and rode away.

As I walked on, I thought how many scars we all carry, physical and emotional, and how we rarely get a chance to really tell the stories to the point of healing. And so, we find ourselves, at whatever age, dragging behind us a sack full or maybe a huge trunk full of old unhealed hurts that weigh us down, depress our joy, sap our confidence, distort our thinking, and otherwise cause us to hide our true goodness. And each of us is just waiting for the right conditions to tell our stories.

Compassion as an Antidote to Suffering

When we look deeply at anything a person does, we can more easily understand why they do it. If we could stand back far enough to see all the causes and conditions bearing down on them, we would see they are doing the very best they can in this moment, in this situation. If they could do better, they would. This is true for you and me. At every moment in the past, we have done the very best we could, so we deserve neither blame nor shame. Compassion naturally flows from this insight.

In the story of the boy who fell off his bicycle, you might have noticed many elements of compassion: I responded to his wounding, knelt down on the same level, acknowledged the hurt, listened to specifics, persisted, remained present, and did not hurry on. I took the time needed, expressed empathy, stayed with him as his stories poured out, appreciated his strength, knew this small hurt was connected to larger hurts, and didn't judge him.

In *The Heart of the Buddha's Teaching*, Thich Nhat Hanh says, "If you really love someone, train yourself to be a listener." He invokes Avalokiteshvara, the bodhisattva of compassion, who has a great capacity for listening with compassion and true presence, can hear the cries of the world, and is not there to "judge, criticize, condemn, or evaluate, but to listen with the single purpose in mind to help the other person suffer less." He goes on to say, "Compassion requires practice. If we are listening to someone and after a while begin to feel irritated or judgmental, then we have lost compassionate listening. Ask if we can continue at another time. We may need to practice mindful breathing and mindful walking to settle our own mind. Even if there is a lot of wrong information or injustice in his way of seeing things . . . try to maintain your compassion within you for one hour."[9]

Compassion also can be expressed in how we speak. We can use wise speech, speaking with care, respect, and the intent to help a person suffer less.

Compassion is also in how we write a letter, an email, a text, or an article. We can know that the reader has suffered. This is enough to feel compassion. Compassion helps us connect with another person. When we write, we try to relieve suffering with our communication. Write with kindness and gratitude. Write what we want to say in a way that the other person can take in. We want the reader to suffer less because of reading what we write. (See "The Fourth Mindfulness Training" in chapter 6 for a description of my love letter to the January 6th insurrectionists, an attempt at compassionate dialogue.)

Individual and Collective Aspects of Compassion

Compassion directly connects us with others, and true connection is essential to creating and sustaining authentic community. Further, compassion connects us with ourselves, which, when we look deeply, reveals our interconnection with the whole. For example, one day I was feeling disconnected and lonely. My internal monologue was some variation of: "I'm all alone. Nobody likes me. My friends never call me. There must be something wrong with me. Who really cares about *me*? I think I'll go eat ice cream." It's embarrassing to admit this, but there it is.

In a moment of mindfulness, I realized I could turn compassion toward myself right then. I asked Dorothy, my life partner, if she would listen for a while. With her tender attention, I allowed myself to welcome any feelings to come up. What was underneath the feelings of alienation and disconnection? First, a sadness that my friends and I were so busy with our own lives that we didn't have time for connection with each other. Then, a deeper grief at living in a society that doesn't care about its people, in an economic system based on greed and exploitation, where so many people are worried about their jobs, debts, health care, and ability to survive, where the wealth gap is obscene, where ill will and meanness come from the pinnacles of power, where money rules and the Earth aches.

I cried and felt the universality of this suffering. It wasn't just *my* suffering. People the world over suffer like that. The conditioning is fairly universal to feel separate, to feel uncared for, to feel we don't belong and no one is there for us. Like the little boy on the bicycle, I discovered that behind the surface hurt, a lot of other hurts were waiting to be listened to.

I saw how this feeling of loneliness had a lot of personal and collective reasons behind it. Ruth King, a Dharma teacher in the Insight Meditation tradition and author of the wonderful book *Mindful of Race: Transforming Racism from the Inside Out*, has a beautiful and succinct mantra that helps me. I heard it from her in a Dharma talk a few years ago: "Not perfect, not permanent, not personal."

Practices for Cultivating Compassion

How do we let things in without drowning in sorrow or anger? We train ourselves to simply be with the truth of things as they are. It begins with learning to understand and embrace our own pain, become intimate with it. The more we do this, the more capacity we have for opening to the pain all around us, the more space we have for others' difficulties and challenges, the more ability we have to be in intimate relations with others. Here are a few compassion practices that have helped me.

Exercise in Self-Compassion

Close your eyes. Relax the body. Try allowing yourself to focus on a continuing source of pain in yourself. Soften and relax into it. Can you feel it in your body? How does it feel? Can you name it—sadness, loneliness, separation, discontent, boredom, anger? Just allow it. Thich Nhat Hanh offers a lovely image of holding our suffering in our arms like a baby, seeing it needs attention. We can say things like: "Hello, dear sadness (or fill in your favorite suffering). I see you. I'll take good care of you. You've been with me a long time. I'll hold you and listen to how it's been for you. Tell me, what makes you sad (or mad or anxious or other distressed feeling)? I'm here for you." Surround the pain with mindfulness, tenderness, and acceptance.

Deep Listening Partnerships

Like the boy who fell off his bicycle, each of us has a storehouse full of stories about hurts that we've never had a chance to fully share and heal. In the sacred space of my weekly deep listening co-counseling partnership, compassion for myself and for my partner has become immeasurable, and the resulting healing has been immense and liberating. I highly recommend developing a deep listening partnership for yourself.

Cultivating Compassion for Others

For whom do we have compassion? Are there limits to our compassion? Are there people for whom we don't have compassion? Practicing loving kindness is one way of connecting with others, but this is easy when I'm not having feelings of aversion, ill will, or active dislike for them. How do we extend compassion to everyone to break societal habits of exclusion and start building more inclusive communities?

I remember reading a story about the Dalai Lama's personal physician, who was imprisoned and tortured by the Chinese government for more than seventeen years. He never got bitter, never hated his captors. How did he keep his compassion alive? He said that he saw that his torturers were also human beings like him; they suffered, they were in adverse conditions, and they were creating unwholesome karma that would bring about their own suffering in the future. This evoked compassion in him.[10]

When I began attending retreats led by Thich Nhat Hanh, I watched in humility and awe how, after coming out of the cauldron of the war in Vietnam, he worked with US Vietnam War veterans and guided them to face their own suffering. He encouraged them to tell their stories, the ones they'd never been able to tell before. He had them face a Vietnamese monk sitting just a few feet from them, and invited them to offer regrets and feel grief. Sometimes the vet might cry or move to hug the monk. Pair by pair, Thich Nhat Hanh was creating a bond between historical enemies. It was healing for the vet and healing for many of us witnessing, who had been impacted by the war, even if not by direct combat.

Ethical Behavior as Compassion

Here too, ethics come into play, for compassion is demonstrated mostly by how we behave: how we treat others, how we speak, how we share resources, how we love, how we consume. Chapter 6 is devoted to this topic.

Outward Discharge, Inner Insight

You might see the complementary healing features in mindfulness practice and the Re-evaluation Counseling practice. Both quieting the mind and releasing emotional pain can bring insight and understanding about our suffering and the suffering of others. Anyone who has sat in silent meditation has probably noticed that just below the surface, as the mind settles, what awaits us is often what Buddhists call "afflictive emotions"—fear, loneliness, unworthiness, sadness, and so on. Anyone who has attended a mindfulness retreat has probably noticed practitioners crying or outwardly discharging. I have observed that in many meditation circles, the discharge process is not emphasized, and is sometimes deliberately ignored or frowned upon, for fear that the practitioner will believe the story and be carried away. In my experience, outward discharge commonly accompanies inner insight and transformation. Through my training in peer counseling and mindfulness, I've learned that the release of painful emotions combined with quieting the mind accelerates the process of liberation from suffering.

Sophea and Children of War: Healing and Empowerment

To close this chapter, I offer a story that illustrates many elements of healing.

When Sophea Suos arrived at the Children of War orientation, she had suffered years of nightmares, migraines, and anxiety. Sophea was a seventeen-year-old survivor of the killing fields of the Cambodian genocide. She escaped Cambodia, spent time in refugee camps, and was eventually resettled in Kansas City by US Immigration. She was selected to be one of sixty-three participants of the 1986 Children of War Tour. I was the adult facilitator for Sophea's small group of seven survivors of conflict and violence. As we traveled the country over a period of three weeks, I witnessed Sophea's impressive healing and transformation from an agitated, tormented, shy young person to an outspoken, courageous truth teller. The conditions that allowed this to happen have relevance to the individual and collective healing needed today.

Children of War was an eight-year-long initiative, from 1984 to 1992. It brought together young people from eighteen war and conflict zones around the world for three weeks to learn from each other and tour the United States talking to youth and community groups and helping catalyze youth peace and justice groups.

Children of War was inspired by Arn Chorn-Pond, a survivor of the Cambodian genocide, and cocreated by Judith Thompson, who worked for the Religious Task Force and helped resettle Cambodian refugees in the United States, and Paul Mayer, director of the Religious Task Force.

The young people in the Children of War programs were ages fourteen to twenty-one. They came from South Africa during apartheid, Namibia in the midst of the War of Independence, Uganda after the murderous Idi Amin regime, Cambodia, Vietnam in the aftermath of the US wars there, the Philippines while recovering from the Marcos dictatorship, the Marshall Islands, site of US nuclear weapons testing, Chile during the Pinochet dictatorship, El Salvador, Guatemala, Honduras during the time of the death squads, Lebanon after the civil war, Palestine and Israel shortly before the first intifada, Northern Ireland during the Troubles, along with young people from US poverty-ridden and racial "war zones" of Black inner cities, poor White Appalachia and rural farmlands, Indigenous reservations, and undocumented immigrant communities.

In the fall of 1986, the Children of War group gathered at a Catholic retreat center outside New York City for a five-day retreat and orientation. It was an incredibly moving time. Young people from each conflict area talked to the whole group about the struggles of their people or country. We met daily in our small tour groups to build trust, learn about what to expect while on tour, and cultivate mutual support.

My small group had young people from South Africa, Palestine, Israel, Northern Ireland, Cambodia, El Salvador, Chile, and the United States. Each person shared their story. By the time Sophea spoke, there was already enough safety to allow her raw emotions to flow. In full tears, she told her story, which included feeling terror, seeing her loved ones killed in front of her, being forced to watch unspeakable horrors, being hunted, running, hiding, escaping, and suffering hardship and loneliness in the refugee camp. Her sharing of pain so deeply touched the pain in the others. Her tears opened our hearts.

For context: the Cambodian genocide was the intentional systematic killing of ethnic minorities, Christians, Buddhist monks, and anyone associated with Western ideas or organizations. Estimates of the total deaths resulting from Khmer Rouge policies, including death from mass executions, disease, and starvation, range from 1.7 to 2.5 million out of a 1975 population of roughly 8 million. One quarter of the country's people had been killed.

Over the weeks of the tour, our group traveled to cities and towns in the northeastern United States. The young people told their stories three or four times a day in schools, town hall meetings, press conferences, community centers, and houses of worship. For the first two weeks, Sophea cried hard each time she spoke, and we noticed that the more she cried, the more details of her trauma emerged. We could see her working her way through deeper and deeper levels of stored pain. This was also true for others in the group, but most dramatic for Sophea. Whenever she spoke, her authentic and poignant communication brought the audience to tears.

After a few weeks of grieving, it shifted to feeling her fear, accompanied by immense shaking and shivering as she related new facets of her experience. Finally, near the end of the tour, the young people were invited to tell their stories from the Sunday pulpit in Greenwich, Connecticut, a wealthy, White, politically conservative community. We were in George Bush's mother's church, hoping for a sizable contribution in the collection plate, which was one of the ways we funded our tour. By now, Sophea's healing had led her to be in touch with anger. When she took the pulpit, she started raging at the US government for selling arms to Cambodia, Laos, and Vietnam, which eventually led to the killing fields in her country. She was on a tear. Part of me was smiling and saying to myself, *You go, girl*! And part of me was wincing, knowing her truth-telling would probably mean a smaller collection plate from people who felt offended by her comments. But it was out of my hands. She was not mincing her words. She was in a zone of power and confidence she had not known before. There was no stopping her. It was awesome to watch. (By the way, the collection plate was still quite generous.)

Sophea returned home from the tour a changed person. She and I stayed in touch over the years. Her nightmares and migraines stopped. She lost the fidgety restlessness that had dogged her for years. She eventually completed college, moved to Minneapolis, married a wonderful partner, and now has several healthy, happy children. She trains people to serve as medical translators for immigrant patients.

O

Because Sophea's trauma was so deep and her transformation was so visible and dramatic, it's important to try to understand the elements that allowed that to happen. It has implications for the trauma-healing work that is urgently needed today.

First, there was a large holding container for Sophea and the other young people. Sixty-three diverse, amazing young survivors had a shared mission to tell their stories as a door of awakening for US youth and adults about appalling human-caused violence in the world. The fact that this was a national tour, highly publicized and covered by the news media, let the young people understand that they were, in a sense, representing their country, their people, and their traumas.

The Children of War consciously included Catholics and Protestants from Northern Ireland as well as Palestinians and Jews from Israel and Palestine. The commonality of suffering created safety and compassion among the young people, no matter the ideology they had absorbed. I recall one example of healing, among many: the Palestinian and Israeli youth initially greeted each other with suspicion, having been taught that the other was their enemy. We deliberately placed pairs of them in the same small tour groups.

Yair would hear Rania talk about how the Israeli military rolled into the Palestinian West Bank and bulldozed the homes of her neighbors. Then Rania would hear Yair share about how scared he and his friends were when Palestinian missiles came roaring into his town, and how Jews had been unwelcome and driven out of one country after another over the past two thousand years. Rania and Yair, and the other Palestinian-Israeli pairs, learned about each other's people and pain, then developed compassion, and some even returned to Israel to facilitate joint Palestinian-Israeli youth peace groups.

For their three weeks together, these young survivors were safe and protected from violence, some for the first time in their lives. This safety allowed them to take off the armor they needed back home to survive. Under the armor, deep suffering was waiting to be shared and healed. Since we knew the participants would be coming with trauma from their experiences, we hired adult staff who were trained in handling deep emotions. As best we could, we wanted to avoid retraumatizing the young people during the tour. But we had no idea how powerful the release of feelings would be.

For example, on the fourth evening of the orientation retreat, it was the Cambodians' turn to share their experiences. Each young person on the tour knew something of the situation facing their own people but didn't know much about the suffering in other parts of the world. As part of broadening their understanding, we often showed a film or had a speaker talk about Central America or South Africa or Northern Ireland or the Middle East. For the Cambodia night, we showed a hard-to-watch documentary about the killing fields. When the Cambodian young people got up to share from their firsthand experiences, they were already crying. Through their tears they beautifully communicated the fear, grief, anger, and pain. Then the collective emotional dam broke open. Touched by the depth of the Cambodians' pain and catharsis, a few others started crying, then a few more. Eventually, throughout the room, groups of young people and staff were holding each other and wailing, sobbing, shouting. An emotional tsunami had been waiting inside each young person for a safe place for years, and it poured out that night. The intensity slowly diminished, and we ended the evening with singing and dancing. Joy and connection were on the far side of pain.

This healing continued on the tour because Children of War often told their story three or four times a day. They were listened to with rapt attention by each group. They were swarmed afterward by folks who were touched by the sharing, who were often in tears, who sometimes shared their own suffering with the Children of War. One impact of this attention was that the tour participants' feelings were valued and welcomed. This was understandable, considering that the key ingredient of successful therapy is that the "client" feels respected, heard, and understood. Warm, caring attention from another person can provide a welcome mat for experiences of isolation, rejection, violence. This attention, experienced multiple times a day, provided a kind of telescoped therapeutic environment that accelerated healing.

Another element was the leadership aspect. The Children of War youth had a platform and a purpose. They were given a spotlight to shine on the unimaginable horrors suffered by young people around the world. Each one rose to the challenge of being a leader, a spokesperson, an organizer, a communicator of important ideas, and a teller of truth. For most of the youth, this process raised their self-esteem and sense of agency. Not everyone had a transformational experience, but most did. For many of them, it lit a fire of activism and civic engagement that continues to this day. In reunions since, person after person has testified how Children of War set them on their path to be a teacher, a journalist, a doctor, a human rights activist, an official ambassador for their country, a social entrepreneur, a leader of constructive change, and more.

For me, Children of War remains the most powerful example I've ever experienced of what we might call "condensed collective healing." It combined the power of personal stories, the universality of suffering, the safety to release pent-up emotions, the collective container and lived experience of Beloved Community, the call to leadership, and the witnessing of human resiliency and recovery. And all this within a three-week period!

It's astounding, and it makes me wonder if these elements might be more widely applied. The persistence of worldwide trauma due to violence, poverty, persecution, oppression, and environmental damage begs for the development of trauma healing methods that are accessible, affordable, applicable across cultures and countries, and both personal and collective. As a species, we have not yet adopted and spread effective methods of collective social healing. The Truth and Reconciliation Commissions that have been tried in South Africa, Northern Ireland, and Rwanda are in the right direction, but such healing work should not wait until people are recovering from war or genocide.

In the West, there is an increasing focus on trauma-informed care, resiliency, self-care, and collective healing. It exists across a wide spectrum: in the Black Lives Matter movement, in climate justice spaces, in youth development organizations, in corporate settings, in social services. There is even trauma-informed mindfulness.

Could some of the elements of the Children of War model be unpacked, combined with recent work in trauma healing and neuroscience, coupled with decades of experience in Re-evaluation Counseling communities, and woven into effective and accelerated healing methods? Such an effort would be an immense contribution to human well-being.

O

In this story, you can clearly see the intersection between oppression and violence as a primary driver of suffering, and community and healing as the balm. Now it is time to turn to our attention to understanding and ending racism and social oppression as a necessary step toward building the Beloved Community.

4

TRANSFORMING RACIAL AND SOCIAL OPPRESSION

The Beloved Community will not be possible until humankind grows beyond oppression-based societies. The current setup, in which a few people own most of the wealth while the vast majority live with economic insecurity, is a formula for pervasive inequality and suffering. The ruling group in any society and in every historical period has gained wealth through exploiting the labor and land of ordinary people. And they have fortified their power by using various forms of oppression to control and divide people. Since all oppressions are interconnected, one group cannot be free without all groups becoming free of oppression. This chapter explores frameworks and practices that have helped me understand and work to eliminate oppression.

My Path to White Awakening and Eliminating Oppression

How did it happen that I—a young White boy raised in a working-poor family in a small military town in the late Jim Crow era in the 1950s—ended up living in Harlem for fifteen years, getting arrested for civil rights protests, working in communities of color, learning from and trying to be solid allies with Black and Latinx people, developing frameworks and tools that have proved useful for healing from racism and other oppressions, and enjoying intimate multiracial, multicultural circles of family and friendship?

Looking forward from my childhood, I could not have predicted this trajectory. But looking back, some of the causes and conditions that shaped this outcome seem clear. I can see how experiences gradually expanded my narrow beginnings to a much larger world view.

My Roots

I grew up in Bremerton, Washington, in a Catholic working-class family. My hardworking parents struggled financially to make ends meet and chose to numb themselves with alcohol, the drug of choice among our neighbors. My mother was a practical, no-nonsense, caring woman who never complained or dramatized her upsets. She always found solutions to obstacles rather than caving in. She had two jobs—one all day with my father's shop, the other all night with the family. She was our rock. My father was kind and humorous when sober but angry, bitter, or maudlin when drunk. He went to work in the morning and either came home drunk or started drinking as soon as he got home. As a young boy, all I knew was that something out there was hurting my dad. And since I saw the same thing happen day after day with most dads in the neighborhood, I made a decision in early adolescence that I was going to help change things so it would be better for my dad and people like him. I didn't understand what I later came to know as class oppression, but I knew something was wrong.

There were only a few Black people in my small town, and I knew none. Everyone I knew was White—my neighbors, barber, store clerks, teachers, priests, police. The men in our neighborhood were shipyard workers, auto mechanics, road pavers, linoleum layers. They were all hardworking men who drank heavily, and some beat their children.

I was inspired by the impressive naval ships that sailed into the harbor, by stories of the Founding Fathers and Revolutionary War heroes, and by great ideals of liberty and justice for all and the pursuit of happiness. I collected small plastic statues of the US presidents. I devoured a series of books for young people on the (White) heroes of our country's early period—Jefferson, Washington,

Davy Crockett. These books were deeply racist and sexist, but I didn't know that then. For me then, they were an exciting way into history. I was so proud of being an American. I loved my country.

Then Came the 1960s

During my coming-of-age years, when I was sixteen through twenty-six, I painfully learned about the underbelly of US history—about the genocide of Indigenous people, slavery and Jim Crow, colonialism, a brutal form of extractive capitalism, and ruthless economic exploitation of people, animals, and the Earth. I felt betrayed and tricked. I felt I had been lied to, that my country was rotten underneath, that I didn't have a home anymore. I was grief-stricken and angry. I got involved in the civil rights, anti–Vietnam War, and student movements. I did civil disobedience and was tear-gassed and arrested numerous times—but only stayed in jail overnight and was only charged with misdemeanors, because I was White.

I learned by reading the liberation thinkers of the day—Frantz Fanon, Paulo Freire, James Baldwin, Ralph Ellison, Martin Luther King Jr., Malcolm X, and others. In college from 1962 to 1966, I majored in Southern US history, studying colonialism, slavery, and the Jim Crow era through the early Civil Rights Movement. I learned more by watching the Southern Christian Leadership Conference (SCLC) of Dr. King, the Student Nonviolent Coordinating Committee (SNCC) of Bob Moses and John Lewis, the Black Panthers, the Black Power movement, and the anticolonial liberation struggles in Africa. This study led me to engage in direct nonviolent civil disobedience, boycotts, teach-ins, and arrests. My education and the events of the early 1960s convinced me that a new social order was needed. My work life ever since has been aimed at helping to provide oases of safety and opportunity for mostly low-income young people in the short term, while contributing to long-term collective change in the overarching structures and belief systems that hold oppression in place.

Teaching High School

I graduated college in 1966, at the start of the huge US military buildup of the Vietnam War. I considered it to be a racist war, so I had to find a way to avoid being drafted. It turned out that teaching high school was draft-deferable work. So, my first professional job was as a high school teacher in Sunnyvale, California, in the heart of Silicon Valley. Most of the White seventeen-year-old students were from middle-income professional families. The war, the Civil Rights Movement, political assassinations, youth uprisings, and hippie culture and music were roiling the United States. Most of my students lived in a comfortable bubble, protected from the harsh realities swirling around them. But it turned out that they were hungry for contact with real-world issues.

Throughout that year, we explored war and the shameful underbelly of US policies of genocide, slavery, and colonialism. I was a young and experimental teacher and brought freshness to their studies. I brought in Hell's Angels motorcycle gang members, Vietnam veterans, women's liberation leaders. Even as we learned about hard-hitting issues, the classroom was interactive, experiential, and fun, and the students were interested and engaged. But I was always getting into hot water with the administration for my unorthodox teaching methods and political views. At the end of that first year of teaching I was fired, or as they called it, "let go," because I was too politically radical for that conservative community.

My Schooling in Harlem

Without a teaching job, I was still facing the Vietnam draft. I wound up hitchhiking to New York City and crossing a picket line of teachers who were striking because parents in low-income communities wanted a say in their children's education. The parents' position seemed fair to me, so I went to work at Intermediate School 201 in central Harlem. It is fair to say that those sixth, seventh, and eighth graders "took me to school."

On my first day in a classroom full of eighth graders, we opened a US history textbook. I asked a student to read aloud the first paragraph, which I had not yet read. He read, "In America, every man is a king, and his home is his castle." Upon hearing it, I winced. There was so much wrong with that sentence. From the back of the room, someone said, "Bullshit!" We closed the book right then, and they began telling me what life was like for them as Black and Latinx young people growing up in America. It was raw, up close, and personal.

It was nothing like the K-12 curriculum guide I was handed when I was hired. That guide was conceptually tight and coherent, outlining what students were to learn year after year, module after module. The problem was that it had nothing to do with the young people, some of whom came to school hungry, or traumatized by violence at home, or distracted by drama on the block, or made to feel stupid in previous years of schooling, or labeled as a "troublemaker," or "learning disabled," or "no good," or worse. Most had been so "dissed"—disrespected, disempowered, disregarded, dismissed—that they now felt discouraged, disheartened, and disengaged.

The teachers and staff were ill equipped to do the healing work that was crying to be done. They also were being pressured by school administrators, politicians, and funders to raise test scores. For many teachers, the job became a management operation, trying to contain the raw emotions of young people acting out their hurts, forcing them to pay attention to subjects that seemed distant from their lives, and punishing them with detention or expulsion when they couldn't obey the rules. The learning that happened was not about the neatly constructed curriculum but about how to survive a toxic and sometimes abusive environment. Nobody was happy with the situation, but the institution reflected the larger economic and cultural world view. It was a setup for high dropout rates among students and high burnout rates among staff. I couldn't address the social and emotional needs of the students while teaching the content I was supposed to teach. So, I left the public school system for good.

The Wonderful East Harlem Block Schools Community

Fortunately, the next chapter of my life as a teacher was profoundly different. The East Harlem Block Schools were created by low-income parents of Black and Puerto Rican children in East Harlem. Empowered by a partnership between Carmen Maristany, a young Latina who was deeply rooted in the community, and her partner and later husband, Tony Ward, a privileged young White Quaker volunteer, parents started a school of their own. They hired staff, recruited students, raised operating funds, and created a beautiful, healthy learning community. It was there that I learned firsthand the importance of people controlling the institutions that affect them. I also saw the power of the alliance between Tony and Carmen, a cross-racial, cross-class partnership that used her neighborhood wisdom and contacts plus his writing skills and outside contacts to organize parents and get the resources needed to implement a new vision.

With the children and parents, we renovated storefronts for classrooms, created exciting learning adventures, and traveled together. We were able to provide safety for emotional healing along with innovative educational methods that made learning interesting and successful. Love was at the center. Relationships and connection mattered, across race and class differences, among children, parents, and staff. We all learned from each other. We valued the different talents and perspectives that each contributed. It was truly a mini Beloved Community.

Those of us who were professionally trained teachers transferred our skills to the assistant parent-teachers who taught alongside us. They grew more skilled and confident, and eventually we came to see our roles as transitional. My partner, Dorothy Stoneman, launched a college-accredited teacher certification program for the parent-teachers, qualifying them to become fully accredited teachers. In the mid-1970s, the White professional teachers stepped back, and the parents, newly professionals, took over the classrooms. This experience was a great lesson for me about the vitality that comes with local folks making decisions about things that matter to them. It was clear that the people living with the issues on the front lines have the most intimate knowledge regarding solutions to those issues. That learning has guided me to this day. The East Harlem Block Schools still exist in East Harlem, more than fifty years later.[1]

A New Political Party

By 1974, the idealistic energy of the 1960s had dimmed and the business class was maneuvering to shift ever more riches and power to themselves. The wealth gap was increasing, mass incarceration was creating a new Jim Crow era, and mutually assured destruction (MAD) was our nation's insane Cold War nuclear weapons policy. Seeing no hope for true social justice transformation from Democrats or Republicans, a group of us—spearheaded by my partner—formed a new political party, the New Action Party for a Human Society. We had a set of party papers and positions, a newsletter, and multiracial, multiclass chapters in New York, Boston, and San Francisco. We wrote a fifty-year plan for taking political power. Yes, the plan was ambitious and bold, and some thought it was presumptuous, preposterous, naive, and even laughable. But we considered those negative attitudes to be expressions of widespread powerlessness that made people feel "You can't fight City Hall," or "That's the way things have always been," or "Poverty (or racism or warfare or environmental destruction) is too big for us to change." We persisted.

One part of the fifty-year plan stated that we needed to create new initiatives and programs to address people's real needs. Such programs, besides being potentially effective ways to relieve suffering and generate collective power, could serve to win hearts and minds—that way, down the road when we would be in a position to run for public office, people would say, "Oh, those folks have done great work. I trust them. They have my vote." We decided to focus on issues facing youth, since a core of us had been teachers and viewed youth as a great but wasted resource for our nation and for social justice work. So, with young people, we created the Youth Action Program in East Harlem, which implemented seven community improvement projects that were the ideas of local young people. One of those projects was to renovate abandoned buildings into affordable housing for low-income folks.

YouthBuild

The housing renovation project eventually grew into a highly successful, publicly funded, national program called YouthBuild.[2] Along the way, the New Action Party faded because creating and expanding YouthBuild became so complex and engrossing that we could not sustain the political party's development.

YouthBuild engages disconnected low-income young adults, ages sixteen to twenty-four, in full-time comprehensive yearlong education and employment training, through which they build affordable housing for homeless and low-income people in their neighborhoods and simultaneously work toward their own high school diploma or GED, while gaining experience and training as community leaders. They prepare for postsecondary education and good paying jobs in construction, while internalizing the twin ethics of national service and leadership for social change.

Inspired by our intention to contribute to the great movement for social justice, we started YouthBuild with a small program in East Harlem. Today there are about 220 programs in the nation's poorest communities, engaging nearly ten thousand young people each year, and supported by an annual federal appropriation of over one hundred million dollars. YouthBuild is now operating in seventeen other countries. Over the last thirty years, more than one hundred eighty thousand young people have built thirty-five thousand units of affordable housing, changing their own lives in the process.

YouthBuild weaves together elements of education and work experience, personal counseling, community service, and leadership development into a comprehensive approach to meet the needs and liberate the highest aspirations of young people. Unifying the YouthBuild program components is a philosophy of respect for the sacred value of every human being and belief that the power of love, coupled with opportunities to learn, earn, serve, and lead, will transform the identity and future prospects of low-income youth.

At YouthBuild, I had the chance to help develop resources, tools, and trainings on various aspects of oppression and liberation for the youth development field. "The Four I's of Oppression" and "Understanding Adultism," (included below) two pieces I wrote to illuminate these topics, have been published in various journals, college curricula, and movement training handbooks. I created the Youth-Build Academy for Transformation, which provided a large variety of trainings for all levels of YouthBuild staff from across the country. Lastly, for over eighteen years, I facilitated eight two-year multiracial cohorts of YouthBuild Directors Fellows Programs that explored race, culture, leadership, power, and healing. I am forever grateful for the learnings and friendships that emerged in these groups.

I stepped away from my work at YouthBuild at the end of 2015, after thirty years. To this day, it remains a vibrant, empowering, and transformative national and international program. I am extremely proud of YouthBuild and have immense gratitude to the young people and staff with whom I had the privilege to work. A more complete description of this amazing program is in my book, *YouthBuild's North Star: A Vision of Greater Potential*.

Expanding My View of Suffering and Healing

A few more experiences were pivotal in my education. My work in developing and serving as a staff person for Children of War—described in chapter 3—vastly expanded my understanding of suffering around the globe. I heard firsthand from young victims of war, genocide, apartheid, hatred, and unspeakable cruelty on massive scales. I learned how young people everywhere are innocent victims of adult madness. Children of War cemented my understanding of the prevalence, pervasiveness, and persistence of worldwide collective trauma that begs for collective healing.

As I also detailed in chapter 3, since 1971 I have practiced and taught Re-evaluation Counseling, an international peer counseling network that has done superb work around healing emotional wounds from racism, white supremacy, and other oppressions. Doing this inner work to transform my own racism has been immensely freeing and rewarding, and has allowed me to be ever more effective in anti-racism work and in building relationships of trust across race lines.

Over the years, I have benefited from racial justice and oppression trainings from the Interaction Institute for Social Change, National Coalition Building Institute, United to End Racism, and more recently, White Awake and East Point Peace Academy. I frequently read the thinking of BIPOC writers and activists and continue learning how to be a better and better ally.

In my role as a Buddhist Dharma teacher, given my background, I've had the opportunity to facilitate retreats and ongoing listening circles for White practitioners on understanding and healing our racism.

Finally, my own family includes my son, son-in-law, and grandson, who are all Chilean Indigenous or Latinx people; four godchildren, now adults, who are biracial—Black and White; and a Puerto Rican foster son, now in his fifties. Discussions of race and whiteness among us are never far away. I am blessed as a White person for the good fortune to have been taught, loved, and challenged by many People of Color in the intimacy of family, friendships, and work.

In reflecting back on my work life, it seems that in each phase I was trying to nurture mini Beloved Communities.

The Four I's of Oppression

Some decades ago, while working with YouthBuild USA, I formulated the following framework, "The Four I's of Oppression." It's not original to me, since I simply combined strands of understanding I gleaned from others into a digestible, easy-to-remember form. It is only one among many such frameworks that others have developed. It has been published in numerous handbooks, diversity manuals, and college curricula. It has been taught all over the world and its usefulness has been gratifying. I offer it as an overview to frame our exploration of this topic.

○

If any random group of human beings had a chance to listen to each other talk about the reality of their lives at a deep level, it would be clear that most, if not all, of them had suffered systemic disrespect and mistreatment simply because they grew up in a particular group in society. Without a choice, each of us is born into a set of intersecting social oppressions.

Looking deeply, we can see that all people are denied or have been denied one or more of the following: safety, justice, opportunity, freedom, or the development of their full humanness. This is not to say that all oppressions are equal, nor to wipe away accountability for damage caused by oppressor groups, nor to elevate suffering of certain oppressed groups as more important than the suffering of others. Oppression is different for each group and each person, and some forms are more damaging and vicious than others. People in some groups are the direct targets of mistreatment. People in other groups are coerced or offered "benefits" for playing oppressive roles toward others. However, all people have been forced into a more limited life by their societal conditioning. All people have had their share of systematic mistreatment, miseducation, and disrespect, and this has warped them to a greater or lesser extent.

Another way to say this is that each person has many social identities, some of which carry privileges and some of which force marginalization. For example, I grew up in a working poor family with a father struggling with a substance use disorder. Money worries and financial insecurity coupled with his emotional volatility created a lot of suffering for me. Being raised Catholic, and educated by strict nuns who told me I was sinful, created guilt and shame. And as a young person, I was subject to arbitrary and unfair discipline from my parents and teachers, with no room to defend myself or object without incurring more mistreatment. Also, as a young person I felt little or no respect from older people, who mostly showed no interest in me or belittled my ideas and accomplishments. In these roles, I was marginalized and subjected to the rule of adults, and had no real decision-making power in the family. I choose to conform to survive, rather than rebel and be further marginalized. From these identities I internalized feelings of powerlessness, unworthiness, and not being important or not belonging. This was a heavy emotional scarring that I'm still healing.

At the same time, I was and am straight, male, and White. Through these identities, as a boy I internalized a sense of being "better" than girls and People of Color. Even though I knew no People of Color when I was growing up, I saw demeaning images of People of Color on TV and in books, comics, and movies. As I grew into adulthood, I had many experiences where being a straight White man gave me distinct advantages. I felt safe to walk alone at night, unlike almost every woman I knew. I was not followed by security guards in stores, unlike many Black people. I generally felt protected by police, unlike most People of Color. As a heterosexual, I was never subjected to the discrimination and violence that LGBTQAI+ people experience. Whenever I was arrested in protest demonstrations, I was not mistreated and was given only a fine, unlike many BIPOC folks who risk jail or worse for protesting injustice. So, life-limiting harm and life-enhancing privilege live side by side in me. Though the details differ, this mix is true for most everyone.

Outlined below are four interrelated aspects of any oppression, which can help us understand how oppression is a system, not just prejudice. For example, when most people are asked what racism is, they say it is prejudice or discrimination against People of Color. This is certainly a part of it, but it is only the most visible, personally experienced part of a vast web of forces.

Ideological Oppression

First, any oppressive system has at its core the *idea* that one group is somehow better than another, and in some measure has the right to control the other group. This idea of being better gets elaborated in many ways: more intelligent, harder working, stronger, more capable, more noble, more deserving, more advanced, chosen, superior, and so on. The dominant group holds this idea about itself. And, of course, the opposite qualities are attributed to the other group: stupid, lazy, weak, incompetent, worthless, less deserving, backward, inferior, and so on.

Institutional Oppression

The *idea* that one group is better than another group and has the right to control the other gets embedded in the institutions of society—the laws, the legal system and police practice, the education system and schools, hiring policies, public policies, housing development, media images, and political power. When a woman earns two thirds of what a man makes in the same job, it is institutionalized sexism. When one out of every four young Black men is currently in jail, on parole, or on probation, it is institutionalized racism. When gay or lesbian folks were banned from the military, it was institutionalized gay oppression. When younger people are excluded from having a voice in almost every area that affects their lives, it is institutionalized oppression of younger people, or adultism.

Interpersonal Oppression

As the *idea* that one group is better than another and has the right to control the other gets structured into institutions, this gives permission and reinforcement for individual members of the dominant group to personally disrespect or mistreat individuals in the oppressed group. Interpersonal racism is what White people do to People of Color up close—the racist jokes, the stereotypes, the beatings and harassment, the threats, the full range of personal acts of discrimination. Similarly, interpersonal sexism is what men do to women—the sexual abuse and harassment, the violence directed at women, the belittling or ignoring of women's thinking, the pornography, the sexist jokes.

Most people in the dominant group are not consciously oppressive. They have internalized the negative messages about other groups and consider these attitudes quite normal.

These kinds of oppressive attitudes and behaviors are reinforced by institutional arrangements. This helps to clarify the confusion around what some claim to be "reverse racism." People of Color can have prejudices against and anger toward an individual White person or White people in general. They can act out those feelings in destructive and hurtful ways. But in almost every case, this acting out will be severely punished. The force of the police and the courts, or gangs of Whites "getting even," will come crashing down on them. Even without acting out, Black and Latinx men in particular are routinely subject to "stop and frisk," being detained without bail, and being killed by police even while unarmed; all of this is carried out by the institutional force of the police and mostly upheld by the court system.

A simple definition of racism, as a system, might be: racism = prejudice + power.

With this definition of the systemic nature of racism, People of Color cannot be racist toward White people. They can have racist attitudes and can act as agents of racism toward other People of

Color. And they can have racial prejudices or animus toward White people. But they don't have the institutional power to enforce mistreatment based on their prejudices. The same formula holds true for all forms of oppression. The dominant group's mistreatment of the target group is embedded in and backed up by society's institutions and other forms of power. In the same way, women cannot be sexist toward men, young people cannot be adultist, LGBTQIA+ people cannot be heterosexist, and so on.

Internalized Oppression

The fourth way oppression works is within the groups of people who suffer the most from the mistreatment. Oppressed people internalize the *ideology* of inferiority, they see it reflected in the *institutions*, they experience disrespect *interpersonally* from members of the dominant group, and they eventually come to *internalize* the negative messages about themselves. If we have been told we are stupid and worthless and have been treated as if we were stupid and worthless all our lives, it is not surprising that we would come to believe it.

Oppression always begins from *outside* the oppressed group, but by the time it gets *internalized*, the external oppression need hardly be felt for the damage to be done. If people from the oppressed group feel bad about themselves, and because of the nature of the system, they do not have the power to direct those feelings back toward the dominant group without receiving more blows, then there are only two places to dump those feelings—on themselves and on the people in the same group. Thus, people in any target group must struggle hard to keep from feeling heavy emotions of powerlessness or despair. They often tend to put down themselves and others, including their own children, in ways that mirror the oppressive messages they have gotten all their lives. Acting out internalized oppression runs the gamut from passivity to violent aggression.

It is important to understand that some of the internalized patterns of behavior originally developed to keep people alive—they had real survival value. For example, many an enslaved mother systematically beat her male child to break his strong will, so he would "submit" to the horrors of the slave master and not be killed. Some claim that the practice of "the dozens"—a game of exchanging ever-sharper insults without losing control—is a direct descendant of slavery conditioning to survive brutal insults.

For illustrative purposes, here are a few examples of internalized oppression: Women attacking a woman leader for stepping out and raising an issue. Bullying among young people. Low-income White people blaming low-income immigrants of color for wealth inequity. Black people calling other Black people names like "Uncle Tom" or "sellout" or "trying to act White." LGBTQIA+ folks disrespecting trans people.

On the way to eliminating oppression, each oppressed group has to undo the internalized beliefs, attitudes, and behaviors that stem from oppression so that the group can build unity among

The Four I's of Oppression

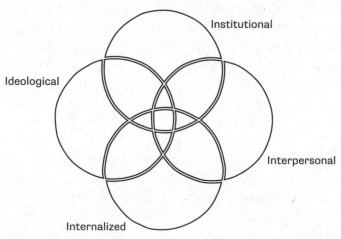

The Four I's of Oppression

people; support its leaders; feel proud of its history, contributions, and potential; develop the strength to clean its own house of cultural patterns that hold the group back; set high standards; oppose corruption; and organize itself into an effective force for social change.

It should be clear that none of these four aspects of oppression exists separately. As the diagram suggests, each is interrelated with the others. It is crucial to see any oppression as a system. Challenging oppression in any of the four aspects will affect the other three.[3]

Ending Racism Is Inseparable from Ending Climate Change

> *It needs to be said that, generally speaking, there is little in the way of clear awareness of the problems which especially affect the excluded. . . . Today, however, we have to realize that a true ecological approach always becomes a social approach; it must integrate questions of justice in debates on the environment so as to hear both the cry of the earth and the cry of the poor.*

—Pope Francis

We are facing multiple social crises that highlight the interconnections between issues previously viewed as separate. For example, climate change is a racial justice issue, a resource extraction issue, a food security issue, a national security issue, an economic justice issue, a public health issue, a population issue, a democracy issue, an immigration issue, a technology issue, a gender equity issue, a species loss issue, a rights of the Earth issue, and so on. Anything we care about is related to climate change and environmental degradation. The silver lining of climate change, if we can grace it with such a positive term, is that we now have the real and necessary mandate of knitting together an integrated awareness that links all these issues into a new understanding of our interconnectedness.

Environmental Injustice

The struggle for racial justice is part of moving toward collective awakening, and it is inextricably intertwined with climate justice. To paraphrase wisdom I heard from Zen teacher Rev. angel Kyodo williams, the reason we continue to degrade the Earth is that we continue to degrade each other. With this insight, she succinctly clarified the link between climate crisis and racism. As we heal the wounds of racism and white supremacy, we will also be healing that which keeps us in unhealthy relationship with the Earth. Acknowledging and healing from the wounds of racism needs to be high on our collective agenda.

The crux of environmental injustice is that the people who have contributed the least to the environmental catastrophe—mostly the Global South, mostly People of Color—are bearing the brunt of climate change. Pacific Islanders are experiencing the effects of rising sea levels. Sub-Saharan West African subsistence farmers are feeling the simultaneous erratic effects of extreme drought and flooding. In the United States, environmental racism is rampant. For example, half of the people who live near hazardous waste are People of Color. Black children suffer from lead poisoning at twice the rate of White children. Black and Brown children have the highest rates of asthma. Frontline communities of color are suffering most from hurricanes like Katrina and Sandy and paying for the cleanup.[4] It is estimated that climate disasters will kill between twelve and forty-five times more people in poorer countries than in wealthy ones.[5]

Hop Hopkins, Director of Organizational Transformation at the Sierra Club, offers a few more concrete examples of environmental racism in his 2020 article, "Racism Is Killing the Planet:"

> When Amy Cooper, a white woman, has an encounter with
> a Black man bird-watching in Central Park and calls the

police   that is white supremacy. When a petroleum pipeline corporation calls in the police to bash Indigenous water protectors at Standing Rock, that too is white supremacy. When a kid in East Oakland gets asthma from car pollution because her neighborhood is surrounded by freeways, that is white supremacy. When the Dakota Access Pipeline is built through Native land because the neighboring white communities fought to keep it out of theirs, that is white supremacy. When the United States pours carbon pollution into the air, knowing that people in countries that have contributed much less to the climate crisis will face the worst of the consequences, that is white supremacy. When big polluters try to buy our democracy so they can keep making money by devaluing the lives of People of Color, that is white supremacy.[6]

When we talk about justice, we need to think about how we can rectify, mitigate, and remedy the tragic impacts of environmental racism and injustice.

Viewpoints about Oppression and Liberation

A Beloved Community is only possible in a context of overcoming and healing oppression.

Following are notions that were developed through working on issues of oppression and that help me hold fast to a long-term vision for liberation. In offering these, I am keenly aware that my views are filtered through my social locations as a cis-gendered White man, raised working-poor but now middle-class. Therefore, these ideas are limited but perhaps offer some clarity.

All people have inherent worth. Buddhists might say that each person has Buddha nature. Christians might say we have Christ nature. Wiccans might call it Divine Mother nature. We all emerge from the same mysterious life force. Therefore, all notions that divide us, cause us to discriminate against each other, or pit us against one another are rooted in fear and ignorance.

All human beings become damaged by oppression. This happens because we were born into an oppressive world, full of suffering, corruption, and separation. Simply by virtue of belonging to a particular social group, we experience mistreatment, discrimination, misinformation, and miseducation. Systemic harm damages every person, not in the same way nor to the same extent, and it prepares us all to take our place in the interlocking worldwide system of institutionalized suffering.

Some results of oppressions are obvious. Clearly, racism has caused irreparable damage to Black people, Indigenous people, and People of Color the world over. Less obvious is that the full humanity of White people has also been damaged by the ugly, cruel legacy of white supremacy. Not in the same way or to the same extent, by any means. But White people have been conditioned to play a role directly or indirectly in maintaining a racist system, and this has instilled fear, guilt, and shame on the one hand, or a sense of superiority and entitlement on the other hand, all of which serves to unnaturally separate White people from People of Color.

Similarly, patriarchy and sexism have oppressed women in horrific ways for millennia. Less obvious is the reality that men are oppressed, not by women but by patriarchy, which warps men's humanity and tells them they shouldn't cry or show fear and vulnerability (at least in Western culture). Men are separated from the fullness of their nature, and out of that fundamental hurt, they hurt women. The oppression of men is not the same as, nor as severe as, the oppression of women. However, all people are damaged by patriarchy and sexism.[7] Every kind of oppression has a similar gradient of damage to all.

Oppressions overlap and reinforce each other. Classism, which existed long before capitalism or white supremacy, is a system based on the false notion that wealthy and powerful people are superior to people with less power and material wealth. This setup has existed for tens of thousands of years. The caste system in India existed long before modern racism. The ruling group in any particular culture or historical time has found many ways to protect and maintain their power and wealth by keeping all other people divided among themselves so they could pose no threat to the rulers' power. All forms of oppression were devised to keep the majority of people suffering and thereby disunited and too weak to threaten the unjust system of the day: slavery, feudalism, and capitalism were economic arrangements that served the owning class in different historical periods. Anti-Semitism has been used for two thousand years to deflect rising popular political discontent away from the owning class and toward Jewish people, keeping them persecuted and insecure wherever they settled. Patriarchy, throughout the world and since time immemorial, has kept most girls and women enslaved, disenfranchised, uneducated, victimized by rape and violence, or marginalized.

White supremacy is a fairly new oppression. According to my understanding, although racist ideas existed in fifteenth-century Europe, modern white racism was not encoded into a legal system until the mid-1600s in colonial America. Back then, no people were called "White" people. European immigrants and their descendants were known by their country of origin: they were English or Irish or French. Until the mid-1600s, working-class Europeans, freed Black people, and Native Indigenous people worked together, intermarried, were good neighbors, and even held elected office. But as these people began to form coalitions and organize against wealthy plantation owners for a fairer share of the wealth, their violent uprisings threatened the power of American colonial plantation owners. These local militia seized plantations, burned down the capitol in Richmond, Virginia, and scared the owning class. So the colonial government of Virginia passed laws that first used the word "White" to identify people. These new laws, which were then

adopted by other colonies, gave White people a few more benefits than freed Black or Indigenous people. For example, Whites
could own property, own guns, and employ Black or Indigenous
people. Black and Indigenous people could not. The government
also made it a crime for a White person to marry a Black person,
and if a White woman had a child with a Black man, she and the
child would become enslaved for the rest of their lives. These laws
drove a wedge between people who had been natural allies.

Today, working people of all races are a huge majority of the population and have many interests in common. But because we have let
ourselves be fooled and fractured into conflicting groups, we remain
too weak and powerless to challenge the rigged system. We need
each other to build the America that I believe you and I both want.

Today, it is clear how this divide-and-conquer strategy is working. All forms of othering keep us divided and powerless while the
owning class stays in power. Furthermore, white supremacy is a
global phenomenon, thanks to European colonialism. A Cambodian friend told me that in Cambodia, Cambodians with lighter
skin were and are treated better than those with darker skin,
because the French brought their brand of racism there. Colonial
powers did that all over the developing world.

**Oppression is maintained by instilling ideas of inferiority and
superiority.** In addition to state power and other structures of
oppression, these systems are maintained by instilling messages of
superiority and entitlement in those who were born or worked their
way into the favored group, and messages of inferiority and unworthiness in the majority of the working-class low-wealth groups or
otherwise unfavored groups. People are conditioned to play their
roles in the system. In my view, the people at the top of the power
pyramid are not naturally greedy, selfish, or cruel. They are inherently good people who have been thoroughly conditioned through
indoctrination, rewards, coercion, social structures, and privilege
to believe they are better than most others, and to believe they are

obligated to obtain ever more wealth and power or they will be worthy of contempt from their parents or peers. Likewise, those who have the least wealth or power are not naturally lazy, ignorant, or unreliable. They have been thoroughly conditioned through discrimination, prejudice, policies, power, and punishment to feel inferior; further, their labor and land have been exploited to enrich the owners in a way that imposes powerlessness on the poor and working classes. And most folks in middle-income classes are conditioned to think that if they work hard enough or act good enough or at least don't cause trouble, they might be able to have some modicum of wealth, status, and power. A few do, but most don't achieve more than minimum security, which is often at risk, given the realities of an uncaring capitalist economy. As outlined in "The Four I's of Oppression" above, this idea of superiority and inferiority gets embedded into social institutions, acted out in personal interactions, and painfully internalized.

Oppression can be eliminated. I hold fast to the goal of liberation of all people from ignorance, delusion, and oppression. Just as racism did not always exist and will one day be a relic of history, the same is true of all oppressions. They will necessarily be transformed on the way to the Beloved Community. It also helps me to believe that there is no inherent conflict between any two people or any races or countries. Distress, misperceptions, hurt, and unwholesome patterns, combined with unjust social policies, cause us to forget our essential relatedness. Even holding out the idea that we have no innate conflicts can make it easier to form alliances.

There are pathways for liberation. It also seems clear to me that no oppressed group can achieve liberation on its own. Women need the active support of men to challenge patriarchy. Black people need White people to be anti-racist. Jews need gentiles to combat anti-Semitism. The same is true for all oppressed groups—we need alliances with people from the oppressor group to the extent possible.

For any oppressed group to attain its liberation, I think at least four interconnected things need to happen:

- Many people in an oppressed group need to heal from the internalized damage done by oppression in order to think and act more clearly, undo feelings of powerlessness, and thereby unleash enormous collective power.

- Members of the group need to create and agree on a program for freedom from that form of oppression. This needs to include working to challenge oppressive laws, policies, and practices in the economic system and the government, as well as advocating for redress of past injustices due to oppression.

- Then they must forge strong relationships with allies and supporters from other groups for their platform.

- Finally, they need to support the ending of oppression for all people.

- Each of these elements is multitiered and complex. Even having this framework sketched can be helpful.[8]

Building unity is necessary. Currently, the powers that be are happy to have us fighting over whose lives matter, or critical race theory, or pronouns, or vaccines. As important as these are, our contentious focus on them keeps us divided and weakened enough to prevent sufficient unity to transform society into a classless Beloved Community that would include, welcome, and value everyone. The concentration of power and wealth is in the hands of very few. Maybe a thousand people, worldwide control more wealth than the overwhelming majority of humanity, and thereby control economies, governments, and power. This is an immoral and inhuman arrangement. Yet it is possible for us to transform it. Why aren't we focusing our collective attention on changing this structure? (I also want to be clear that those in the owning class are human beings who had to be miseducated, conditioned, trained, and hurt enough to play their roles as agents of oppression. In addition to being stopped from harming more, they need healing too.)

Building relationships, alliances, and common cause across racial lines is necessary for the big work of transforming classism and economic oppression. We need to end racism, and I believe it will end in this century. But we need to end racism in the context of the liberation of all people. When one person suffers, all people suffer, and no place is safe until all places are safe, as great teachers such as Thich Nhat Hanh have taught.

Today in the United States, racism goes hand in hand with classism, sexism, and all the other "isms." There have been ongoing debates about which one is primary or most important. These debates are fruitless. All need transformation. All serve the overarching economic oppression.

Tools toward Collective Liberation

On the way to realizing the Beloved Community, what is required is radical transformation at the base of our civilization. This means creating an economy that promotes well-being and happiness and is not based on greed. It means realizing a vision of social fairness, compassion, and cooperation where the "isms" have been healed and eliminated. It means reintegrating humans with the rest of the natural world and knowing our place in the family of life. It means cultivating a human culture that encourages contentedness, sufficiency, caring, curiosity, and creativity.

This transformation seems like a dream, given the current trends. Yet, slow and incremental reforms will not do it. As Greta Thunberg, the young Swedish climate activist, says about the governmental climate crisis approach, "This is not sufficient; our house is on fire."[9] Hoping that technology or the market or human decency or enough political will can save us from the worst is not sufficient either. The required change calls for a radical shift in consciousness coupled with deep systemic changes in our behavior, policies, and institutional structures, as well as correspondingly deep inner changes in our feelings of powerlessness, the unconscious biases that make us feel superior or inferior, and the underlying conditioning that makes us feel separate. Those of us from non-Indigenous cultures can learn much from the resistance and ancient wisdom of Indigenous people all over the world who have tried their best to remain in harmonious relationship to the natural world despite the colonialist destruction of their cultures.

Down through history, poor and working people have led periodic uprisings to oppose their mistreatment. Often these uprisings were crushed by state power. Some turned into revolutions that shifted the political power. But because the new leaders did not have safety or methods for healing their past hurts, and the transformation of consciousness was incomplete, they tended to recreate new forms of tyranny, so the oppression continued, even if in slightly less severe ways. In the twentieth century, this cycle has played out in Russia, China, Cuba, and South Africa.

I often heard Thich Nhat Hanh say that humans are not the enemy; ignorance is the enemy. As a Catholic boy, I was taught to hate the sin but love the sinner. Re-evaluation Counseling (RC) taught me to separate the person from their patterns, or in Buddhist terms, their irrational, unwholesome habit energies. Harvey Jackins, the founder of RC, taught me that there are no oppressor humans; there are only oppressor patterns, and inside each oppressor pattern there is a good human being doing stupid or evil things that he or she can't help.

What follows are two approaches I have found extremely useful in liberation work.

1. A Framework for Personal Liberation Work

In YouthBuild, we developed practical methods to address oppression. In 1992, Richard Henry, director of a YouthBuild program in San Francisco, said to me that if we were not deliberately helping young people deal with the effects of racism on their lives, we were wasting their time. As we thought about what this would mean in a program setting, I found myself expanding this challenge into a four-part framework for doing personal change work around all oppressions. Originally meant for youth programs, it fits many groups in society. The version here is a generalized framework.

In short, the framework says that to deal with oppression holistically, people need ways to *inform* themselves about oppression issues, *heal* from the emotional hurts caused by oppression, learn effective ways to *cope* with ongoing daily oppression, and *get involved in efforts to eliminate* all forms of oppression and injustice.

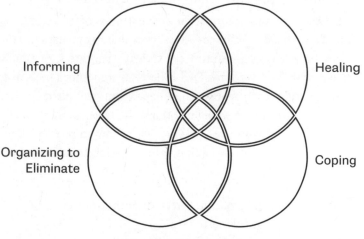

Liberation Framework

Inform: Create a Coherent Understanding of Oppression

There is much truth in the adage that knowledge is power. Knowledge helps us understand ourselves and others and navigate the world. From a certain perspective, the history of the world has been shaped by the mistreatment and disrespect of one group after another; by tyranny, slavery, oppression, injustice, and cruelty; by humans hurting other humans, causing untold suffering. Probably most of the ways people feel bad about themselves come from having been raised in a particular group, gender, race, religion, class, or nationality. It helps to develop a clear understanding of what oppression is as a whole system, as in "The Four I's of Oppression" outline: ideology, institutional components, interpersonal dynamics, and internalization. An analysis should also break down in simple graspable terms how different oppressions are related to each other, and what, if any, are their common roots. It also would include some history and facts around oppression and sketch out the key elements of a process of liberation from oppression.

Heal: Release the Emotional Hurts of Oppression

No matter how much information we have, most of us are walking around with huge loads of emotional hurt due to oppression. This weighs heavily on us; we must try to learn and grow, or simply survive, while carrying this load. The pain sometimes boils over in rage or stifles us in depression or hopelessness. It makes us less effective in life than we would be otherwise. In our work with ourselves and other people, we need to learn how to provide times and spaces to release some of that pain, to create enough safety to share the feelings.

Manage: Develop Effective Ways of Handling Oppression in the Moment

No matter how good our analysis is or how much healing we have done, oppression is waiting for us just around the corner, every day, in real-life terms. We live and work in an oppressive society. There are many ways we can learn to deal more effectively with oppression. For example: learning to handle sexually harassing behavior; studying one's legal rights in cases of discrimination; learning to act or dress counter to stereotypes; practicing different ways to interrupt an oppressive joke or comment; role-playing various ways of handling a racist boss without getting fired; strategizing how to build relationships with personal allies who will defend or speak up for you; and so on. We need to get increasingly skilled at challenging the legitimacy of oppression while surviving and managing our lives.

Organize: Engage to Eliminate Oppression

Certainly, we must understand, heal from, and survive the current oppressive system, but we also need to organize to eradicate all forms of oppression. It is useful to hold a firm position that oppression can and must be eliminated. It may not happen in our lifetimes, but we have to hold out this vision as an eventuality. The question is: how can we become more skilled, committed, and engaged in eliminating oppression, and in helping others to do the same? Tending to the first three steps above will help, but what kind of organizing can move it beyond survival to action for change?

2. A Safe Process for Learning about and Healing from Oppression

Over decades of my healing work within the Re-evaluation Counseling community, I had the opportunity to learn a great deal about people who were different from me through a simple but elegant approach. When we gathered in conferences or workshops, we participated in the following three-part process.

Separate Caucus Groups

During the first evening, in the whole group, we collectively wrote a list of every identity anyone wished to name. Then each person chose the one that was most pertinent to them at that time, and we all gathered in self-chosen identity groups. Mindful that each person had more than one identity, over time, people chose other identities to explore in the same way. In their groups, each person had a turn to respond to four questions about their chosen identity:

1. What do I love about being a _____ person?

2. What has been difficult about being a _____ person?

3. What do I never want to hear, see, or experience about _____ people from others who are not a _____ person?

4. How can others support _____ people in their liberation?

Sharing in the Whole Group

The whole group reconvened, and a panel composed of representatives from each group was invited up front to share their answers to these questions. A respectful listening atmosphere was created so the whole group could listen and learn in a relatively safe setting. Many tears of loss, expressions of anger, or light bulbs of insight resulted for the people sharing and listening. It was a profound learning and healing process that built awareness across groups.

Writing and Agreeing on a Program for Liberation

The separate identity groups reconvened and began drafting a program for their group's liberation, which was shared widely for feedback and elaboration. This was an iterative process because there was no final program. However, envisioning a world free from racism, for example, and outlining concrete steps to get there stimulated thinking, hope, and focused action.

Several factors helped this process work, and they are replicable. One is a shared understanding that all people suffer from oppression in different ways. This needs to be understood and agreed on early in the process. Another factor is that the process begins with sharing within one's chosen identity group. This provides safety for being honest and opening up to healing internalized hurt and trauma, which is more difficult to do in groups that include people from other dominant groups. Then, sharing in the larger group in a safe facilitated process allows for deep listening without the listeners becoming defensive. When folks from a particular identity group receive the respectful, warm attention of the whole gathering while they share, they often cry about the pride they feel in having a certain identity or the hurts they've endured. This, in turn, can open the minds and hearts of listeners. It becomes clear to everyone listening how much all people have suffered, and how nearly universal are the experiences of feeling or being mistreated, misunderstood, disrespected, and excluded. Naturally, compassion arises in all directions. We can see each other as beautiful beings who have been hurt and who are trying to find a way home. The desire to help with each other's liberation comes more easily. As one leader put it, "We can't make it all the way home without all of us."

This simple, elegant, and safe process can be adapted to many groups—within our religious congregations, at work, in trade unions, in our social justice organizations. In any group, there are many identities and dynamics of oppression to explore, even when people in the group appear to be similar. For example, within any racial grouping there are diverse cultures, religious and political beliefs, immigration backgrounds, gender issues, visible and invisible physical disabilities, and so on. We have much to learn about each other.

Adultism: A Foundational Form of Oppression

I'd like to highlight a little-known form of oppression called "adultism"—the systematic mistreatment and disrespect of young people just because of their youth. Although it is not widely understood, adultism is a nearly universal human experience that shapes and damages all young people, who then carry that damage into adulthood. It is critical to identify and challenge adultism as a pervasive force that conditions humans to participate in interlocking systemic oppressions.

In the YouthBuild leadership program that I helped guide for over thirty years, in order to create conditions for young people to transform their lives, we had to comprehend and counteract adultism. We trained program staff and young people to recognize it and to develop a culture of respect and inclusion, which contradicted many of the conditions of disrespect they met in their schooling and environment.

Understanding Adultism

Most of us care about young people. Those of us who are educators, youth workers, or parents want to be effective and have good relationships with young people. We are satisfied when things go well. We feel bad when our relationships go sour. Sometimes we scratch our heads in dismay when, despite our best efforts and concern, we find ourselves in conflict with our children or students. We sense that larger dynamics are at work that we can't quite see. To be successful in our work with young people, we must understand a particular condition of youth: young people are often mistreated and disrespected simply because they are young.

Adultism refers to behaviors and attitudes based on the assumption that adults are wiser and better than young people, and are entitled to control young people and generally do whatever they want to young people without their agreement. This mistreatment is reinforced by social institutions, laws, customs, and attitudes.

Except for incarcerated people and a few other institutionalized groups, young people are more controlled than any other group in society. Most children are told what to eat, what to wear, when to go to bed, when they can talk, which friends are okay, when to be in the house, and that they must go to school. Even as they grow older, their ideas and opinions are not valued; they are punished at the will or whim of adults; their emotions are considered immature. In addition, adults reserve the right to punish, threaten, hit, take away privileges, and ostracize young people when such actions are deemed instrumental in controlling or disciplining them.

If a group of adults were treated this way, we would all agree that their oppression was almost total. However, for the most part, the adult world considers this treatment of young people acceptable because we were treated in much the same way, and we internalized the idea that "this is the way you treat kids." We need to hold adultism up to a bright light.

The Heart of It

The essence of adultism is disrespect of the young. Our society typically considers young people to be inferior to adults, and less important. It does not take young people seriously and does not include them as decision makers in the broader life of their communities.

Obviously, adults are enormously important and necessary in the life of every young person. This fact may make it difficult to understand adultism. And not everything the adult world does in relation to young people is adultist. It is certainly true that children and young people need love, guidance, rules, discipline, teaching, role modeling, nurturing, and protection. Childhood and adolescence are a steady series of developmental stages, each of which has a distinct set of needs, issues, and difficulties. For example, a three-year-old needs a different amount of sleep than a fifteen-year-old does; what works to physically restrain a seven-year-old will not work with an eighteen-year-old; and how you explain conception and birth to an inquisitive toddler is quite different from how you explain these to a sexually active teenager.

Differing cultural, ethnic, gender, class, and religious approaches to these developmental stages can further complicate the identification of adultism. For example, public signs of affection between boys may be normally practiced in one culture and almost forbidden in another culture. Adults' responses may be considered either appropriate or oppressive, depending on the cultural lens through which we view the boys' actions and the adults' reactions.

The point is that no single act or policy or custom or belief, in itself, is necessarily adultist. Something can be labeled adultist if it involves a consistent pattern of disrespect and mistreatment that has any or all of the following effects on young people: an undermining of self-confidence and self-esteem; an increasing sense of worthlessness; an increasing feeling of powerlessness; a consistent experience of not being taken seriously; a diminishing ability to function well in the world; a growing negative self-concept; increasingly destructive acting out; increasingly self-destructive "acting in" (getting sick frequently, developing health conditions, attempting suicide, depression, and so on); feeling unloved or unwanted.

Certainly, these serious conditions do not entirely stem from adultism. Other factors, such as sexism, racism, poverty, and physical or mental disability, may also contribute. But systematic, prolonged disrespect and mistreatment simply because of being young are major sources of trouble.

Evidence that Adultism Exists

Unlike well-documented, widely acknowledged "isms" such as racism and sexism, the concept of adultism is not widely understood or accepted as a reality. There is certainly much research and literature on children and youth, but extraordinarily little of it concludes that young people are an oppressed group in our society, with parallels to other such groups. Therefore, I would like to draw forth examples, primarily from the United States, to point to the reality of adultism.

Consider how the following comments are disrespectful. What are the assumptions behind each of them? "You're so smart for fifteen." "When are you going to grow up?" "Don't touch that, you'll break it!" "As long as you are in my house, you'll do it." "You're being childish." "You're so stupid (clumsy, inconsiderate, etc.)." "Go to your room!" "You are too old for that." "You're not old enough." "Oh, it's only puppy love." "What do you know? You haven't experienced anything." "It's just a stage. You'll outgrow it." Yelling: "Don't ever yell at your mother like that!" Saying about a baby: "She doesn't understand anything." Innumerable similar comments reflect adults' low expectations of young people.

Reflection Questions

Do you remember hearing any of these statements as a younger person? How did it make you feel?

Disrespect toward young people takes many forms. There is explicitly oppressive treatment in the form of physical and sexual abuse; the US Centers for Disease Control report that one in seven children in the United States has experienced childhood abuse or neglect in the past year.[10] There is also a range of nonphysical punishments or threats: being routinely criticized, yelled at, invalidated, insulted, intimidated, or made to feel guilty, with the effect of undermining a child's self-respect; and being arbitrarily or unfairly grounded or denied privileges. If young people protest their mistreatment, they are often subjected to more punishment.

Young people are denied control and often are not even allowed influence over most of the decisions that affect their bodies, their space, and their possessions. For example, most adults think they can pick up little children or kiss them or pinch their cheeks or touch their hair without asking, or without it being mutual. Adults can often be seen grabbing things out of children's hands without asking. Would you do these kinds of things to an adult peer?

Most young people know that in a disagreement with an adult, their word will not be believed over the adult's. Most adults talk down to children, as if children could not understand them. Adults often talk about a young person in the young person's presence as if he or she were not there. Many adults lay down rules or give young people orders to do things with no explanation. Adults, in general, do not really listen to young people, do not take the concerns of a young person as seriously as they would an adult's concerns, and have a hard time perceiving young people's thinking as worthy of adult respect or on par with the quality of adult thinking. Yet young people are expected to listen to adults all the time.

Adolescents are frequently followed by security guards in stores, chased by police from parks or gathering places for no good reason, and assumed by passing adults to be "up to no good." The media often promote negative images and stereotypes of them, especially of urban youth and Black youth.

Adultism plays out in our educational system, as young people in the United States are forced to go to school for twelve years whether school is an effective learning environment for them or not. They are forced by the law and by their parents, except for those who exercise the demanding option of home schooling. If their spirit, energy, or learning style does not dovetail with the prevailing teacher, school, or educational philosophy, they begin to fail, have "special needs," are tracked, and may eventually leave and be labeled a dropout. Throughout the twelve years, students have little to no voice, no power, and no decision-making avenues to implement changes. While society's motivation of providing education for all its young people is laudable, the school system as an institution perpetuates adultism.

Some young people do well in school; some find school to be a safe refuge from a dysfunctional home; some flourish and excel. And schools are staffed by many creative, caring, courageous teachers who love young people and love sharing learning. But it is more typical that schools subject students to rigid control through the use of hall passes, detention, suspension, expulsion, and other penalties, and in recent years, having police in the schools. Any community needs rules to live by, but the rules in most school communities are *imposed* on young people and enforced by adult staff. Students are forced to accept the grading system, which causes them to internalize a lifelong view of themselves as "smart" or "average" or "dumb"—with profound impacts on many aspects of their lives. However, students do not get to officially grade teachers. If a student receives an F, it is assumed the student failed, not the teacher.

Adultism also manifests in multiple societal institutions. For example, young people do not have the same legal rights as adults. There is a separate set of laws for them. Of course, some laws specifically protect young people from mistreatment, but other laws unduly restrict their life and freedom. Many communities have curfew ordinances that apply to young people but not adults. In divorce cases, until a recent landmark custody case, young people were not permitted to have a voice in deciding which parent, if either, they wished to live with.

Another institutional example is the absence of socially responsible, productive, and connected roles for young people in most societies. In the United States, they find few jobs, no policy-making roles, few influential youth councils, no positions of political power, and no high expectations of their contributions to society. On the other hand, the youth market is exploited for profit as the manufacturing, alcohol, social media, and entertainment industries manipulate styles, fads, popularity, and other aspects of mass youth culture.

The Emotional Legacy

Most of these examples were reported to me by young people. Consistently, they say that the main message they get from the adult world is that they are not as important as adults; they do not feel they are taken seriously; they have little or no power. They say the emotional legacy of being treated this way for years is a heavy load, and it can include any or all the following: anger, feelings of powerlessness, insecurity, depression, lack of self-confidence, lack of self-respect, hopelessness, and feeling unloved and unwanted.

How do these feelings impact young people's behavior, especially as they grow into adolescence and early adulthood? Some act out by bullying, being prone to violence, rebelling against the "norm," running away from home. Others "act in" by becoming self-destructive through alcohol and drug abuse, depression, suicide. Some gain a sense of belonging or safety by joining a gang, a clique, a club, teams. Some isolate themselves, feel lonely, don't ask for help, don't have close relationships, don't trust. Again, adultism is not the only source of such behaviors, but it surely plays a major role.

Many adults lay on young people their own accumulation of disappointments, losses, smashed dreams, unaccepted love, and other painful experiences. For example, out of his hurts, my father repeatedly told me, "Growing up is giving up. You'd better get used to it." And, "Don't talk too loud or walk too tall, and if you have any dreams, better keep them small." Many of us have heard older people express similar statements to us or other young people. Hearing such crippling messages time after time, young people gradually come to believe them.

A Link to Other Forms of Oppression

There is another important reason for understanding and challenging adultism. The many ways we were disrespected and mistreated, over time, robbed us of vast amounts of our human power, access to our feelings, confidence in our thinking and ability to act, and enjoyment of living. The pain we experienced as young people helped condition us to play one of two roles as we got older: to accept further mistreatment as women, as People of Color, as workers; or to flip to the other side of the relationship and act in oppressive ways toward others who are in less powerful positions.

A simple illustration might help make this clear. Imagine a sixth grader is humiliated by the teacher in front of the class for not doing a math problem correctly. He feels disrespected. The recess bell rings. He is fuming. He goes outside and picks on someone to get his feelings out. Who does he pick on? Someone smaller or younger. So it goes: the sixth grader picks on the fifth grader. The fifth grader turns and knocks down the third grader. The third grader goes home and picks on his little sister. The little sister kicks the cat.

Mistreatment is passed down a line of physical power, bigger to smaller, and often older to younger. The significance of this early experience becomes clearer when it is generalized to other forms of abuse of power. It is a clinical truism that men who were routinely beaten as little boys often grow up to beat their partners or children. Similarly, White people, disrespected as children, turn the same attitude—embellished with misinformation and institutionalized white supremacy—on People of Color. If a person had not been disrespected and mistreated repeatedly in their youth, they would not willingly accept being treated that way as they got older, nor would they willingly heap disrespect on others. Those who have been bullied often become bullies. Those who have been abused often become abusers. This is a pervasive and lasting effect of adultism.

Adultism, racism, sexism, and other "isms" reinforce each other. The ways young people are treated or mistreated are inseparable from their class, gender, and ethnic background. But being disrespected simply because of being young has similar impacts across diverse backgrounds.

Adultism is a pervasive and difficult form of mistreatment to identify, challenge, and eliminate precisely because every human being has experienced it. Whatever the degree of severity or cultural variety, most people consider adultist behavior to be natural and normal.

Implications for Adults Working with Young People

The set of behaviors, attitudes, policies, and practices we have labeled adultism gets in the way of effective youth-adult partnerships. It is useful for adults to reflect on our interactions with young people for signs of unintended disrespect in tone, content, or assumptions. For those of us who work in schools or youth programs, I recommend that we reexamine the program practices, policies, and power relationships through the lens of noticing adultism, and make needed adjustments.

These guidelines might improve our relationships with young people and counteract the effects of adultism:

○ Listen attentively to young people. Listen when they talk about their thoughts, experiences, and feelings.

○ Ask questions. Ask what they think about everything.

○ Step back. Curb the inclination to take over. Support the initiatives of young people.

○ Validate their thinking. Welcome their ideas.

○ Be willing to accept that they will make mistakes. Putting their ideas into practice will bring mixed results. They will learn. We need to learn to support their process of taking leadership.

○ Change the power relationships wherever appropriate. As an adult, find ways to refrain from using authority, making the final decision, or being the real power behind a decision.

○ At the same time, do not thrust young people into decision-making and leadership positions without training, practice, and understanding of their responsibilities. Otherwise, they will be set up for frustration, confusion, failure, and humiliation.

○ Always respect all young people, no matter what their age, and expect them to respect each other at all ages. This is the starting point for reversing internalized disrespect.

○ Have high expectations of their potential and positively assess their current abilities. Never sell them short and always be prepared to lend a hand if they face a difficulty.

○ If you are angry about them, do not take it out on them. They get this from adults all the time. It only adds more hurt. We need to take care of our upsets about them some other way.

○ Give young people accurate information about the way the world works, our experiences, relationships and sex, the contributions of young people to humankind, and other issues that interest them. Never lie to them.

○ Be patient with yourself when you unconsciously slip into old adultist habits. It will take time to undo them. Always appreciate how well you are doing.

○ Stop asking young people, "How old are you?" Although it may seem like an innocent icebreaker, this question serves a tendency to sort them into categories. For example, if a child says she is seven years old, we put her in our box of assumptions about seven-year-olds and forget that Mozart was creating amazing music by age six. Instead of inquiring about their age, we can get to know their uniqueness in other ways.

Good Policy

In our efforts to create solid relationships with young people, we inevitably come up against adultism: theirs, ours, or society's. Teachers in schools and staff in youth programs need to avoid two extremes. One is the permissive attitude that says, "Anything the young people want is okay." The mistreatment of and disrespect for young people have left them, to varying degrees, with irrational feelings, misinformation, and tendencies to act out their hurts. Adult staff must not abdicate their responsibility to provide effective leadership and good policy. The other extreme is the adult authority running the show. Adults, likewise, have their share of irrationality, which is often the legacy of the adultism visited upon them as youth. Young people need policies that protect them from adultist leadership.

A sound policy for behavior in our work together needs to include agreeing to treat each other with nothing less than complete respect; to think independently and not just react; to act to improve the situation; to be trustworthy, honest, and reliable in relations with each other; to think about the well-being of the whole group; to care about each other; and to struggle against everything that keeps us divided among ourselves.

Envisioning a World Without Adultism

It is inspiring and sobering whenever I ask young people to imagine a world in which young people are completely respected and never suffer from mistreatment because they are young. It's inspiring because they talk about how education could be more related to them as learners, and how they would help hire teachers and help develop curriculum. They would use schools as community centers to provide services and opportunities. They would treat their siblings and friends with much more care. They would have open and trusting relationships with adult family members and others. They would help decide how to get things done. They would help end conflict between racial and cultural groups. They would feel smart and effective, feel confident and loved, feel part of their community. They would be leaders.

It is sobering because present reality is so far from that. However, each of us, as parents or in schools and youth programs, can help create conditions that support young people to develop their vision, practice decision making, exercise judgment, and grow in leadership, and thereby help us evolve into a world without adultism.

An Encouraging Message for White People

In this section, I'd like to talk directly to White people, as a White man with unearned privileges. I cannot presume to include a comparable section for People of Color because I do not have their lived experience, but can encourage all of us to access the resources that are available written by People of Color. Living and working in communities of color for the past fifty years, I have been taught, challenged, and loved by People of Color; I have been forced and invited to do a lot of work on myself as a White person. This has been a powerful journey of liberation for me, helping me shed some of my conditioned racism, release my fear, guilt, and feelings of powerlessness, become a more effective ally in the movement to end white supremacy, and deepen my capacity for close, intimate, genuine relationships with People of Color. I am not finished by any means, since this work is a lifelong process, but what a difference it has made for me!

Listening Circles for Inner Healing of Racism

In June 2020, within a week of George Floyd's murder by Minneapolis police, one hundred White mindfulness practitioners from the Plum Village Community of Engaged Buddhism responded to my online invitation to a Listening Circle for Healing Our White

Racism. In pairs and four-way structured listening sessions, people explored two questions: "What breaks my heart about the current racial suffering?" and "What in me needs healing around race?" They opened their hearts, listened deeply, shed tears, and experienced their anger and acceptance.

As a result of that first ninety-minute session, a bare beginning, seventy people committed to three more sessions to continue exploring their own white racism, hoping to become familiar enough with the format of the Listening Circle model so that they could offer something similar to their White friends. It turns out that White people are fairly eager to do this inner work. After the first four introductory sessions, about twenty people continued to meet monthly for several years, and many of them began their own local listening circles.

Similar to the teachings of the Four I's of Oppression and the discussions on racism above, the following key points emerged in our work together.

Racism has done incalculable damage to People of Color the world over through slavery, apartheid, colonialization, genocide, mass incarceration, exploitation, and discrimination. The horrors of racism challenge all norms of human decency. Sufficient repair and restoration are impossible. And the more we uncover, the more we learn that the damage is even worse than we could imagine.

Racism, not to the same degree or in the same way, has also damaged the humanity of White people who have been conditioned to act as agents or silent witnesses of racism. And it has damaged the Earth and its creatures through genocide, European colonialism, resource extraction, and the pursuit of profit over well-being.

Racism has been incorporated into a system of white supremacy that permeates much of Western culture and is most pronounced in the United States. White supremacy includes extremist groups of racists who express vile, hateful rhetoric and violent racist behavior, such as' the Ku Klux Klan, neo-Nazis, skinheads, and

White nationalists. But most extremists act as individuals. Deeper examples of white supremacy are baked into official policies and practices like the redlining of neighborhoods for housing, disproportional mass incarceration of Black and Brown people, de facto school segregation, and discriminatory hiring. White "privilege" is a set of unearned advantages White people have that BIPOC people do not have, based solely on skin color.

Racism did not always exist, and it will not always exist. In the American colonies in the mid-1600s, it solidified into a system to exploit low-income people and keep working people of African, Indigenous, and European descent divided among themselves.[11]

I have a firm conviction that racism as a system will be eliminated within this century. Racism did not always exist, and so it can be ended. To end it, we must do the following: change racist ideas and policies, stop racist behaviors, redress the injustices from racism, end all other interlocking oppressions, and help all people recover from the damage done to them by racism. Adding a Buddhist perspective, it will also require coming to understand the interbeing nature of peoples and cultures.

Healing the emotional damage of internalized racism that White people have inherited is key. Healing is not a substitute for action to change the structures of racism and white supremacy, and this is not intended to be an escape for White people to center on our own pain. However, healing is a vital component in a long and noble human struggle to end racism. White people need to do this work separate from People of Color. (A more current term is Black, Indigenous, People of Color, or BIPOC, which acknowledges that distinct groups have different experiences of racism.)

It is vital to heal the inner damage done to individuals by racism, which is different from ending racist policies and behaviors. If racist policies and behaviors magically stopped overnight, the damage from past racism would not disappear. Many people who had been targeted would still feel attacked, worthless, mistreated, ignored, self-doubting. Many people conditioned to function as agents of racism would continue to feel superior, entitled, and deserving, or guilty and confused about our roles. Only by healing the inner damage done to individuals can we be confident that racist attitudes and behaviors will not continue and that racist policies will not reappear in other guises. Without this healing, our thinking is clouded, our relationships are distressed, and our unity work to end racism is slowed.

Here is a sampling of common race-related distresses among White people:

○ Feelings of grief and anger at learning about or witnessing past and current injustices.

○ Feelings of guilt or shame as we consider our complicity and times we may have caved in to racism.

○ Feelings of loss and grief about being cut off from easy, natural relationships with our siblings of color.

○ Feeling bad about our past ignorance or clueless about racism and its damage.

○ Feelings of confusion about the story of the United States—the *ideals* of liberty, equality, democracy, and the *reality* of white supremacy.

○ Feelings of fear of retribution from BIPOC people for centuries of mistreatment, and vulnerability to rejection by BIPOC people who resent our privilege.

○ Feelings of fear about what we may have to give up if we acknowledge our white privilege.

○ Feeling powerless if we decide to really organize to end racism.

These and all other emotional effects of racism can be healed if given enough time, attention, understanding, and safety to release the stored emotions. Such healing is not a substitute for organizing and taking action against institutionalized racism, but it is an essential component in acting powerfully to end racism.

It has been liberating and energizing for me to engage in this inner healing work around racism. Over time, having safe spaces to surface, acknowledge, and release the pain of my own vestiges of conscious or unconscious racism has been a fruitful practice. I have intentionally done this healing work in interactions with other White people, rather than People of Color, in order to avoid exposing People of Color to my racism. As mentioned elsewhere, for almost thirty-five years I have maintained a weekly deep listening partnership that has been a profoundly safe container in which to explore and heal hurts related to racism. As Thich Nhat Hanh says, "No mud, no lotus." Out of our racist mud can grow deeper solidarity, right action, closer relationships across racial lines, and an engaged, courageous commitment to liberation for all human beings.

Listening Circles for Healing Our White Racism: Key Ideas for Facilitators

Structured listening sessions offer a safe space for White people to do the work of healing emotional damage.

Some guiding viewpoints. It is important for Listening Circle facilitators to hold out a noble vision of human beings along these lines:

All people have inherent worth and goodness. In Buddhism, we say that everyone has Buddha nature, that our true home is in the ultimate dimension of unbroken wholeness.

All people get hurt. There is suffering; this is the First Noble Truth of Buddhism. We get broken. The Second Noble Truth is that there are causes of suffering—understandable roots that include family life, personal experiences, generational trauma, historical narratives, oppression, greed, hatred, ignorance, and the conditioning to feel separate.

All people can regain access to their true nature. There is a promise of an end to suffering. Buddha said that healing is possible, liberation from suffering is possible. This is the Third Noble Truth.

Practices of mindfulness, concentration, and insight lead to transformation and liberation. This Fourth Noble Truth, also called the Eightfold Noble Path, is a rich and varied process that blends personal and collective awakening, meditation on the cushion and action in the world, individual commitment and Sangha refuge, and ethical living at all levels.

No one is born a racist. Young White people must be taught, conditioned, miseducated, and mistreated in order to act as agents of racism. Harvey Jackins, the founder of Re-evaluation Counseling, likened racism to dog poop on our sneakers. At workshops, he would tell us to notice three things: it's not an inherent part of your sneaker; it's really hard to scrape it out of all those crevices; and everywhere you go, it stinks the place up.

In addition to the visible and invisible system of oppression, racism and white supremacy are also held in place significantly by unhealed hurt. A White child who is treated with respect, taught compassion and connection, educated with an inclusive version of US history, and allowed to feel their feelings as they grow up, would never willingly participate in or agree to the oppression of anyone. But most White children never get that upbringing. Instead, we are born into an oppressive system that pits all against all for the purposes of protecting the wealth and power of the few. Racism and other oppressions keep us fighting among ourselves rather than unifying to transform a corrupt, unjust system based in greed, fear, and insecurity.

Suggested Framing Comments for Facilitators

Welcome the participants as White people. Their humanity is not in question. Validate their courage and commitment to do this uncomfortable liberation work. It's not easy, but they are choosing integrity. Invite them to look around, smile, and offer each person a bow of gratitude for being here. White people are deeply good human beings who have been conditioned to be agents of oppression. This conditioning has separated us from each other and from People of Color. Racism has warped our humanness and damaged us, not in the same ways nor to the same degree as it has for People of Color. We have been conditioned to feel superior and entitled, but if we are half awake, we also have taken in the monstrous effects of racism, and this in turn can generate feelings of guilt, shame, and powerlessness in us. The people gathered are making a decision, in part, to use our white privilege to help dismantle white supremacy.

Acknowledge other identities. Each of us inhabits more than one identity, including our gender, class, religious background, ethnicity, sexual orientation, and physical differences. In some of those we have experienced discrimination or mistreatment, which also needs healing. However, for this Listening Circle we are focusing on white identity.

Explain the purpose of the Listening Circle. This group provides a safe, structured space for White people to listen and be listened to about their emotional, heart-level experiences related to racism and white supremacy. It assumes that each person is at a different place in their awareness of and engagement with racial issues. This type of Listening Circle accepts each person as they are and assumes that being listened to in a safe, structured context will allow each person to explore their racism at their own pace, in their own way. It assumes that each person moves toward their own well-being and awakening as best they can, given all the causes and conditions in their life, and that everyone deserves neither blame nor shame, but rather acceptance and appreciation. Information and action, as important as these are, are not the point of these sessions. Understanding, releasing, and healing of painful emotions is the point.

Use "equal time turns." The two main formats of these Listening Circles are two-way listening partners and small-group listening circles, both of which use equal time turns. Equal time tends to help people relax, helps them listen better because they know they will get a turn, and honors each person equally. Each person chooses when to speak and can choose to pass or simply remain quiet during their turn while enjoying the presence of the listeners.

Explain how to listen. When I'm working with a Buddhist group, I often say that while you are the listener, please listen as if you were the Buddha. We have notions of how Buddha would listen: see the Buddha nature of the person speaking; offer warm, relaxed, respectful attention, no advice, no judgment, not even questions; hold the person with unconditional kindness and acceptance. We honor confidentiality. Obviously, these are not Buddhist methods but are universal qualities of deep listening. When we intentionally offer this quality of attention, the speaker may notice the difference from ordinary conversation; this can allow them to make contact with a deeper place inside. Being aware of our breathing, calming concentration, or attention can help us listen more deeply.

Allow for emotional release of feelings. Sometimes, the speaker may well up with emotion, whether it is fear, anxiety, sadness, or anger. Allow feelings to surface uninterrupted. Whether we are aware of it or not, most of us are carrying deep wells of pain around racism. These feelings have been waiting for the right conditions to surface. Be willing to be uncomfortable. Black, Indigenous,

People of Color (BIPOC) are being drowned in whiteness. They *have* to see it. They *have* to pay attention to whiteness to navigate treacherous and often dangerous territory. What we White people take for granted and don't even notice is toxic for People of Color. Remember that feelings of hopelessness or powerlessness or discouragement are mostly rooted in old unhealed feelings. As we release old feelings, we will have more attention, more courage, and more capacity to engage in ending racism.[12]

Beginning Anew with Our White European Ancestors

In his Plum Village monastic community, Thich Nhat Hanh created a process for regaining harmony when relationships are frayed, which he called Beginning Anew. When two individuals (and sometimes members of a group) find themselves experiencing tension between them, they engage in a respectful four-part process. First, they appreciate each other; this is called "flower watering" of the other person's positive qualities. This grounds them in a container that is larger than the conflict. Next, they each apologize for ways they may have hurt the other, or for things they are sorry about; this is called "expressing beneficial regrets." Third, each person tells the other how they themselves are hurting. And fourth, each shares how the other could concretely help diminish that suffering.[13]

In my work with White people who are just beginning to understand whiteness and white supremacy, I adapted a structure called Beginning Anew with My White European Ancestors, which seems to work as an accessible ramp into the territory. Our generational trauma of white-on-white oppression began hundreds of years ago in Europe; it conditioned European colonists to take up oppressive roles toward Indigenous people and People of Color early on, and it continues to infect most White people today.

In pairs, each White person shares about three things:

1. Appreciations

What do I appreciate about my European ancestors or heritage? What are the positive contributions my people have made to humankind? Examples can be mentioned, such as ideas about human rights, individual liberty, democracy; classical Western musicians like Mozart; ballet; the Western scientific method; the courage and fortitude to flee oppression and find a new home; White abolitionists and anti-racist activists. All cultures have contributed good things. This round helps counteract white guilt and validates positive aspects of our history.

2. Regrets

There are two sides to this step. First, I acknowledge and offer apologies for how my White ancestors hurt other White people through centuries of wars, tyranny, violence, witch hunts, and public hangings. This includes how White people killed six million White European Jews. Then, because I carry this legacy, I explore the ways my European or White-heritage ancestors harmed People of Color, and name the harm for which I am specifically sorry. What are White people still doing today that is profoundly harmful? What breaks my heart in relation to all of that? This round often brings up grief or anger.

3. Making Amends

What do I vow to do personally from this point forward to help heal the harm that my European ancestors and dominant white culture have done to People of Color? And to Jews? What do I vow to do to help change the systems that perpetuate that ongoing harm? Try to be specific. This round asks for personal change.

Each of these rounds can evoke deep feelings. In this work with White people, I've discovered that underneath white defensiveness or guilt is usually brokenheartedness. Why? There are various reasons. Some Whites, as children, had friends of color whom they loved, and from whom they got separated because of racism. Some had a babysitter who was a Person of Color, whom they loved as much as they loved their parents, or sometimes more, and from whom they were later separated. Many young Whites saw unjust treatment of People of Color but could not stop it because they were too little and powerless. Some White folks carry the inner shame of times they caved in to peer pressure and didn't speak up against a racist joke or other racial mistreatment. Some White people were raised in such a segregated world that they never had a Black or Brown friend and therefore feel ignorant and separate. Many White people feel a lack of ease in their relationships with People of Color, a discomfort, maybe fear, maybe guilt born of the legacy of racism and white supremacy. Many White people know at some deep level that the privilege we enjoy because of our skin color is inherently unfair and wrong, and is built on generations of brutal exploitation and oppression, but we don't want to give up our own safety and security, so that creates guilt.

Furthermore, White people fear putting attention on the injustices of racism because we are confused about the extent of our responsibility for correcting it. Are we obligated to give up our home? Our money? Give it all away because it came from privilege and exploitation? How much of our time and energy do we give to ending racism? Do we need to get arrested? What is required, to be fair? When you open your heart, what do you have to do? These are not easy questions.

However, underneath these fearful or defensive reactions, if the conditions are safe enough, what most White people find is that broken heart. We find a deep well of grief and loss at being separated from People of Color in our lives, of feeling betrayed by miseducation, of feeling disillusioned about our country, whose ideals of life, liberty, and the pursuit of happiness were incomplete and built on genocide and slavery. And we feel inadequate to change conditions.

Transforming racism and white supremacy is a long, multilay-ered, complex struggle. One necessary piece is healing both our individual and collective suffering from racism. For me, it has been an honor and a relief to recover part of my humanity. This has included facing and releasing my own pain due to racism, read-ing and studying, and learning to be an ever more effective ally of BIPOC folks in challenging structures of racism. In the safety of my weekly co-counseling sessions, I have been able to acknowl-edge and heal much of my white racism and understand how I have ignorantly perpetuated harm by acting out my unearned white privilege.

Most social justice activists understandably focus their work on the external structural policies and practices that they think need changing. While we do this, it is also crucial to put atten-tion on healing the inner personal habits and hurts that limit our humanity, dull our thinking, and keep us divided and acting small. These patterns include feeling unloved or disrespected, the pres-sure to succeed, the vulnerability to criticism, the insecurities of being not enough, our conditioning to feel separate, and our igno-rance, powerlessness, and internalized trauma that prepare us to take our place in the oppressive structures that are waiting for us. The process of healing also includes loving ourselves as inher-ently worthy human beings, while increasingly coming to love and respect all others.

To transform the system, individual healing is not sufficient without stopping the harm, gaining political power, and imple-menting structural changes. But if we do not do the inner heal-ing work, then our rigid and irrational old habits and patterns of oppression will infect the new world we are working so hard to build.

Through years of doing my work of healing and rooting out internalized racism (still in process), it has become an energizing and uplifting journey—though it is still angering and frustrating as I continue to learn how bad things were and still are. I have come to understand in my bones that anyone's liberation is linked to the liberation of everyone. People of Color cannot end racism and white supremacy by themselves. Nor should they have to. The active participation of White people is required. In simple terms, I see this as having two major parts that go hand in hand. One part is recovering our full humanity from wrong views, miseducation, and hurtful actions around race. This is the inner healing journey. The second part is to unite and act in concert with others around a strategy to challenge and eventually dismantle white supremacy. The racial upheaval of recent years is a cry of suffering and a surging call to us White folks to join wholeheartedly in this monumental and heroic human struggle for freedom.

Below are some steps for White people to move toward becoming allies to end racism.

Steps Toward Becoming White Allies[14]

There are many ways for White people to be allies in eliminating racism. Some of these include:

Taking visible stands against all forms of racism by backing anti-racism organizations led by People of Color, as well as standing independently as a White person against racism.

Working to eliminate our own racism and healing the places we have been silent and passive about racism.

Actively and vocally supporting People of Color when they want to gather together, and educating White friends who do not support those groups or who view them as "exclusionary."

Actively seeking correct information and healing from the ways we have been unaware and uninformed.

Sharing our money with People of Color we love, those in our community; donating to organizations led by People of Color; and paying land tax to Indigenous groups looking to rematriate land.

Donating to funds that allow People of Color to rest, receive mental health care, afford child care, and so on.

Building a life that contradicts racism, which includes being in close contact with and building long-term friendships with People of Color and challenging the racist messages of superiority, separation, difference, and fear.

Training and building groups of White allies committed to eliminating racism by assisting other White people to heal the damage done to us by racism.

Understanding that being allies to People of Color is also for our own benefit, since it involves reclaiming our full humanity and having a world that is right for everyone, a world where everyone matters.

For more information about White people healing the damage done by racism, see the pamphlet "Working Together to End Racism," a publication of the organization United to End Racism (*www.unitedtoendracism.org*).

5

BUILDING DEEP LOCAL COMMUNITY

Community Is Essential for Liberation

It is possible that the next Buddha will not take the form of an individual. The next Buddha may take the form of a community, a community practicing understanding and loving kindness, a community practicing mindful living. And the practice can be carried out as a group, as a city, as a nation.

—Thich Nhat Hanh

When you wake up and you see that the Earth is not just the environment, the Earth is us, you touch the nature of inter-being. And at that moment you can have real communication with the Earth. . . . We have to wake up together. And if we wake up together, then we have a chance. Our way of living our life and planning our future has led us into this situation. And now we need to look deeply to find a way out, not only as individuals, but as a collective, a species.

—Thich Nhat Hanh

When author and climate activist Bill McKibben was asked, "What is the best thing an individual can do for the climate?" he said, "Stop being an individual."[1] We cannot end racism, or reverse the process of global warming, or eliminate oppression and exploitation, or renew democracy, alone. While we honor and support each individual's efforts to heal and protect, we also need to nurture deep intimacy and closeness in community.

A community, a Sangha or meditation group, a listening circle— this kind of support group is where we learn patience, tolerance, and compassion; it's where we practice peaceful conflict resolution, relationship repair, and cooperative planning; it's where we find refuge, solidarity, and healing. Ananda, the Buddha's beloved disciple, once asked his teacher if having good friends or spiritual companions was half the path. The Buddha told him that having good friends was the entire path.

Although we sometimes have trouble living together, we need each other. It's impossible for us to live alone. Even a hermit in a cave is provided food by other beings. We are inexorably connected and can't live without each other. But more than that, nurturing our togetherness serves many purposes on the path toward realizing Beloved Community.

Counteracting Individualism

Our society's emphasis on individualism gives rise to separation. We get pitted against each other through discrimination, oppression, and competition for respect and limited resources. We often feel the need to protect our own, to go it alone, to compete. We blame and shame others. Our families and social networks are diminished by these divisive behaviors. Nurturing community, on the other hand, allows us to find ways to unite across issues, create multiracial and multiclass organizations, and develop strong groups of practice as refuges, as sanctuaries, as think tanks, as renewal spaces.

Healing Oppression

Most of us have been so soaked in white supremacy, patriarchy, and other oppressions that they often show up in our organizations, including our spiritual communities, and undermine our collective efforts for social justice. The urgency of the climate crisis asks us to get on with healing and reunification work. Environmental impacts will affect everyone, not equally or at the same pace or time, but no place will be untouched. The coming generations depend on us repairing long-festering historical systems of exploitation that have kept us separate and damaged the Earth. This is deep and necessary work that requires the safety of caring community.

Providing Refuge

Nurturing deep community strengthens our ability to provide a refuge of support for climate activists and climate refugees, to help each other maintain loving kindness and compassion as climate stress and chaos mount, and to be able to resist voices of separation and demonization when fear is present. Strong community helps us deepen our skills in listening, healing, and reaching harmony—skills that will be increasingly needed.

Resisting State Power

Another reason for building deep and local community is to nurture strong bonds to resist the use of state power or violence leveled against social justice efforts. As authoritarianism rises and divisions harden, there may be an increase in government or militia-based surveillance, repression, and attacks on people engaged in social activism. Marginalized groups know this all too well. Social solidarity can be a bulwark against institutional repression.

Healing Trauma

Yet another reason for safe community is that the trauma and hurts we carry are not just individual; each of us was born into a world shaped by trauma through centuries of violence and abuse. Many people tend to think a messed-up world is just the way it is, and if we suffer, it is our fault. Collective traumatization has become normalized.

In the 1960s, I learned that when women began to gather in groups to share their stories and support each other, it became clear that each woman's mistreatment and hurtful experiences were similar to other women's. The insight grew that women's suffering was systemic and collective, and it had deep roots in an ancient patriarchal structure. Being in a small, safe community allowed for this understanding to emerge and for healing to happen within that shared understanding. Deep community is key for collective healing.

Deepening Awareness of Challenges to Community

As much as we need togetherness, building and maintaining a peaceful community can be daunting. People bring all their "stuff" into community—their gifts, talents, unhealthy habits, irrational needs, irritating personal traits, and unhealed hurts—and it's difficult to manage all of this elegantly and skillfully. There is also a perennial dynamic tension between individual and collective needs. As a result, living in community can be fraught with confusion and suffering. It is worth reflecting on some of these complexities to shine light on the potential difficulties and begin understanding how to work through them.

Examining Ideas of Freedom

Diverse beliefs, cultures, and contexts influence the ways people envision and create community. For example, notions of freedom differ. The great freedom tradition of the modern Western world is individual liberty, freedom from tyranny and oppression, freedom from external constraints to individual happiness. On the other hand, the great freedom tradition of the Eastern world is inner liberation and individual enlightenment; it is freedom from craving, ill will, and the delusion of separateness. For example, Thich Nhat Hanh taught that true freedom is freedom from the delusion of a separate self. The Eastern tradition includes deep meditation, mindfulness, living an ethical life, and deep strains of compassion, kindness, and acceptance of the present moment. It elevates the goal of awakening as the ultimate freedom.

In my opinion, each of these great freedom traditions is incomplete, has fault lines, and needs the other for a full realization of freedom. If you are living in a society that guarantees and even enshrines individual rights but hasn't dealt with desire, hatred, insecurity, and feelings of separation, it can lead to consumerism, unbridled greed built into capitalism as an economic system, and the glorification of individual rights over the well-being of the community. Yet, if you think you can live in a safe, enlightened, private cocoon unaffected by the troubles of the world, and that if you just change your thinking you can be happy, then you are colluding with the external oppressions that contribute to immense suffering for the majority of your fellow human beings.

The monk and the revolutionary need each other. Combining the best of both traditions can help a more complete freedom to emerge. Also, both types of freedom require community, which represents the possibility of belonging, of not being alone, of connecting with something larger than ourselves.

Nurturing Awareness of What We Bring to Community

People have different motivations for being in a specific community, whether that community is a family, a neighborhood association, a bingo club, a workplace, a sports team, a religious group, a political party, or an army unit. If belonging to a community is a choice (and sometimes it is not, as with one's family or racial group), a person might come to the group to enjoy the camaraderie, or the socializing, or a sense of meaning, or joy and laughter, or safety and healing, or getting attention, or a chance to lead, or a refuge from the storms of life, or the intensity of a focus, or a sense of being accepted and loved, or many other motivations.

From time to time, it can be good to review our reasons for being part of any group.

We may also bring to the community our irrational behavior and attitudes, our unmet needs, our longing for or fear of closeness, our unhealed childhood and ancestral wounds, and our judgmental and competitive impulses. This "stuff" can create tensions, conflict, and lack of harmony in a group. Having agreed-on ways of handling "stuff" can help create trust.

Additionally, few people receive training in the art of nurturing community or how to manage this heady mix of "stuff." Sometimes this results in lack of clarity about the purpose of the community, or loose adherence to community norms, or unresolved hurts among community members. It can be useful to learn some basic understanding of group dynamics and skills in meeting facilitation.

To make things even more dicey, most people have issues with leadership and authority, which get acted out in community. Some people like structure with clear leadership and rules. Some have an allergy to authority, often for understandable reasons, such as past mistreatment or disrespect from authorities like parents, teachers, police, government officials, religious figures, or gurus. They might prefer leaderless communities with flat hierarchy and no titles. Other people prefer "leaderful" groups where many people share in leadership functions and decision-making. Leadership is necessary, but it can be shared, developed, and rotated. It also can have an individual component and a collective component. Building awareness of people's preferences and needs in relation to leadership can be helpful.

To complicate things even more, the collective suffering of our wider society can show up in our community. I often say about groups I'm part of, "If it's out there in society, it's in here too." Community members come not only with what they think of as their personal suffering, but also their share of widespread suffering engendered by isolation, competition, oppression, financial issues, climate change, natural disasters, death and dying, and on and on. This can manifest in the form of unaware racial or class bias or other oppressions, acting out of anger, jealousy, or other troublesome behaviors, and even certifiable mental illness. These stressors can disrupt group harmony and diminish the quality of belonging. Cultivating ongoing awareness around these dynamics is vital for maintaining harmony.

In the face of the complex challenges at play, it is beneficial to continually explore what our community is for, and look deeply into how it's doing. We can ask: How does the community mirror aspects of the wider society—for instance, in terms of individualism, or white privilege, or private pursuit of happiness? How does the community offer alternatives to the unsupportive or divisive aspects of dominant culture? For example, are the community members committed to each other's well-being, or do they feel responsible for assisting others with their suffering? What are the members' responsibilities toward each other? The right mix of individual liberty and accountability to the community needs continual fine-tuning.

Thich Nhat Hanh imagined that the next Buddha would emerge as a community—a peaceful, harmonious, just, kind, and cooperative collective. That sounds like the Beloved Community, doesn't it? If this is to be, we have much to learn about nurturing ever-deeper community.

Be the Change

"Be the change we want to see in the world." This quote is often attributed to Gandhi. It is good advice, but it is not what he said. He actually said:

> We but mirror the world. All the tendencies present in the outer world are to be found in the world of our body. If we could change ourselves, the tendencies in the world would also change. As a man changes his own nature, so does the attitude

of the world change toward him. . . . A wonderful thing it is and the source of our happiness. We need not wait to see what others do.[2]

The invitation is to live now in ways that nurture the direction we wish to go. In chapter 3, on healing and resilience, we touched on a two-part process of recovering our full humanity out from under patterns and distress. The first part is healing the emotional hurt through processes like discharging afflictive emotions in safe settings with the warm attention of another person, or mindfulness practices in the silence of meditation, or feeling held by nature. The second part is holding a direction toward our full humanity, even if we don't yet believe it is true about us.

Collectively we are living inside a hurting and hurtful society. Part of the transformation we need is actively engaging with others to change laws, policies, and unjust practices. And part of it is living each moment as if we are free. Thich Nhat Hanh often taught about living as a sovereign person, walking as a free person, not being caught in the delusion of a separate existence. I'm reminded of the title of a book, *We're All Doing Time*, by Bo Lozoff, a Buddhist teacher who started the Prison-Ashram Project. Most of us are living in a kind of prison. For some, there are actual bars and locks. For most of us, it's a prison of our negative habit energies, destructive patterns, and self-loathing. We are not free.

The invitation is to model and live *into* the way we would like our world to be. Since society and many communities are immersed in age-old dynamics of domination, our work needs to deliberately, diligently use processes that counteract and transform these unwholesome social patterns. The ways we develop our community will affect how we show up in mindful action.

In our groups, how we *are* is the foundation for what we *do*. Attention to our relationships and processes is part of building a new culture inside the collapsing environment. Here are some ways I have found useful to deepen personal relationships and nurture community in a group setting:

- Early on and periodically in a group, take turns telling each other your life stories. At various times, tell stories from the perspective of your race, gender identity, class background, or any social identity.

- In one of the first meetings of a group, it can be helpful for folks to share what you need from the group in order to show up fully and create a space that is both brave and safe.

- Make a regular habit of appreciating one another, deeply and with specifics.

- Regularly enjoy grounding exercises with the group, like praying, sitting or walking meditation, or guided visualizations.

- Cocreate a holding container for folks to be vulnerable, to express deep emotions, to explore the roots of suffering, to become comfortable with and welcoming of each other's tears, fears, and vulnerabilities.

- Try to notice and counteract habits of separation—ways your conditioning has you withdraw, hold back, feel inwardly critical, distance yourself, and keep others out. Learn to gently welcome each other back in.

- From time to time, consider having separate sessions for various identity groups, such as different gender identities, cultural and racial identities, or age identities. As appropriate, share out from these groups to the whole community. This can help surface strengths to be acknowledged or tensions to be resolved.

- Create effective ways of resolving inevitable relational conflicts with compassionate dialogue, restorative circles, kind speech, checking of your perceptions, and listening deeply.

○ Related to conflicts, develop ways to acknowledge and resolve the inevitable microaggressions—the comments or actions that come out of an oppressor group's conditioning and are experienced as hurtful—and to say some form of "ouch" when it hurts or some form of "oops" to acknowledge the mistake and make amends.

○ Hold periodic reviews to reflect on your relationships, surfacing anything that may need to be addressed. Be sure to include appreciations of each person.

○ Socialize from time to time. Enjoy dinner or tea with the whole group and one-on-one. Deliberately build relationships. Attend each other's events and important milestones.

○ Be as present as possible for a group member who has a serious illness or death in their family or other distressing event. Show up for each other in times of need.

Ideally, these kinds of practices will deepen people's trust, understanding, and love for each other. In this way a group can evolve into a powerful, heartfelt, strong circle that each member can turn to, depend on, contribute to, feel connected to, and gladly take bold action with. Many of these practices can be introduced and enjoyed in the wider circles of our lives.

Someone Committed to Your Spiritual Development

In moving toward making the Beloved Community real and operational, we can benefit by deepening our commitment to each other's spiritual development. In most traditions, the ultimate fruit of spiritual practice is awakening from the narrow confines of a small identity and into the spaciousness of true freedom. That means freedom *from* suffering, from fear, from disconnection and dissatisfaction. And it means freedom *to* love, create, connect, and be at home and at ease. It is being present to the miracle of this moment.

What would it look like if someone were committed to supporting you on your spiritual path? What would it be like if you had a skillful spiritual companion who personally cared about your liberation? How might that facilitate your development?

In addition to practices such as meditation, prayer, retreats, and rituals, there is also spiritual mentoring. For example, in the Buddhist tradition of Thich Nhat Hanh, at the monasteries there are structured mentoring relationships among monastics; each person has a specific elder sibling who helps guide their development. Other traditions also have built this relational piece into their practices. If you are in a twelve-step program, you have a sponsor with whom you talk on a regular basis. If you are in psychotherapy, you have a therapist who listens deeply and asks important questions that you might not ask yourself. In the Re-evaluation Counseling community, at least one person is committed to your "reemergence" or "awakening," and actively assists you to identify and shed unwholesome habit energies.

Another way to explore the usefulness of spiritual mentoring is to reverse the question: *What would it look like if I were committed to someone else's awakening?* When I ask myself this question, my aspirations for a caring personal spiritual relationship become clear.

○ First, I have to be committed to my own full awakening! I want to ask myself regularly: Do I really intend to be free, or am I just going through the motions? Am I willing to recognize and embrace my own suffering in order to realize true peace, or am I wanting to stay comfortable and comforted? How do hindrances such as desire, aversion, laziness, restlessness, and doubt operate in my own practice? Knowing that I can only truly assist another to the extent that I have freed myself, such questions motivate a more sincere effort, sharpen my practice, and increase my ability to be present for the person to whom I'm committed.

○ With the person I am supporting, I want to practice the four kinds of love, which Buddhists call the Four Immeasurable Minds: loving kindness, compassion, joy, and equanimity. This means I want to deepen those qualities in myself more and more. I also want to be active in learning about the person and their struggles, showing them love, and giving them my best attentive presence.

○ I want to check any ego tendencies to "help" or "save" the person, to create dependency, or to pat myself on the back for feeling wiser or more advanced or better than they are.

○ I want to continually study and practice my ethical guidelines as the ground for my behavior. Any ways that I am not walking the talk will show up in the relationship.

○ I want to accept the person's expression of deep emotions, since their suffering will arise during their liberation process. I want to be present when suffering comes up, even urge it up and out, if appropriate. I know from my own experience that full *release* of feelings can cleanse and permanently relieve long-stored suffering. The more I do my own emotional work, the more capacity I have to accept the emotions of others without either of us getting confused or overwhelmed. This capacity to be present for their emotional discharge is also cultivated through mindfulness, concentration, and insight.

○ I want to continually add to my toolkit of skillful means so that I can think about the person from many perspectives. To paraphrase an old saying, I want to avoid having only a hammer so I don't treat everything as a nail. A person's journey to inner freedom is sometimes subtle, nuanced, nonlinear; sometimes wild, roaring, ecstatic; sometimes depressing, confusing, scary. A hammer won't do for all these!

o I also want to ask for help when I don't know what to do. This is where it's supportive to call on a person committed to *my* full awakening—a trusted adviser, spiritual friend, or teacher. I also want to seek guidance in sacred texts, Dharma talks, and other sources of wisdom.

Reflection Question

Which of these points are easy for you, and which ones might need more development?

There are risks in setting up such committed relationships. Since human beings can get hooked by all sorts of unwholesome behaviors, sticky situations might arise. For example: the mentee could feel judged or shamed; the mentor could feel unskilled or unsuccessful in their role; the two could cross boundaries and cause further suffering. It is good to be aware of these possible traps. Yet the benefits go two ways: If I commit myself to *your* full awakening, that intention will encourage *me* to grow. True love is never one-way.

Certainly, some individuals benefit from a personal and sustained relationship with a wise, skilled teacher. But most practitioners do not have such an up-close and personal connection with a teacher. For example, in the United States, there are millions of Buddhist practitioners but only hundreds of ordained qualified teachers. Not everyone wants a spiritual mentor, but for those who do, could spiritual mentoring be deliberately structured?

For example, after someone has attended a meditation or practice group for a sustained period of time, they could ask a more experienced member to be their mentor. The mentor could check in regularly with the mentee, inquire about their life and meditation practice, and encourage attendance at community practice sessions and retreats.

If an experienced mentor is not readily available, an alternative is for two community members to pair up with each other and agree to check in regularly. They ask each other what they've learned and what has challenged them in their practice since they last talked. They offer each other reflections, feedback, and suggestions. They might attend workshops or retreats together, or occasionally check in with a more experienced practitioner if they feel stuck in their relationship. This kind of peer mentoring, or paired practice, encourages mutual deep listening.

Spiritual mentoring relationships, or practice partnerships, call for a crucial shift in the community: the idea that each individual who shows diligence in practice over time is thought about in a personalized and ongoing way. Each serious practitioner feels specifically known and cared about by their support person, and feels their practice is deepening partly because of the support person's commitment to their spiritual development. While it is true that we are all connected and safe in the ultimate dimension, it is most helpful to feel the connection and love on a personal level.

In the United States, many of us are steeped in notions of individualism and separation. Common practices reinforce this: we put babies in a separate room to sleep apart from their parents; we set up Individual Retirement Accounts; we pursue individual happiness; we draw lines around parts of the Earth and call them separate countries; we see nature as something to exploit and control for profit. We even use language that embeds notions of separation deep in our psyche. For example, we say, "Look at those two seagulls *separated* by ten feet of water," instead of "*joined* by ten feet of water." There is a subtle but significant difference. In our culture, we are so thoroughly conditioned into separateness that we rarely experience what it is like not to feel separate. We can develop habits of going it alone, of not asking for help, of personal achievement or failure, of being the lonely hero or heroine.

This can infect our spiritual practice. We can get stuck in thinking, "This is *my* path," or "*my* practice," or "*my* liberation." We are individuals doing the practice, but no one awakens by themselves. Believing that we become enlightened on our own is just another delusion, a version of wrong view. Buddha didn't awaken on his own. An infinite number of causes and conditions gave rise to his enlightenment. He had many teachers and fellow practitioners on the spiritual path. He had an early life of privilege and freedom from material want, a protected learning environment, and the influences of the cultural world view of his historical period. He had a deep aspiration to understand the nature of things.

Thich Nhat Hanh said that the next Buddha would be a Sangha. For me, this has several meanings. One is that a community of great depth, integrity, caring, and skill is developing, and it will generate so much collective concentration, ethical behavior, and wisdom that awakening will become more common. Secondly, we are being challenged to develop more collective responsibility for each other, all living beings, and the Earth—partly as a necessary counterweight to the rampant greed-fed individualism currently devouring the Earth's wealth, energy, and resources, and partly as a natural evolution within an increasingly clear awareness of interconnectedness.

Reflection Questions

Have you ever had a spiritual mentor or been one? What was your experience? How might you benefit from having a spiritual mentor? How might you develop a mentoring relationship?

6

LIVING ETHICALLY ON
A DAILY BASIS

You are me, and I am you.
Isn't it obvious that we "inter-are"?
You cultivate the flower in yourself,
so that I will be beautiful.
I transform the garbage in myself,
so that you will not have to suffer.

—Thich Nhat Hanh

If interbeing is real, meaning that everything is interconnected and nothing has an independent or separate existence, then what we do in our thoughts, words, and deeds ripples outward infinitely. How I speak impacts you, and your words affect me. We experience the positive and negative fruits of our actions. Jesus said we reap what we sow. Buddha said karma is real and inescapable. The modern version says what goes around comes around. Neuroscience has confirmed that every thought has a corresponding internal correlate. In other words, I can't say one thing and do the opposite without it registering as "does not compute" in my complex body-mind awareness. It literally causes dis-ease. Being aware of this interdependence makes me want to take good care of my actions.

The truth of interbeing shows us the necessity of living an ethical life. How we show up in our everyday life is where the rubber of mindfulness meets the road. We can reduce a lot of suffering by trying to live by a collective ethic along the lines of the Five Mindfulness Trainings offered by Thich Nhat Hanh. We can visualize them as intersecting circles, each impacting the others.

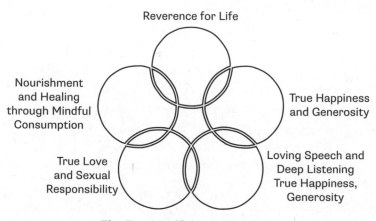

Reverence for Life

Nourishment and Healing through Mindful Consumption

True Happiness and Generosity

True Love and Sexual Responsibility

Loving Speech and Deep Listening True Happiness, Generosity

The Five Mindfulness Trainings

Every community, large or small, needs a set of guidelines to navigate human relations. I've chosen to focus on the Five Mindfulness Trainings because they apply to so many aspects of daily life. The trainings are not about being perfect; instead, they are considered practices. They are not moral absolutes or even absolutely attainable. They are like the North Star: using the star as a compass, you never actually get to it, but you are guided along a beneficial path. It helps me to remember that we're always practicing something, whether we know it or not. The question is whether what we are practicing is leading to wholesome results.

For each of the five ethical practices, I have included Thich Nhat Hanh's formal wording. I encourage you to read it in full, since each training is power-packed. Each one begins with "Aware of the suffering," then moves to "I am committed" and "I am determined" to express the intention to live in a wholesome direction. After each one, I offer comments or examples from my own life.

The First Mindfulness Training: Reverence for Life

Aware of the suffering caused by the destruction of life, I am committed to cultivating the insight of interbeing and compassion and learning ways to protect the lives of people, animals, plants, and minerals. I am determined not to kill, not to let others kill, and not to support any act of killing in the world, in my thinking, or in my way of life. Seeing that harmful actions arise from anger, fear, greed, and intolerance, which in turn come from dualistic and discriminative thinking, I will cultivate openness, nondiscrimination, and nonattachment to views in order to transform violence, fanaticism, and dogmatism in myself and in the world.

Having reverence for life means trying to do as little harm as possible. This points to nourishing gratitude for all of life and noticing the goodness and beauty all around, even amid suffering. It means cultivating compassion for all beings, and being kind and nonviolent in our relationships with all humans, the Earth, oceans, rivers and lakes, and animals, fish, and plants. It means eating in a way that causes minimal suffering to animals and plants, growing or buying organic foods as means allow, conserving water and energy, and making other choices that help sustain life.

I do my best to practice reverence for life in various ways. I catch spiders and flies in the house and put them outside. I pick up street litter to help beautify the environment. To save water, I wash the dishes using a small stream of water, don't flush the toilet after each use, and turn the faucet off when brushing my teeth. These are small things. You have your own such practices. These are not virtuous acts. They simply flow naturally when we are aware of the preciousness of everything.

A favorite poem illustrates reverence for other species. It was written by Joseph Bruchac, of Abenaki Indigenous ancestry. Perhaps he was named "Birdfoot."

BIRDFOOT'S GRAMPA

The old man
must have stopped our car
two dozen times to climb out
and gather into his hands
the small toads blinded
by our lights and leaping,
live drops of rain.
The rain was falling,
a mist about his white hair
and I kept saying
you can't save them all
accept it, get back in
we've got places to go.
But, leathery hands full
of wet brown life
knee deep in the summer
roadside grass
he just smiled and said
they have places to go to
too.[1]

A vow to practice reverence for life is also linked to healing the wounds of white supremacy and patriarchy, which has caused such violence. This training asks us to stick up for all people, to interrupt racist, sexist, anti-Semitic comments and jokes, to join the efforts to undo discriminatory laws and practices, and to insist on justice and restoration of dignity for all human beings.

Reflection Questions

For you, when has reverence for life been easy to practice? When has it been challenging?

Reverence for life also implies respect. For example, in the YouthBuild program, we worked with young people who grew up in low-income communities, had dropped out or had been pushed out of school, and were thoroughly disrespected by the systems of white supremacy. The YouthBuild program was specifically designed to contradict the systemic lack of reverence for their lives. We tried to communicate respect coupled with high expectations. The piece below is a summary in content and tone of how staff tried to communicate these values to young people in the program.

The Door

You came to the door for good reasons. Maybe you were lost and wanted to find your way back. Maybe you were suffering and needed healing. Maybe you were addicted and wanted help. Maybe you aimed to flip the script of your life and become somebody admirable. Maybe you knew you were smarter than your school records, or more caring than your criminal records, or more capable than your work records. Maybe you were sick of a messed-up world and wanted to help change it.

If you open the door, you will be met with respect and kindness. You will be deeply listened to about your journey and why you want to come here. Out there, maybe you are viewed and treated as undeserving, assumed to be worthless. In contrast, in here you will be told that you are a sacred being, worthy of love and respect, to be treated with caring and compassion, patience and faith. You will also be told that you must want to be here, that it will not be easy, that much will be asked of you, that you will have to be self-disciplined and courageous, that you will have to keep at it even when you don't feel like it. This is a hero's journey, not for the faint of heart. You are capable of great things, even beyond your imagining, but it will not be handed to you. You will have to work hard, with no guarantees. You will have to make and remake your own decision to be here.

If you decide to come in, you will find a welcoming and safe place, a community of like-minded people, a positive, encouraging culture. You will find people who believe in you, don't hold your past against you, and will be there when things get tough. You will be expected to learn your ABCs and learn to love learning itself. You will be expected to be a leader here in everyday things, and gradually to serve the community and take responsibility for ever larger circles out into the wide world. You will be expected to learn how to love and be loved, how to accept and show caring and appreciation, how to cultivate compassion and forgiveness. And you will be expected and supported to face your inner demons, and to liberate yourself from limiting beliefs, old fears, and unworkable habits. You will be assisted and expected to create healthy practices for your body, mind, heart, and spirit.

You will be asked to explore questions like: Who am I? What is my purpose in life? What am I called to do? What are my gifts and talents? You will be told: you are not just someone who needs help getting your schooling, or getting a job, or getting ahead, or getting yours. It's about not settling for a small vision; it's about rising up to who you really are. So much is possible for you, if you believe it and if you work for it. Are you ready for this? The door is open.

Adapted from *YouthBuild's North Star* by John Bell

The Second Mindfulness Training: True Happiness

Aware of the suffering caused by exploitation, social injustice, stealing, and oppression, I am committed to practicing generosity in my thinking, speaking, and acting. I am determined not to steal and not to possess anything that should belong to others; and I will share my time, energy, and material resources with those who are in need. I will practice looking deeply to see that the happiness and suffering of others are not separate from my own happiness and suffering; that true happiness is not possible without understanding and compassion; and that running after wealth, fame, power, and sensual pleasures can bring much suffering and despair. I am aware that happiness depends on my mental attitude and not on external conditions, and that I can live happily in the present moment simply by remembering that I already have more than enough conditions to be happy. I am committed to practicing Right Livelihood so that I can help reduce the suffering of living beings on Earth and reverse the process of global warming.

One of the causes of the climate crisis is that we humans have been "stealing" the future from our descendants. The stealing has not been intentional, but our extraction of natural resources for our comfort and profit has essentially robbed our descendants and millions of species of a quality environment. Similarly, greed, hatred, and insecurity have caused humans to oppress, enslave, imprison, or otherwise steal from other humans through much of history. How do we cultivate nonstealing and deep generosity, refusing to take what is not ours, offering our time and material resources to those in need, creating a widespread culture of giving and sharing? As seas rise, food shortages increase, and climate refugees flood across international borders, how can we practice opening our hearts and extending our hands instead of putting up walls?

Generosity comes in intimate and gigantic versions. Small and personal examples are: respecting other people's things; not taking credit for other people's accomplishments or stealing the spotlight; freely sharing our knowledge and skills with others; sometimes stepping back so that others can step up; showering people with love and appreciation; and letting go of having to be "right."

In my personal life I've had opportunities to share my time, energy, and material resources with those who are in need, and have been blessed with a fuller life as a result. For example, in 1980, thirteen-year-old Freddy Acosta came to my partner and me and asked if we would adopt him. He was part of the Youth Action Program, the precursor to YouthBuild that we had started in East Harlem. When we asked why, he said he loved his family, who lived in the projects, but they had a lot of problems that kept dragging him down, and he wanted to get his life going in the right direction. We were touched and impressed by his self-awareness, boldness, and sincerity. We talked several times more and finally said that we couldn't adopt him because he already had parents, but that we could discuss this with his parents, and if they agreed, he could come live with us as his second chosen family. They agreed, and Freddy moved in with us. He's now fifty-seven years old and has been part of our extended family over these decades.

This began a family trend or tradition or practice—I'm not sure what to call it. Freddy was the first of six or seven young people who stayed with us for extended periods of time, when they became homeless, or had just been released from prison, or needed a temporary safe landing place. It was not always easy or convenient. These relationships required attention and resources, and sometimes they were not comfortable for our own children. But they taught us much about resilience and perseverance in the face of hardship. To this day, we remain close with of most of those people and continue to reap the blessings of true intergenerational and cross-cultural relations.

Occasionally, friends have said how generous we've been to open our home and hearts to these young folks. Although those friends have good intentions, I think this is a mistaken notion rooted in the delusion of separateness. When I hold our experience in a larger frame of interbeing, I know that Freddy and the others are my fellow human beings who have suffered through no fault of their own, because of systems of poverty and racial discrimination, the same systems that privilege me. I also know that caring for them is caring for me; being "generous" to them is being "generous" to myself. No discrimination.

Beyond the personal, there are also examples of generosity on a larger world stage. A few years ago, I heard Van Jones tell a moving story in a recorded speech about the first time Nelson Mandela met with F. W. de Klerk's National Party government in South Africa. Jones said:

> Nelson Mandela didn't just believe in the beauty of his own people. He believed in the beauty of his opponents. You've seen the picture of him with his ANC [African National Congress] comrades sitting on one side of the table, and the government that had imprisoned him and tortured his friends and murdered people on the other side of the table. And Mandela would have been justified recounting every single injustice and indignity, and letting them know that the time is going to

change, and get ready. He didn't do that. What Nelson Mandela did is, in the language of his oppressors, recounted every great achievement of the Afrikaners. He named and recited by heart, in their language, and said, "With a people as magnificent as you, I know that a just peace is possible." He didn't call his enemies out. He called them up; he called them in.[2]

Mandela had a vision for them that was higher than a vision they had for themselves. This was an invitation of enormous generosity. Mandela wrote in his autobiography, *Long Walk to Freedom*:

> We did not want to destroy the country before we freed it, and to drive the whites away would devastate the nation. I said there was a middle ground between white fears and black hopes. . . . "Whites are fellow South Africans," I said, "and we want them to feel safe and to know we appreciate the contributions that they have made to the development of this country." Any man or woman who abandons apartheid will be embraced in our struggle for a democratic, nonracial South Africa.[3]

The Third Mindfulness Training: True Love

Aware of the suffering caused by sexual misconduct, I am committed to cultivating responsibility and learning ways to protect the safety and integrity of individuals, couples, families, and society. Knowing that sexual desire is not love, and that sexual activity motivated by craving always harms myself as well as others, I am determined not to engage in sexual relations without mutual consent, true love, and a deep, long-term commitment. I resolve to find spiritual support for the integrity of my relationship from family members, friends, and sangha with whom there is support and trust. I will do everything in my power to protect children from sexual abuse and to prevent couples and families from being broken by sexual misconduct. Seeing that body and mind are interrelated, I am committed to learning appropriate ways to take care of my sexual energy and to cultivating the four basic elements of true love—loving kindness, compassion, joy, and inclusiveness—for the greater happiness of myself and others. Recognizing the diversity of human experience, I am committed not to discriminate against any form of gender identity or sexual orientation. Practicing true love, we know that we will continue beautifully into the future.

The MeToo Movement that erupted in 2017 was the latest exposé in the long sordid history of patriarchy, sexual exploitation, and abuse. The massive outpouring of women saying MeToo was both heartbreaking in its scope and encouraging in the bravery and solidarity it showed—twelve million uses of MeToo on social media in the first twenty-four hours, according to various reports.[4] Commentators rightly said we needed to change the culture of male power, elect more women into public office, and enforce sexual harassment laws.

What are the root causes of sexual suffering? What has happened to make sexual misconduct so pervasive? What happened to men that they support a ninety-six-billion-dollar pornography industry that produces, by some estimates, thirteen thousand films a year (compared to Hollywood's six hundred films), has twenty-five million websites,[5] and sees sixty-eight million search engine requests for porn every day?[6] No one is born a rapist, a sexual abuser, or a porn addict; even the most dangerous of these men began as sweet little boys. What happened?

The strutting of male power, the images of violent masculinity, the glorification of the warrior starts in childhood. Most boys are taught not to cry, never to show fear, to shake it off, to suck it up. They are commonly shamed for being soft or kindhearted. Furthermore, homophobia plays a huge role in male conditioning. When I was growing up in the 1950s as a White, working-class, heterosexual, Catholic boy, the message was to be a Marine, not a "homo." On playgrounds then and today, boys typically compete in sports, show off, fight, or isolate themselves on the edges. Violent video games, heavily marketed to boys, further contribute to a macho male culture.

For many boys and men, the beckoning archway of human need for closeness and love gets bricked up, brick by hurtful brick, until the only pathway for those real needs narrows to a small keyhole called sex. Add testosterone, unrelenting sexual advertising and media images, and systematic training to feel superior to women and expect women to serve men in exchange for protection. Learning to act fearless, to repress emotions other than anger, and to be aggressive and even violent to get what you want reinforce this training to "be a man." As little boys, we fought against this conditioning as best we could, but eventually we surrendered. How many parents have watched our sweet toddler sons slowly lose their capacity to cry or hide their tenderness in order to fit into the harsh teenage boy culture?

Most of us men grow up being cut off from our feelings, our true loving nature, our natural compassion. Many of us feel isolated, competitive, insecure, lonely, and fake. We can rarely admit it, and usually only in the safe embrace of a lover. I have had men tell me privately that the only time they can allow their feelings and completely relax is after an orgasm with someone they trust, who welcomes them. Men are easily manipulated by the sexualized culture to find closeness through sex.

For some men, sex can become a compulsive acting out in the form of sexual harassment or abuse. Sexual behavior without love and respect is a misuse of power that masks men's insecurities and hurt. In addition to being distanced from our natural compassion and cooperativeness, many men were also abused as boys, physically, emotionally, or sexually. It is a clinical fact that most abusers were abused. Without opportunity to heal from mistreatment, we often pass it on. In this way, abuse can continue down the generations. To be fair, most men are not sexual predators or abusers. Most boys who have been hurt don't grow up to hurt others.

In our commitment to address sexual harassment and abuse, hold perpetrators accountable, and clean up male misuse of power, we should not turn our backs on men and leave their trauma intact.

Ending sexual harassment and abuse of women requires healing and preventing the hurts of men as part of ending patriarchy. In a real way, men are also oppressed, not by women but by cultural and economic systems based on greed and individualism, which teach men to be competitive, aggressive, and capable of being cruel and even willing to kill fellow human beings, as in war.

The damage done to men's humanity leads to the damage they do to women's humanity. To break that chain, we must unite in a broad long-term commitment to challenge sexist social structures and do the personal work of healing our individual hurts. This requires that we transform our society to one that embraces each person's full humanity.

In addition to challenging the structures of sexism, the personal work required is reconnecting with our essence to recover our innate security and contentment that doesn't depend on anyone else. When people so attuned to their true nature come together, there is not exploitation or abuse but true expression of love. And true love by its nature is relational, mutual, respectful, and caring.

I was once asked to offer a workshop for a network of educators on the topic of ethics in the classroom. I explored how the Five Mindfulness Trainings might help create beautiful, safe, respectful learning environments for students. And since sexuality for adolescents and young adults is often a fraught topic of concern, I offered these statements as reflection prompts and even possible guides for young people to consider:

- I will respect my body and the bodies of others.

- If I engage in sexual activity, I will try to do so only with love and commitment.

- I will refuse hookups and I will treat sex as sacred.

- I will try to prevent sexual abuse and try to stand up to sexual harassment.

○ I am determined not to use sex to cover my bad feelings of loneliness or worthlessness.

○ I aspire to practice safe sex and pregnancy prevention.

The Fourth Mindfulness Training: Loving Speech and Deep Listening

Aware of the suffering caused by unmindful speech and the inability to listen to others, I am committed to cultivating loving speech and compassionate listening in order to relieve suffering and to promote reconciliation and peace in myself and among other people, ethnic and religious groups, and nations. Knowing that words can create happiness or suffering, I am committed to speaking truthfully using words that inspire confidence, joy, and hope. When anger is manifesting in me, I am determined not to speak. I will practice mindful breathing and walking in order to recognize and to look deeply into my anger. I know that the roots of anger can be found in my wrong perceptions and lack of understanding of the suffering in myself and in the other person. I will speak and listen in a way that can help myself and the other person to transform suffering and see the way out of difficult situations. I am determined not to spread news that I do not know to be certain and not to utter words that can cause division or discord. I will practice Right Diligence to nourish my capacity for understanding, love, joy, and inclusiveness, and gradually transform any anger, violence, and fear that lie deep in my consciousness.

Given the corrosive public discourse that permeates public life in much of the Western world, how can we practice kindness and solidarity in our speech so we don't add to ill will, blame, and demonizing? Conversely, how can we listen well to people who disagree with us? How can we keep their inherent goodness in mind even as we dialogue respectfully to help understand and transform the situation? Can we offer compassionate listening with a wholehearted intent to help relieve suffering and find common ground?

Sometimes our speech is unkind in subtle ways. For example, when I began working with this practice, I realized that my use of sarcasm was a type of unkind speech. I used to enjoy indulging in sarcasm, especially about public events or politicians. But I came to see that this was a form of verbal violence, disrespect, not caring, dismissing the person, splitting them off into an "other" category, creating dualism and separation. As I noticed this more often, I asked myself where my impulse to be sarcastic came from. I realized it covered over my great disappointment in those public figures. Sarcasm prevented me from feeling the separation, the disconnect, and the anger. So now I try my best not to use sarcasm, even when it is very tempting!

In his essay "Falling in Love with the Earth," Thay says that Earth nourishes and protects all people and all species *without discrimination*.[7] This includes all buddhas and great beings. It also includes political leaders of all stripes. It includes the Black protesters and the neo-Nazis in the streets of Charlottesville, Virginia. Treating the continuum of people with equanimity may be challenging, but it can be a very beneficial practice. A few examples:

○ Once, during a presidential primary here in the United States, I invited people in our meditation group to say which of the many primary candidates they had the most compassion for, and which ones they had the least compassion for, and why. It was a challenging exercise that surfaced some of our biases and reactivity.

○ I have practiced loving kindness meditation for all political candidates, for all the sitting politicians, and for all the advocates across the political spectrum. I've offered this wish for them: "May you be happy, healthy, peaceful, safe, and free from fear." While doing this practice, I was able to imagine their positive qualities. I remembered that each of them was once a five-year-old child. This practice, over time, can help us develop compassion toward others. It doesn't mean we don't challenge bigotry, untruthfulness, or dangerous talk, but we engage in compassionate dialogue while trying to keep the person's essential wholesomeness in mind.

We can practice having conversations with people who have differing viewpoints. We can learn how to have compassionate dialogue and reach for common understanding. We can listen well. For example, the week after January 6, 2021, I wrote a kind of love letter to the people who stormed the US Capitol. In the United States, unkind speech dominates much of public discourse. The vitriol and meanness are toxic, divisive, and counter to true communication. When trying to engage with people whose views we disagree with or disapprove of, presenting them with facts or attacking them personally does not cause them to change their minds. It might serve as an emotional release for us, but it doesn't move the conversation. A more reliable approach is to try to speak to their hearts, reach for our shared humanity, treat them with respect, and be interested in them.

In my letter, I tried to identify with the insurrectionists' passion and love of country, to reach for common ground despite our different views, and to invite a civil dialogue. I sent the letter to two very politically conservative friends of mine and asked for their feedback. We had several rounds of cordial emails until I asked each of them what they would do if they were in charge. This was a bridge too far for them, and they each stopped communicating. Although I did not send the letter to any others, I shared it on my website (*https://beginwithin.info*) and found the process of writing and sharing it to be a very helpful practice for me.

The Fifth Mindfulness Training: Nourishment and Healing

Aware of the suffering caused by unmindful consumption, I am committed to cultivating good health, both physical and mental, for myself, my family, and my society by practicing mindful eating, drinking, and consuming. I will practice looking deeply into how I consume the Four Kinds of Nutriments, namely edible foods, sense impressions, volition, and consciousness. I am determined not to gamble or to use alcohol, drugs, or any other products that contain toxins, such as certain websites, electronic games, TV programs, films, magazines, books, and conversations. I will practice coming back to the present moment to be in touch with the refreshing, healing, and nourishing elements in me and around me, not letting regrets and sorrow drag me back into the past nor letting anxieties, fear, or craving pull me out of the present moment.

Every time I read this mindfulness training, I see how powerful it is and how intertwined it is with the other four precepts. In its implication and aspiration, it is both daunting and encouraging. Trying to practice this training touches on deep, lifelong habit energies such as feelings of loneliness, disappointment, discouragement, isolation, and hurt. I realize that if I break this vow, break my determination, then I am like most everyone who breaks their own internal promises. This fact can help me feel deeper compassion for others who break precepts, laws, bonds, or relationships. Practicing this Fifth Mindfulness Training calls forth both vigilance and compassion.

In addition to being entwined with the other four trainings, the fifth one is unlike the others in one key respect. The first four are about what we put out, what we direct toward others. Said negatively, they are: no killing, no stealing, no sexual misconduct, and no lying. Said positively, they are: respect all life, be generous, have loving relationships, and speak with good purpose. The fifth training is about what we take in. Said negatively, it is: don't take in toxins from anywhere. Said positively, it is: cultivate good health, both physical and mental; consume mindfully.

If we are feeling blue, lonely, discouraged, angry, unloved, or hopeless, unless we bring mindfulness to these mind states, we often do things we think will make us feel better. If we eat or drink something that contains unhealthy ingredients and that clogs the arteries, grows fat tissues, or floods the blood with too much glucose, then our bodies get more tense and stressed. If we sit and play a violent video game or watch sports or TV programs that portray anger, vengeance, and hurtful actions, then those images and distress build up in us. If we turn outward for relief from our bad feelings, we might talk trash or gossip about someone. If these don't give us enough temporary relief, we might feel pushed to hurt someone sexually, steal, or become aggressive or even murderous toward others. What we take in greatly conditions what we put out.

So, what messages do we consume or take into our consciousness that lead us to feel bad?

Once I was facilitating a workshop on diversity and identity. Around the room I placed sheets of newsprint. Each sheet was labeled with a different social identity: immigrants, Black people, gays and lesbians, working-class people, rural folks, rich people, Latinx people, people with disabilities, women, overweight people, Jews, Muslims. The participants were asked to write up negative things they had heard about each group. Afterward, they were invited to look at what was written up. It was horrifying. There were so many hate-filled messages. When I asked the participants how it would affect them if they were in one of those categories of people, many insights and lots of compassion arose.

Most of us have received our own versions of these messages. Perhaps most of the ways people feel bad about themselves are rooted in having grown up in a particular group and having been subjected to negative societal judgments about that group. It is an example of interbeing: this is, because that is. Thay says that happiness is not an individual matter. Unhappiness also is not an individual matter. Much of people's dysfunction, addiction, and neuroses is linked to the toxic societal messages we have consumed throughout our lives.

In many ways, it is obvious that what we consume impacts us. "We are what we eat" is one truth. If we eat junk, our body gets unhealthy. If we eat whole foods, our body gets happy. Likewise, what we feed our minds shapes our bodies, our thoughts, and our actions. And so much of the edible food and mental food that we ingest has harmful effects below our consciousness.

I remember reading about a practitioner who was doing a ten-day meditation retreat. Around day three, after her mind had settled a bit, what arose were terrifying images from a movie she had seen when she was a little girl. It disturbed her calm. As she investigated the images over the next few days, her conscious awareness was flooded with other scenes from horror movies and monster movies she had watched throughout her childhood. She was a solid enough practitioner that she was able to watch the parade of terrifying images pass through. But it was striking to her that they had been stored in her subconscious all these years, below awareness, taking up a certain psychic space. Who knows how that vault of scary scenes had influenced her life. She reported feeling lighter and more fearless because of surfacing and facing these memories.

Another aspect of consuming is that in our capitalist society, we are offered individualistic solutions for collective problems. For example, much of our food is filled with chemicals and additives that cause sickness and disease. In the last fifty years, rates of obesity have tripled in the United States.[8] What is offered as a solution? Dieting. The dieting industry is a multibillion-dollar enterprise that profits off people's distress. People who are overweight often feel ashamed, blame themselves, and pay gobs of money for one diet program after another, even though experience shows that diets usually don't work. What is not challenged is the huge shifts in our food production system over the last fifty years: monocropping; the use of glyphosate (Roundup); genetically modified seeds; increased use of food additives, corn syrup and other sugars, processed food, and fast food; food deserts in low-income communities; and junk food everywhere. Even our schools have become purveyors of malnutrition to young people by contracting for vending machines stuffed full of junk food.

Our consumption habits are hurting the Earth. With our thirst for more, we extract, clear-cut, overfish, deplete resources, dump toxic waste into the waterways and oceans, and poison the land and air with chemicals. Looking deeply helps us examine our desires, and as we become increasingly aware, we realize that our personal and collective consumption is part of addressing climate change.

Less obvious objects of consumption include the media, news, entertainment, conversations, and jokes we take in. Which ones are wholesome and which are toxic? How can we protect our impressionable consciousness from unwholesome consumption? This inquiry can help guide us, individually and collectively, toward simpler, more wholesome, mindful, and responsible living. Thich Nhat Hanh suggests a three-part approach for practicing mindful consuming: (a) make a list of the kinds of toxins that we already take into our body and mind; (b) be mindful of what we ingest into our bodies and consciousness today; (c) prescribe a healthy diet for body and mind, make a list, and begin following it.[9]

Buddhist teacher Jack Kornfield suggests this practice: "Undertake for one week or one month to refrain from all intoxicants and addictive substances, such as wine, marijuana, even cigarettes and caffeine if you wish. Observe the impulses to use these, and become aware of what is going on in the heart and mind at the time of those impulses."[10]

I've also found it useful to practice saying these sentences:

"Aware of the suffering caused by internalized hurt, I am committed to loving myself deeply and completely in each moment of daily life. This will mean . . ." I complete the sentence and repeat it as many times as needed.

"I am determined not to engage in intentional destruction of life, stealing, sexual misconduct, hurtful speech, or mindless consumption, which mainly arise from not loving myself. To cultivate deep and complete loving of myself, I vow to . . ." I complete the sentence and repeat it as many times as needed.

Likewise, transformation of suffering happens in interconnected ways and ripples out in many directions. For example, let's imagine that I notice a tree in bloom and allow myself to stop for a few minutes, take in its beauty, and feel grateful for the wonders of spring. This makes me feel happy and light as I go into a grocery store. I say kind words of appreciation to the store clerk, which helps her feel better about herself, and that motivates her to choose a healthy lunch instead of her usual diet of junk food. She enjoys the fruit and hummus so much that she is inspired to shift her family's diet to include more whole foods. Eventually, this decision leads to reduced sickness and lower health care costs for her family, as well as diminished support for the industrial food system. Her children learn to care for their bodies through healthy plant-based food, and they eventually pass these values on to their own children.

○

Each of the Five Mindfulness Trainings is interconnected with the other four, and practicing deeply with one will inevitably impact the others. When I use kind speech, I am increasing reverence for life. When I protect my mind and body from toxins, I am being generous toward myself and those I love. When I appreciate a store clerk, I add energy to collective well-being. And on and on in endless circles.

7

ENGAGING IN MINDFUL SOCIAL ACTION

The World is perfect as it is,
including my desire to change it.

—Ram Dass

Seeing and acting go together.
Otherwise, what is the point in seeing?

—Thich Nhat Hanh

"Don't Shoot!"

Sometimes life thrusts us into a situation that demands quick action. One time, I faced a challenge that made me realize the importance of training to handle interpersonal conflict as effectively as possible.

Cynthia and Rocco lived on the third floor of our communal house. They were a Puerto Rican couple in their early twenties. I had known Cynthia since she was an elementary student at the parent-controlled freedom school in East Harlem where I taught for years. I did not know Rocco well but saw that he was a hardworking young guy trying to make it out of poverty. We lived with a group of neighborhood schoolteachers in a brownstone in Central Harlem, a

Black neighborhood in New York City. It was the 1970s, when collective houses were fairly common.

One morning about 3 a.m., I was awakened by Cynthia screaming, "Don't shoot! Don't shoot!" I impulsively jumped out of bed and ran up the stairs in my bare feet and underwear to find Rocco with a handgun, trying to force his way into their room, and Cynthia struggling to keep him out.

Without thinking, I stepped between them. The gun was up against my bare belly. In a flash, I had the presence of mind to say in a calm voice, "Rocco, you must really be upset, because I know you don't want to hurt Cynthia!" Immediately, he dropped the gun, leaned into me and started crying, pouring out his pain and suffering.

My wife, scared of potential violence, had called the police while I was running upstairs. So as Rocco and I sat on a bed, with him crying about the disrespect and hurts he'd experienced in his life that had been triggered by his fight with Cynthia, suddenly two very large police officers arrived at the front door and clumped their way up the two flights of stairs. I tried my best to explain the situation, but they were responding to a domestic violence call, and Cynthia indicated that she needed some space from Rocco to calm down. The police officers took him into custody overnight. Cynthia didn't press charges but wanted time to recover from that scary incident.

The whole scene with the gun happened in a flash. I am not recommending that anyone should or could do anything similar to what I did. I acted intuitively, almost impulsively. I put myself at risk, acknowledged Rocco's pain in a kind way, spoke to his humanity, offered him respect, and stayed close to listen to his story. It wasn't a thought-out response or a deliberate strategy. But it may be worth noting some elements that helped prepare me for this intuitive moment.

First, Rocco and I knew each other; we already had a relationship. Though we were not close, I sensed that he would not shoot me. But I didn't know for certain, so it was risky. I probably would have done something quite different if I had not known him. I made a split-second decision to trust our connection. Second, I think the fact that I stood in front of him in my underwear and bare feet made me appear somewhat vulnerable and unthreatening. Third, I arrived in that moment with years of training in two deep practices that I have shared about in this book. One practice was mindfulness meditation, which conditioned me to slow my racing mind, nurture compassion, and feel interconnected with everyone. The other practice was Re-evaluation Counseling, a method of peer counseling that provided me with regular opportunities to heal my inner wounds and taught me how to hold a loving space for others who were experiencing deep distress. In the heat of the situation with Rocco, I didn't have to think about what to do. My instinct coupled with these long-term trainings gave me some automatic skillfulness.

The peer counseling training assumes that people are inherently good and worthwhile, but the suffering that happens to us covers our awareness of our wholesome nature. When we are upset, when our old wounds get restimulated, we can very easily get knocked off our center, lose our usual reasonableness, and act out in ways that often cause more harm.

That night, a deep unhealed wound in Rocco got touched, and he flipped out. What he needed in that moment was a way to drop underneath the reactive behavior to the hurting part inside him. I provided a calm presence, a safe space, an acknowledgment of his hurt, and a voice speaking to his essential goodness. When I said, "Rocco, you must be really upset, because I know you don't want to hurt Cynthia," he felt seen. Someone saw that he was hurting, didn't judge him for being upset, and pointed to the deeper reality of his love for Cynthia. Important healing happened for him as he cried about his early hurtful experiences. In our Western culture, it is rare for us to have a safe space to express our feelings: to cry, or shake with fear, or rage with anger in a safe way, or grieve at life's losses. It's especially rare for men.

My training in mindfulness was completely in sync with this counseling approach. Training the mind is a seminal task and instruction of many spiritual traditions. Why? Because the mind shapes our thoughts, which shape our words and our actions. In Buddhism, for example, it is taught that if we think impure, hateful, or unwholesome thoughts, unhappiness will result. And if we think pure, loving, wholesome thoughts, happiness will follow us.

Here are some elements of training the mind that I have found useful:

I try to see the person's sacred inner being as separate from their unwholesome behavior, no matter what they are doing. If I hold fast to a belief in their true, good nature, it helps me see their harmful habit energy as a distortion caused by wounding or wrong ideas. This training helped me assume Rocco was truly a good person, even though he appeared angry and violent in that heated moment. My training in mindfulness also informed me that deeper truths underlie any conflict. A conflict is a broken relationship crying out to be mended.

I calm my own mind with concentration and mindfulness. If my mind is racing or restless or jumping from thing to thing uncontrollably, then my words and actions are also likely to be unfocused, restless, and even chaotic. The mind tends to take on the energy of whatever it thinks about. That's why many spiritual traditions ask the practitioner to slow their mind by focusing on a single object of awareness, like the breath, a mantra, or a prayer. From a quiet, concentrated mind can arise deeper truths about the nature of things, which a busy mind misses. Over time, my regular meditation practice helped me recognize my reactive thinking, embrace and heal some of my inner wounds, and nurture a level of emotional steadiness that allowed me to stay calm with Rocco. This capacity to stay calm was not a conscious decision in the moment but a deeply internalized habit of mind.

I practice seeing everything as interconnected. There is only one indivisible reality that holds everything. We are related to each othcr, depend on each other, and cannot be separate from each other, even if we feel separate. This is not my belief; it is a universal truth of reality. What hurts you hurts me, and vice versa, even when we are not aware of this. So, violence anywhere sends shivers out across indivisible reality and makes all beings less safe. Likewise, loving kindness anywhere reverberates across indivisible reality and increases well-being for all. I *knew* what Rocco was feeling, because I also had felt angry and violence prone. I *knew* he had inherent worth because I had it too. I *knew* he needed to feel validated and connected in that desolate moment, because I had been there too. My training to see and experience interconnection helped me connect with Rocco. Again, it was not a conscious decision but a honed practice.

I try to hold an open mind without preconceptions. Thanks to my training to question assumptions and not act hastily, I was curious—I wanted to know what was going on with Rocco rather than assuming he was up to no good. If I had not engaged in this type of training, I might have heard the scream, seen the gun, and reacted aggressively without asking what was provoking this scene. In other situations, I have had to use force to stop someone from harming themselves or another person. Sometimes fierceness is necessary. Discernment is key. Because of years of training my mind, in an instant I was able to think there might be danger, assume Rocco was hurting, trust our relationship, respond softly and lovingly and calmly to counteract his upset, and act to protect him and Cynthia by reaching for his heart, not his gun.

In truth, I do not know which parts of my response to Rocco were simply intuitive and reflexive, and which ones were conditioned by having trained my mind over years. I suspect both were at play. Also, I think it's important to note that even the best training may not prevent violence in all cases. But it can greatly increase the likelihood of a peaceful, positive resolution.

To this day, I am grateful for all the conditions that allowed a potentially tragic moment to turn into a healing moment.

Training and preparation are essential for effective action engagement. Let's explore the action dimension.

> **Practice Suggestion**
>
> What are some ways you are training your mind? How would you like to refine these? What's one new way you would like to train your mind, and how can you go about it?

Framing the Social Action Dimension

Why Action?

The Beloved Community will not come into existence by itself. At minimum, it requires all the conditions explored in previous chapters and diagramed below, plus a huge dose of good fortune.

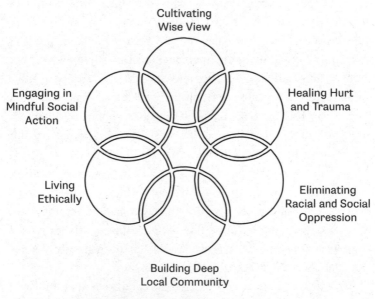

Cultivating
Wise View

Engaging in
Mindful Social
Action

Healing Hurt
and Trauma

Living
Ethically

Eliminating
Racial and Social
Oppression

Building Deep
Local Community

Conditions for the Beloved Community

In this chapter we come to the last element or pathway: social action. Realizing the world we want requires action—individual and collective, visionary, nonviolent, multidimensional, worldwide, sustained over time, aimed at transformation at the base of society.

None of these six elements explored in this book stands alone, and all of them are intertwined. Action elements have already been mentioned in each of the previous five chapters. So, it is somewhat artificial to pull social action out and focus on it as a separate piece. After all, authentically engaging in mindful social action is inseparable from cultivating wise view. It necessitates healing trauma, must include transformation of oppression, is much more powerful with an engaged community, and will be hollow if not grounded in the integrity of daily ethical behavior. This chapter explores both inner and outer engagement, and it focuses primarily on actions in the wide world that is hurting badly and calling us to heal what we've harmed.

Reform or Transformation?

In all honesty, I am pulled in two directions regarding social action. On the one hand, it seems presumptuous to prescribe specific actions. There are more than enough ways to engage. We don't need to waste time debating which issue is most important, like whether we first need to eliminate racism or curb climate change or secure democracy or end capitalism. For me, seeing that interbeing is true, it doesn't much matter where we begin acting. If we imagine society like a piece of fabric and begin pulling just one thread, since all the threads are interdependent, eventually that entire fabric will unravel. In fact, renowned writer, activist, and Buddhist scholar Joanna Macy uses the term "the Great Unraveling" to point to the likelihood of systems collapse if we continue our present course.[1] My main guidance for myself and others is to begin where we are and do what we love. If we come from love, then our values, motivation, and energy will be more aligned than if we are acting from some "should."

On the other hand, as I said in chapter 1, I think our current economic system, which pursues profit above all else, is the major *external* source of individual and collective suffering. Piecemeal reforms at the edges are valuable and necessary, but these are Band-Aids to stop the bleeding. They are not undoing the structures that cause the bleeding. Until our brutal, extractive, corporate economy is transformed into a caring, cooperative, fair, and sustainable economy, the Beloved Community is not attainable.

Which is it—patiently reforming by doing what we love, or upending capitalism? Actually, both. We can follow a middle way. Ideally, we do what we love, wholeheartedly, to move toward a more humane society because love can overcome hate and ill will, and love will sustain us longer. And we do what we love within a larger aspiration of transforming society and the current greed-based economy.

Taking this middle way means I ask myself questions like these:

○ How is the issue or problem I'm addressing caused by our current economy?

○ How is capitalism perpetuating racism or any other systemic oppression? Why?

○ When we work on one issue—whether it is immigration, or criminal justice reform, or voting rights, or wetlands preservation, or LGBTQIA+ rights, or reproductive choice, or protesting a fracked gas pipeline, or growing a community garden, or building opportunity structures for low-income youth—how does this effort help us move toward a new, caring, cooperative economy?

○ How does what I'm doing help generate conditions for the transformation of our economy?

○ How can I make explicit the connections between climate change and racism and the economy? And ask others to consider the connections?

○ How can I invite others to envision living in a Beloved Community?

○ How can I speak with relaxed confidence about our future in the face of discouraging news?

○ No matter what work I'm doing, how can I find ways to make friends with folks quite different from me, or at least engage in compassionate dialogue?

Practice Suggestion

Try asking yourself some of these questions and reflect on what arises.

For example, if we focus on climate change, we know the evidence is mounting that we are crossing planetary boundaries by creating loss of biodiversity, diminished fresh water, soil depletion, ocean acidification, and global warming.[2] We know that environmental damage is monumental, and that humans' and other species' suffering will deepen immensely. Obviously, the Earth is calling us to act. Doing nothing is unacceptable and immoral because it ignores the damage humans have done. But what exactly do we do? In my view, we must do many things at once, which is both daunting and exciting. We preserve the forests, soils, water, and oceans from further deterioration. We transition off fossil fuels to renewables quickly. We draw down carbon from the atmosphere. The wealthy countries fund mitigation and clean technology transfers to the developing countries. And so much more. As necessary as all these actions are, they address the symptoms but not the root causes. Therefore, simultaneously, we must engage in transforming two underlying causes of the symptoms: a global economy based on greed, and collective consciousness steeped in the delusion of separateness. Without transformation of these two, those other efforts will not suffice.

Mindfulness and Social Action

The realm of social action is a vast field for mindfulness practice. We want some things in the world to be different. We judge other things to be wrong, unjust, or hurtful. Still other aspects of life, we don't pay much mind to. These three can be spoken of as desire, aversion, and ignorance. Whether we get attached to things going our way, or we can't get rid of undesirable things, we can feel frustrated, powerless, angry, or sad. We can be so agitated that we act with urgency, haste, unskillfulness, maybe even violence. Or we withdraw, go numb, give up. All these responses result in more suffering.

These are the opening verses of the classic Buddhist text the Dhammapada:

> Mind is a forerunner of all actions.
> All deeds are led by mind, created by mind.
> If one speaks or acts with corrupt or impure mind,
> suffering follows,
> As the wheel follows the hoof of an ox pulling a cart.
> Mind is the forerunner of all actions.
> All deeds are led by mind, created by mind.
> If one speaks or acts with a serene mind,
> happiness follows,
> As surely as one's shadow.[3]

Unless our mind is clear, steady, peaceful, and compassionate, our actions can be the cause of more suffering, even if we have the best of intentions. The starting place is within us. However, self-transformation is a lifelong process, so we can't wait—indeed it is impossible to wait—until we are completely healed and free from suffering before we act. We show up in each moment with our imperfect selves, and we act as best we can in that moment. As our awareness increases, our actions give us exquisite feedback about where we might need more inner work. Likewise, our continuing inner work guides us ever more accurately to wise action.

Ram Dass's quote at the top of this chapter tickles me: "The World is perfect as it is, including my desire to change it." It captures the seeming paradoxes that arise as we consider improving the world. For example:

How do I accept things as they are while trying to change the things I view as unwholesome?

How do I act for justice without blaming and demonizing others?

How do I let go of my notions of right and wrong while still acting to right the wrong?

How do I act with all due haste to stop hurt and harm without being urgent and hateful?

How do I nurture social justice without getting rigidly attached to my notions about justice?

How do I make action plans and not get attached to the outcomes of those plans?

It is worth reminding ourselves of some elements of mindfulness from chapter 1:

For me, applying a mindfulness lens means trying to be awake to what is happening in the present moment as best I can; trying to see the impermanent and interconnected nature of reality; questioning common dualistic thinking of "us" and "them;" aspiring to look at all beings with eyes of compassion; seeing the universality of suffering and the irrepressible human aspiration for happiness; connecting the links between individual and collective struggle and liberation; always looking for root causes that underlie present conditions; grounding myself in the fact that everything changes; and striving to offer perspectives and projects that nourish the flourishing, well-being, peace, and joy of all beings and the Earth.

Two points are essential to keep in mind:

The path of personal transformation is not separate from the path of social transformation. It is delusion to think that I can be genuinely happy while the world is messed up. We can't have a private paradise while the world around us is on fire. In other words, transformation of external social structures and inner consciousness go hand in hand. And as long as we continue to be divided around race and class, we are unlikely to transform systems of injustice. To use a crude image, in our orientation to a particular identity or issues, we are trying to move society on skateboards, bicycles, and golf carts—this is good, but it's not the locomotive that pulls the train forward. To truly advance, what we need is a broad swath of working people, poor people, trade unions, and their allies. Without dismantling the class society and transforming capitalism into a caring, just economy, we are tinkering at the edges, and individual suffering will keep piling in. Realizing this, I commit ever more to working to change the social conditions that give rise to suffering, while I also continue to heal my personal hurts.

Nonviolence is the means and the end. Reverence for life is a guiding principle for social action. This is huge, demanding, complex, and challenging to embody.

Let's dig a little deeper into nonviolence as a bedrock approach to social action.

> ### Reflection Question
> Which of these mindfulness elements might you need to cultivate more?

Relevance of Nonviolence to Today's Civil Unrest

Civil unrest is on the rise around the world. In 2019 and 2020 alone, there were huge sustained social justice protests in Hong Kong, Chile, Lebanon, Sudan, Venezuela, Iran, the United States, and other countries. Massive global "climate strikes" took place on September 20, 2019, with visible actions coordinated by young people and Extinction Rebellion. Then the murder of George Floyd in 2020 ignited the largest protest in US history, with millions of people filling the streets all over the country for days. The spark, or issues, or goals of these protests differed: economic justice, political freedom, democracy, racial equity, dignity and human rights, Earth justice. But all of them have touched into a deep sense held by many people that the system is rigged and that there needs to be transformation at the base, not just reform at the margins.

Most of the demonstrations and protest movements are primarily focused on government or corporate policies or actions that are seen as repressive, unjust, or harmful. These movements have many brave and creative facilitators with tons of experience, savvy, and deep values. The call and response for civil unrest and nonviolent resistance seems to be an alternative to inaction or slow change from the powers that be. And civil disobedience may become increasingly compelling and necessary as one approach to confront intransigent forces standing in the way of fundamental change. There is much truth in this approach.

A companion truth is that the roots of social and ecological suffering also lie deep in our individual and collective consciousness—namely greed, hatred, and the conditioning to think we are separate beings. Unless these roots are transformed, the external structural changes will not hold. For example, the twentieth-century revolutions in Russia, China, Cuba, and South Africa all turned sour partly because structural change, by itself, was not enough. Changing the faces at the top is not sufficient for true transformation. To be sustainable, it needs to go hand in hand with the healing of emotional damage and a shift away from greed, hatred, and competition.

When people think of nonviolent civil disobedience, we often think of Gandhi or Martin Luther King Jr. I first read about Gandhi when I was sixteen. He became one of my early teachers. For Gandhi, the great marches—like the Salt March of 1930, which marked the beginning of the end of British rule in India, although it took until 1947 to become official—were the smallest part of the work, the tip of the iceberg.

The largest, most important part of Gandhi's nonviolent way of being was what he called "self-purification." This is the deep

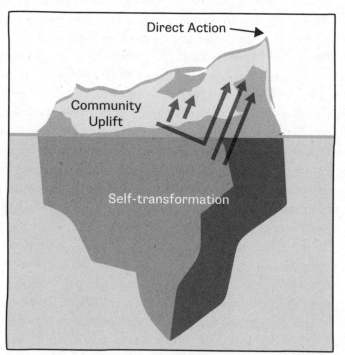

Graphic courtesy of Fierce Vulnerability

The Gandhian Iceberg

work of healing from emotional wounds, addictions, and internalized oppression; eliminating toxins from our diet, speech, and behavior; letting go of ego; and living an ethical life. Gandhi developed communities, ashrams, and rigorous practices to support this kind of deep personal and collective work. The second-largest part of Gandhi's nonviolent way of life he called the "constructive program." This was intended to develop self-sufficiency, sovereignty, self-rule, and service. People lived in communities, spun their own cotton, made their own clothes instead of buying British-made textiles, grew their own food, schooled their children, served those in need, accepted the "untouchables" (now called Dalits) into their communities, uplifted the role of women, and followed a vegetarian diet. Many of us have spent our lives in various constructive programs. I always thought of the organization that I helped build, YouthBuild USA, as a constructive program.

Under Gandhi's approach, only when people had done sufficient work on their own personal transformation and had served the constructive program enough were they ready for *satyagraha*—translated as "truth force," a direct action campaign. In fact, for the Salt March, Gandhi chose seventy-eight people as the core group to provide stability to the movement. These seventy-eight had engaged in serious spiritual practice and rigorous training in nonviolence, and had spent an average of fifteen years in the ashram, internalizing the way of nonviolence.

Even then, two weeks before the Salt March, knowing they were going up against British state power, Gandhi wrote in a letter to his followers, "Not a single believer in nonviolence as an article of faith for the purpose of achieving India's goal should find himself free or alive at the end of the effort."[14] He wanted them to know what they were signing up for. Because of Gandhi's central principle that the means generate the end, he insisted that every step of the march would be a spiritual practice furthering self-purification and consciousness change.

Dr. Martin Luther King Jr. was inspired by Gandhi. King was thrust into social action as a twenty-six-year-old newly minted minister of a Baptist church when he was asked to lead the Montgomery bus boycott in 1956 and 1957. He did not have the decades of preparation and training in nonviolence that Gandhi had, but he had his Christian faith and Jesus as his model of loving one's enemy, turning the other cheek, and willingness to suffer for a larger purpose—marks of principled nonviolence. Over time, he and his colleagues built an organization and a movement that engaged millions of people in direct nonviolent campaigns, which helped change the face of racism in the United States. Here are the elements of his approach to nonviolence:

Martin Luther King's Fundamental Philosophy of Nonviolence

From the King Center.

Principle 1: Nonviolence Is a Way of Life for Courageous People

It is not a method for cowards; it does resist.

It is active nonviolent resistance to evil.

It is aggressive spiritually, mentally, and emotionally.

Principle 2: Nonviolence Seeks to Win Friendship and Understanding

The outcome of nonviolence is the creation of the Beloved Community.

The end result of nonviolence is redemption and reconciliation.

Principle 3: Nonviolence Seeks to Defeat Injustice, or Evil, Not People

Nonviolence recognizes that evildoers are also victims and are not evil people.

The nonviolent resister seeks to defeat evil, not persons victimized by evil.

Principle 4: Nonviolence Holds that Unearned, Voluntary Suffering for a Just Cause Can Educate and Transform People and Societies

Nonviolence is a willingness to accept suffering without retaliation; to accept blows without striking back.

Nonviolence is a willingness to accept violence if necessary but never inflict it.

Nonviolence holds that unearned suffering for a cause is redemptive and has tremendous educational and transforming possibilities.

Principle 5: Nonviolence Chooses Love Instead of Hate

Nonviolence resists violence of the spirit as well as the body.

Nonviolent love is spontaneous, unselfish, and creative.

Principle 6: Nonviolence Believes That the Universe Is on the Side of Justice

The nonviolent resister has deep faith that justice will eventually win.

Nonviolence believes that God is a God of justice.[5]

It is clear from this statement of principles that nonviolence is a deep and challenging practice. This is not a part-time job. Living by this code asks us to move into wholeness, cleanse our hearts of hate and ill will, heal our emotional wounds so we are not reactive, overcome feelings of powerlessness, be willing to take on suffering for a higher purpose, and practice love and compassion even in the face of violence.

To practice nonviolence like this essentially asks us to live as if we were already in the Beloved Community, because we truly have no chance of realizing the Beloved Community without embodying these principles.

Practice Suggestion

What is one way you can begin to pay more attention to one of the Kingian principles in your daily life?

O

Down through history, much nonviolent civil disobedience has arisen in the heat of struggle, not from training and preparation. Sometimes it has been successful, sometimes not. In 2011, Erica Chenoweth and Maria Stephan released their book *Why Civil Resistance Works: The Strategic Logic of Nonviolent Conflict*, a study of 323 mass actions and uprisings since 1900. They had expected to find that violence was more successful as a method of regime change, but the data proved otherwise: Countries with repressive regimes were ten times more likely to transition to democracy when the protest campaigns were nonviolent. Nonviolent campaigns prevailed in some of the anticolonial freedom struggles in Africa, played a huge role in ending apartheid in South Africa, and helped overturn repressive governments in the Arab Spring, even if temporarily. Harking back to Gandhi's "constructive program," Chenoweth says in an interview that Poland's Solidarity

Movement "built its own newspaper, its own schools, and even its own self-governing coalition in areas of resistance." Their book clearly points to the reality that even if a resistance campaign begins spontaneously in response to injustice, to succeed it needs to be sustained over time, and "it's hard . . . and it requires imagination and creativity. It requires organization. And it requires courage and discipline."[6]

True practitioners of nonviolence such as Gandhi, Martin Luther King Jr., and Thich Nhat Hanh have been very clear that nonviolence is not only a tactic or a skillful means. True nonviolence is a way of living and being. If we have real reverence for life—the first of the ethical precepts described in the previous chapter—it includes all life: every human, animal, plant, and mineral. No exceptions. Therefore, nonviolence is required in thought, word, and deed. Nonviolence is not just the absence of violence but also the active practice of peace. As peace activist A. J. Muste said, "There is no way to peace. Peace is the way."[7]

I believe that all beings have value and are emanations of the great Life Force, and this belief leads me to the practice of nonviolence toward all life forms. Though perfect nonviolence is impossible (for example, we kill grass and insects just walking across a field, and we kill vegetables to eat), the intention is to treat all life forms with respect and reverence. Nonviolence in my social action work is not just a tactic but a way of being. For example, with comrades and opponents alike, I try my best to practice kind speech, compassionate dialogue, and deep listening. I try to act with kindness and compassion toward everyone, even in a conflict situation. This also means that while I support stopping people from harming others and I support holding them accountable for the suffering they may be responsible for, I do not support demonizing opponents or seeking retribution, punishment, or exile. When people are causing harm, they need healing and restoration even as they are held accountable or relieved of the power that allows them to inflict harm.

Advocacy Principles of YouthBuild USA

Here is a practical application of a nonviolent, respectful approach that we used in YouthBuild (described in chapter 4), written by Dorothy Stoneman, founder and president. The set of attitudes and principles that have made YouthBuild's approach to community organizing effective thus far have been:

1. We have organized people on the basis of vision, caring, and responsibility, not on the basis of anger.

2. We have motivated people toward the common good, not for self-interest.

3. We have encouraged people to propose solutions, not to protest wrongs.

4. Our objective has been to win, not just to be morally right.

5. Our approach has been consistently to persuade and win over ever more allies, never to identify so-called "enemies" or to attack or embarrass the opposition.

6. Our advocacy work has had people who benefit from the campaign, such as youth in low-income communities, in the forefront of speaking and lobbying as well as participating in planning and policy-making.

7. We have organized for broad diversity, bringing as many relevant perspectives into the thinking as possible.

The result has been that we have produced no "enemies." We have attracted extremely responsible people who are able to sustain their energy over time, and we have achieved many of our objectives so far. We have followed these principles since 1988.

With this brief background on nonviolence, let's get more specific about action.

Discerning What to Do

Probably most of us ask ourselves repeatedly: What more can we do to help make things better? What are we to do in the face of nearly certain types of collapse? As I've made clear, we need transformation at the base. Piecemeal reforms at the edges will not transform our collective suffering. Refusing to look directly at the seriousness of our situation gives us false hope that somehow we can avert the worst, and keeps us numb enough to go along with accepting things as they are, or just advocating for mild reforms, thereby sealing our fate. In reality, both reform and transformation are needed.

A Helpful Framework

I find it important to have a framework to locate what I'm doing and how it fits into a larger picture. Joanna Macy offers a three-part framework that I like.[8] She says any deep social transformation involves three intersecting, nonlinear buckets of work. One is **holding actions**. This is where we are called to protest, to stand up against injustice, to say "No!" We march, we affirm that Black lives matter, we block pipelines, we challenge hate, we live in trees to stop the clear-cutting of forests, we protect the vulnerable. This is crucial work, and it can save lives. However, it doesn't change systems of harm.

Another circle of activity is **creating new structures inside the old**. On the edges of the corrupt society is where we create new ways of being. We create schools for girls in Afghanistan; we plant millions of trees in Africa to stop desertification; we promote the use of renewable energy; we experiment with regenerative agriculture, community banking, alternative medicine; we build nonprofit organizations to foster home ownership, neighborhood services, community policing, opportunities for low-income youth, reentry supports for returning citizens. We engage in electoral politics and legislative reform. YouthBuild is an example of this bucket of work. These kinds of activities are important for two reasons: they provide social benefits for people and the environment, and they point the way toward a humane and just social system.

However, these efforts are vulnerable to being swept away by changes in political power unless there is a strong third circle of activity: **consciousness shift**. The reforms made by building the new inside the old will not hold unless consciousness has evolved enough to inform public opinion to create unwavering support and foster collective awakening. In his book *The World We Have: A Buddhist Approach to Peace and Ecology*, Thich Nhat Hanh is clear about this:

> We need a kind of collective awakening. There are among us men and women who are awakened, but it's not enough; the masses are still sleeping. They cannot hear the ringing of the bells. We have built a system we cannot control. This system imposes itself on us, and we have become its slaves and victims.[9]

Changing our consciousness is a many-layered process, but it is absolutely important as part of realizing the Beloved Community. It is implied in Jesus' instruction to love thy neighbor, in Gandhi's self-purification requirement, in Thich Nhat Hanh's goal of waking up from the delusion of separateness. It is what we do when we embody the deep insights of impermanence and interbeing. Consciousness evolves as we heal from internalized hurt and trauma, as we make common cause with all groups to end oppression, as we refine our daily ethical practices. Consciousness shifts when, in community, we move from "me" to "we."

Action Menu

There is no shortage of ways to engage. This illustration mentions just a few.

A Wide Range of Mindful Actions
A Sampling

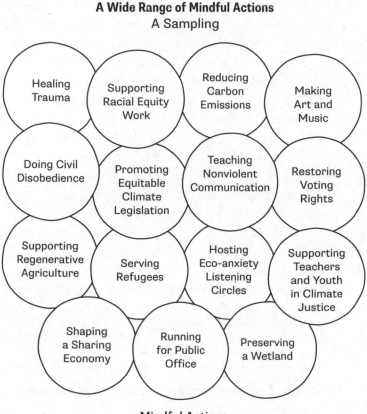

Healing Trauma

Supporting Racial Equity Work

Reducing Carbon Emissions

Making Art and Music

Doing Civil Disobedience

Promoting Equitable Climate Legislation

Teaching Nonviolent Communication

Restoring Voting Rights

Supporting Regenerative Agriculture

Serving Refugees

Hosting Eco-anxiety Listening Circles

Supporting Teachers and Youth in Climate Justice

Shaping a Sharing Economy

Running for Public Office

Preserving a Wetland

Mindful Actions

I am often asked, "What should I do to make a difference?" First, I generally don't think a "should" is a helpful motivation. We don't want to come from obligation or guilt but rather from love and reverence for all of life. Much of our suffering comes from trying to live the "shoulds" that were imposed on us. There are many sources of "shoulds"—including the expectations of parents, the criteria for belonging and not belonging in groups, religious ideals of what a "good" person does, definitions of success, dictates of cultural styles and beliefs. It can be challenging to find one's own voice and direction in such a mix.

Secondly, what we do is contextual. Sometimes we are called to be on the front lines, and sometimes we need to be on retreat. What we might have energy for in our twenties is quite different from what we might do in our seventies. Sometimes our actions are more limited than we'd like by our job requirements, our financial situation, our need to avoid being victimized by racist institutions, and so on. To illustrate, imagine a long-time leader in the climate justice movement whose mother has developed a terminal illness, and she has to decide whether to continue her key leadership role or devote the bulk of her energy to her mother. What is the "should" here?

Social engagement requires discernment. It is a deep practice that might include searching inside for our own truth, cultivating patience, undoing feelings of powerlessness, and loving ourselves more fully. Earlier I said that my general guideline is that we do what we love, knowing that everything is interrelated, and we continually ask how what we are doing contributes to the well-being of all. If you are trying to figure out your sweet spot for social action, you might try the exercise in the sidebar.

Practice Suggestion: Doing What You Love

Ayana Elizabeth Johnson, a marine biologist and climate activist, suggests this process for discerning where to put our efforts.[10] Ask:

a. What am I good at? What are my skills, experience, talents, expertise?

b. What do I see that needs doing? What are the issues in the public arena that I can see need attention?

c. What brings me joy in life? What reliably renews my energy and brings me alive? This process can help clarify what we can do that embraces all three questions.

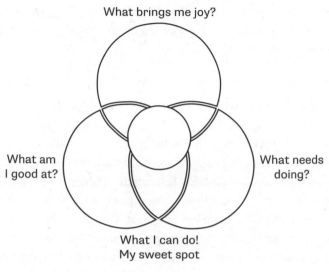

What brings me joy?

What am
I good at?

What needs
doing?

What I can do!
My sweet spot

Discerning Where to Put Our Efforts

Sustaining All Life (*www.sustainingalllife.org/resources/climate -change*), the climate justice initiative of Re-evaluation Counseling, has lists of things people can do in ways that integrate self-care with care for the environment.

Ongoing Study, Visioning, Skill-Building, Organizing

If we have determined how we want to contribute to the action dimension, there are some obvious next steps.

Study, Research, and Learning

We need to continue to educate ourselves and connect the dots so we increasingly see how issues like racism, climate change, war, and trauma intersect. In addition to this general background, members of a social action group will want to be informed about specifics of the issues they have decided to focus on, whether it is direct civil disobedience to stop a fracked gas pipeline, support for human immigration reform, creation of opportunities for marginalized groups, or another arena.

Visioning

As the saying goes: without a vision, the people perish. We do not want to be only protesting, or only expressing grievances about injustice, as necessary as these are at times. We want to be working toward "the more beautiful world our hearts know is possible," to use social thinker Charles Eisenstein's phrase.[11] I have found that engaging in visioning sessions from time to time helps me to become clearer about what I wish for. One of the tactics in any long-range social justice campaign is articulating and inspiring people about the benefits of a changed situation—for example, a world without racism, or an environment powered by clean energy, or a city where no one has to be homeless or folks do not have to worry about health care. (See "A Vision of Beloved Community" in chapter 8 below for an example of a visioning exercise.)

Reflection Questions

What is your vision for a better world? What skills would you like to deepen for your social justice engagement? What further study might you need?

Growing Our Skills

Ongoing training in new skills will help us become ever more effective in our engaged action. There are plenty of organizations that provide excellent training in social action skills.

Love Letter Writing Practice

One skill we can cultivate, and one type of action we can take, is kind speech. In the United States, unkind speech dominates much of public discourse. The vitriol and meanness are toxic, divisive, and counter to true communication. When trying to engage with people whose views we disagree with or disapprove of, presenting them with facts or attacking them personally does not cause them to change their minds. It might serve as an emotional release for us, but it doesn't move the conversation. A more reliable approach is to try to open their hearts, speak to our shared humanity, treat them with respect, and be interested in them. These are skills we can cultivate.

Among the many skills that could help, we could train ourselves to use kind speech and compassionate listening in conflictual situations. My friend Emma told me about a time that this training made a difference. She shared:

> It was election day in 2000. I was canvassing with many others, holding a sign supporting John Kerry for president. On the opposite corner of the intersection, there was a woman holding a sign for George W. Bush. Her husband had died in the Vietnam War, and she hated Kerry because of his work against that war. She kept saying, "When Kerry lied, people died," and talking about "Hanoi Jane" [Fonda]. She was pretty confrontational, and other Kerry canvassers were ending up in big arguments with her. She kept mentioning her husband dying in the war, so at one point I interjected and said I was so sorry her husband had died. She stopped, looked at me, and said, "No you're not. None of you people care about any of that." I said, "No, I really do. I care a lot about people dying because of war. That's why I think we shouldn't have wars." She answered, "Well if we hadn't entered World War II, we'd be walking around with slanted eyes speaking German." A bunch of canvassers heard that and started arguing with her more. I kept eye contact with her and just said that maybe sometimes certain wars are necessary, but I think we have more than we need to have. When other canvassers tried to get in on the conversation, arguing various points, she cut them off: "I'm only interested in talking with this lady, not you." She kept talking to me. She told me

about how terrible it had been to have her husband die and listen to Jane Fonda be a traitor, and Kerry was just the worst. I mostly listened. I don't know that I changed her mind about Kerry, but her tone softened significantly. I had been holding a bullhorn, and when a cop car drove over to check on us, she said to me, "Honey, hide your bullhorn, you don't want them seeing that," which I took as a sign that she felt connected to me.

Emma was more equipped to do this because she had been trained in deep listening as a co-counselor and recognized that the woman was hurting and needed acknowledgment of the heavy grief she was carrying. Emma's empathy created a small moment of connection that de-escalated a conflictual situation.

Thich Nhat Hanh teaches about writing love letters to officials as a form of mindful action:

> In the peace movement there is a lot of anger, frustration, and misunderstanding. The peace movement can write very good protest letters, but they are not yet able to write a love letter. We need to learn to write a letter to the Congress or to the President of the United States that they will want to read, and not just throw away. The way you speak, the kind of understanding, the kind of language you use should not turn people off. The president is a person like any of us.
>
> Can the peace movement talk in loving speech, showing the way for peace? I think that will depend on whether the people in the peace movement can *be* peace. Because without being peace, we cannot do anything for peace. If we cannot smile, we cannot help other people to smile. If we are not peaceful, then we cannot contribute to the peace movement.[12]

Here are suggestions for composing a love letter regarding a social justice concern.

1. Bring to mind the person or group you want to write to. Sit and contemplate what motivates you to write. Create a strong image of the person in your mind's eye, seeing what

you appreciate about the person, and what opens your heart regarding this person. You might imagine sending wishes for their well-being, like: "May you be happy, peaceful, healthy, safe from harm, and free from suffering." Even if you have a strong dislike of the person, wouldn't things be better if they *were* happy, safe, and free from suffering?

2. Write an affirmative and positive love letter to that person, sharing from your heart about what concerns you, trying to reach them with language they might respond to. Be as kind and respectful with your words as you can. You can note areas of disagreement and inquire about their thinking, with a sincere desire to understand the source of their viewpoint. If possible, you can also appreciate them for areas of their work that you genuinely respect.

3. Ask a friend to read your letter and offer you feedback.

4. Wait a couple of days, then incorporate the feedback and try to express even more compassion. Then send the letter.[13]

In a previous chapter, I referenced my attempt to write a kind of love letter to the people who stormed the US Capitol on January 6, 2021. My letter tried to communicate that I identified with their passion and love of country, that I too believe that the system is rigged against the well-being of the majority of citizens, that we have more in common than in conflict with each other, and that I'd like to engage in a civil dialogue to try to reach for common ground despite our different views.

Years before that, I wrote a letter to President Clinton urging him to make ending poverty a cornerstone of his administration. This letter is available on my website: *https://beginwithin.info*.

Organizing Ourselves

There are innumerable ways we can individually contribute to realizing the world we want to live in. For example, we can move our money from big banks that invest in fossil fuels to credit unions that invest in local communities. We can support farmers markets and eat more plant-based food. We can vote for candidates who are aligned with our values and vision. We can write to public officials using kind speech. We can practice abiding by the ecological motto of the Shakers: "Use it up, wear it out, make do, or do without." And on and on. And because big change requires collective action, each of us can take initiative for organizing ourselves into action pods, as described in the next section.

Beloved Community Circles

There is a real need to bring Buddhism into the
life of society, especially when you find yourself
in a situation of war or social injustice.

—Thich Nhat Hanh, *The World We Have:*
A Buddhist Approach to Peace and Ecology

As a contribution to the noble efforts to build the Beloved Community, here is a specific model for socially engaged action called "Beloved Community Circles."[14] This model was first developed and is being implemented by practitioners in the Plum Village Community of Engaged Buddhism. However, the model can be adapted for many other faith-based, justice-oriented communities.

A Lotus in a Sea of Fire

Many people are doing amazing and beautiful things to relieve suffering in the world, at all levels, from caring for an aging parent to working to end racial injustice to providing pivotal leadership for the Paris Climate Accords. It is also true that many folks want to engage in more direct mindful action under the umbrella of their spiritual community but either don't know how or don't want to do it alone.

"A lotus in a sea of fire" is a phrase Thich Nhat Hanh used to describe the cauldron of suffering during the wars in Vietnam, as well as the essence of our true nature that sits unharmed and upright in the midst of the flames. Today we are in our own sea of fire. The climate is hot. Racial turmoil in the United States is deep. Viral epidemics are deadly. Democracy is imperiled. Our economy is unfair and failing most people. In those war years in Vietnam, Thich Nhat Hanh told his followers that it was not enough to sit in the temple cultivating peace when the world around them was in flames. Mindful action to relieve suffering was also needed. He said, "When I was in Vietnam, so many of our villages were being bombed. Along with my monastic brothers and sisters, I had to decide what to do. Should we continue to practice in our monasteries, or should we leave the meditation halls in order to help the people who were suffering under the bombs? After careful reflection, we decided to do both—to go out and help people and to do so in mindfulness. We call it engaged Buddhism. Mindfulness must be engaged. Once there is seeing, there must be acting. Otherwise, what is the use of seeing?"[15]

He developed the School of Youth for Social Service, which engaged tens of thousands of young practitioners in education, health care, and agriculture in local villages. Like Thich Nhat Hanh, today we are called to respond to our suffering world, and to respond with compassion, courage, and mindfulness.

What Is a Beloved Community Circle?

In brief, a Beloved Community Circle (BCC) is a group of three to eight people, geographically local to each other, who engage in spiritual practice together, care for each other's well-being, and engage in mindful action of the group's choosing.

It's small and personal. A BCC is intended to be a small, intimate group of practitioners—not too few and not too many. They can go deep with each other, forge strong bonds of love and support with each other, train together, and become a dependable, reliable, courageous cohort for mindful and socially engaged action to meet the challenges of the day. Under certain circumstances, a BCC might be virtual rather than local and physical. For example, there might not be enough BIPOC practitioners in a particular locale, so BIPOC from various locations might form a virtual BCC.

It has a threefold purpose. A Beloved Community Circle's purposes are: (1) personal liberation: to practice deepening mindfulness for further liberation from personal suffering; (2) community building: to actively come to care about the well-being of the others in the BCC; and (3) social transformation: to collectively engage in application of practice in the wider world on issues of one's choosing or of importance to the whole group, somewhere on the axis of racial, social, and climate justice, for the purpose of protecting and preserving all living beings and the Earth in a way that is equitable toward all races, ethnicities, and species.

There is a self-chosen focus. Each Beloved Community Circle determines its own action focus somewhere in the territory of racial and climate justice. A BCC might want to organize around a particular identity marker or vocation, such as a BIPOC BCC, a queer BCC, or a BCC of healers or artists or vegans. A BCC can be focused more generally on social justice or can be organized around the specific interests of its members. One BCC may comprise folks who want to work on community resilience and apply those skills to their local community. Another BCC may focus on shutting down a coal-fired power plant in a low-wealth neighborhood. Another BCC may be interested in a specific advocacy project, like a carbon tax. Still another BCC may choose to support Indigenous leadership in water protecting. Still another may be engaged in protecting voting rights.

It is self-organized and autonomous. Each Beloved Community Circle is free to act on its own, organize itself, and call itself a BCC as long as it is in harmony with the basic what, why, and how of the initiative.

There is a six-month commitment. Each member of the Beloved Community Circle commits to participate for at least six months. This minimum commitment helps create consistency, stability, and trust among the members. At the end of the time commitment, each member assesses the impact of the experience and discerns whether or not to continue, with mutual agreement among all the members of the BCC. The assessment helps illuminate what worked and how the experience might be more inclusive and effective moving forward.

It includes ongoing training. Each Beloved Community Circle receives initial on-boarding training and periodic trainings to enhance skills, spread throughout the year, all online for easy access. Over time, trainings might include skill development in good group process, healing around racial and social inequities, nurturing a strong community, Kingian nonviolent direct action, personal healing and resiliency, deep listening partnerships, nonviolent communication skills, awareness and applied ethics, and mindful action pathways. Such trainings bolster our mindfulness skills with other effective abilities and methods.

It belongs to a network. Local Beloved Community Circles are linked into a global village through electronic platforms for sharing resources, experiences, and questions, connecting across Circles, and inspiring each other with mindful actions.

Members help sustain the network. The Beloved Community Circle network requires a certain level of funds and other resources to function well. For example, funds might be needed to support trainers to develop and facilitate trainings, to provide financial assistance for retreats and trainings to members who need it, to cover costs of electronic platforms, and possibly to cover the wages of a future part-time BCC coordinator. The BCC network aspires to live into a gift economy model,[16] trusting that each BCC member or BCC supporter will offer what they can from their wallets, resources, and hearts in a collective experiment of mutual support.

Spiritual practices are relevant. Wisdom traditions and Indigenous teachings have much to contribute and are exquisitely relevant to our collective efforts to face our situation, manage the grief, numbness, and fear, and attempt to curb the worst suffering. For example, my Buddhist mindfulness practice and Thich Nhat Hanh's teachings offer elements of wise view; a deep understanding of the key sources of suffering; practices of developing our love, compassion, sympathetic joy, and equanimity; a centering of community building as a necessary refuge; a specific set of ethics for everyday life; and a history of socially engaged practice as modeled by Thich Nhat Hanh.

The development of a network of Beloved Community Circles deliberately and purposefully organizes people to offer these or other spiritual practices in the wider world of suffering, by embodying the teachings through action to help bring forth healing, justice, and liberation of all.

For those who have not yet found their path or group for mindful action, perhaps being part of a Beloved Community Circle is a practical entry point because it provides a clear sense of purpose (practice, community building, and action), an intimate group as a home base, useful training, and local action in the context of a coordinated network.

Belonging and the Beloved Community

The Beloved Community is not just a group of our closest people who share our values. True Beloved Community, as envisioned by both Dr. King and Thich Nhat Hanh, excludes no one, sees no enemies, and creates a place of belonging for each and every person. Othering and exclusion of some folks from the favored group is one of the oldest and most persistent divisive habit energies that human groups manifest. The separation that results is one of the deepest wounds that people can experience, and it becomes institutionalized through systems of oppression like racism, sexism, classism, anti-Semitism, heterosexism, ageism, and others. A Beloved Community Circle deliberately works to create a place of belonging so that the Circle does not slip into recreating these dominant culture inequities.

Here is a beginning list of ways a BCC can work toward that ideal, while knowing this work is always evolving:

1. Incorporate basic awareness of the dynamics of oppression and conditioning around separation into the DNA of the BCC network.

2. Engage all BCC members in on-boarding trainings on racial justice, environmental racism, and climate justice.

3. Explore individual and collective self-audits of income, wealth, and resource status and possible ways to shift some resources.

4. At climate justice actions (like protesting a fracked gas pipeline), highlight the ways the issue is also a racial justice issue. At racial justice actions (like advocating for immigrants at the US southern border), highlight the ways the issue is also a climate justice issue. Keep connecting the dots.

5. If the BCC is based on affinity groups, make sure they are cultural sanctuaries and they stay connected to the larger BCC network for mutual learning and actions.

A Beloved Community Circle provides an entry point for folks who are wanting or waiting for an organized, safe, personalized, and collective way to engage in the issues of the day under the umbrella of their spiritual community. The small size of a Circle is manageable in terms of caring about each other, decision-making, resolving conflicts, and determining a common action or project. The BCC network, as of this writing, is in the early stages of expansion. The vision is to develop a large, robust, coordinated network of local mindful action teams that add more mindfulness, kind speech, caring and nonviolent action, nondualistic thinking, deep listening, and compassion to humanity's noble effort to protect and preserve Mother Earth and her beings.

○

For more information about how to start a Beloved Community Circle, write to *belovedcommunitycircles@gmail.com*.

Love. Heal. Act.

The beauty of our planet and its beings is beyond words. And the current suffering of our planet and its beings is heartbreaking. It makes me want to alternately celebrate and mourn, give gratitude and organize. Because the environmental crisis impacts everyone everywhere, and because it is interconnected with so many other crises, I'd like to explore three questions related to the climate situation.

- ○ How do we fall in love with Mother Earth over and over to nurture connection with the natural world?

- ○ How do we face the immensity of climate suffering and let our hearts break open without getting overwhelmed?

- ○ How does each of us take full responsibility for protecting and preserving our beloved Earth?

Falling in Love with Mother Earth Over and Over to Nurture Connection with the Natural World

When we were small, many of us had a secret or magical place in nature where we went for refuge, where we felt safe or renewed or in awe. I lived on Puget Sound, in a town across the bay from Seattle, with water and mountains all around. When I felt lonely or lost, I climbed the willow tree and looked out at the Olympic Mountains. Their solidity and calm soothed my agitation. When I was thirteen, I built a kayak and floated for hours, watching seagulls and clouds. I felt whole, embedded, happy. Do you have such a memory?

Across the political spectrum, most environmentalists started their action because of love. When asked what makes them care about the environment, they talk about memories of beloved places: a creek they fished that's now polluted, a forest they roamed that was cut down to build a shopping mall, or cypress trees in a bayou they call home, now dying because of oil sludge.

Finding ways of renewing our love for the natural world is the starting point that helps us look squarely at the climate catastrophe facing us. I try to take daily opportunities to pause my hurried pace. I might take a slow walk in the woods or even around the block to look at the trees, or sit by a stream, letting Earth elements penetrate the cells of my being. Years ago, my partner and I did a thirty-day hike in the Cascade Mountains in Washington State. With only what we carried in our backpacks, we were totally immersed in the natural world, walking slowly, drinking deeply the sights, sounds, and feel of the forest, the alpine meadows, the snow fed streams. Forty years later, the memories still sustain us.

There's a simple reflection by Saint John of the Cross about connection:

> I was sad one day and went for a walk.
> I sat in a field. A rabbit noticed my condition and came near.
> It often does not take more than that to help at times
> to just be close to creatures who are so full of knowing,
> so full of love though they don't chat.
> They just gaze with their marvelous understanding.[17]

Even though I have been conditioned to feel separate from nature, it is impossible for me to be separate. My actual relatedness is infinite. In an earlier chapter, I told the story of how Thich Nhat Hanh asked his students if we could see all the elements that were necessary for a piece of paper to manifest: the sun and the rain that nourished the tree from which the paper was made, the microorganisms under the tree, the soil, the logger, the food that sustained the logger, and so on, without limit. Take any of these elements away and the paper would not exist.

Likewise, each of us is dependent on an infinite number of causes and conditions. A famous quote from Martin Luther King Jr. beautifully captures this web of connection:

> You get up in the morning and go to the bathroom, and you reach over for a bar of soap, and that's handed to you by a Frenchman. You reach over for a sponge, and that's given to you by a Turk. You reach over for a towel, and that comes to your hand from the hands of a Pacific Islander. And then you go on to the kitchen to get your breakfast. You reach on over to get a little coffee, and that's poured in your cup by a South American. Or maybe you decide that you want a little tea this morning, only to discover that that's poured in your cup by a Chinese. Or maybe you want a little cocoa, that's poured in your cup by a West African. Then you want a little bread, and you reach over to get it, and that's given to you by the hands of an English-speaking farmer, not to mention the baker. Before you get through eating breakfast in the morning, you're dependent on more than half the world. That's the way reality is structured. So let us be concerned about others because we are dependent on others.[18]

I sometimes sit and feel into how the forest is in me, and I am in the forest, or the ocean, or the sky, or the desert. We are descendants not just of our human ancestors, but also of plant, earth, mineral, and star elements.

An immediate step in renewing a right relationship with the Earth is to pay attention. Be present. Start where we are. Whatever we really give our attention to, we come to care for. That calls up compassion. We feel for the clear-cutting of the forests where we grew up, or the destruction of the wetlands where we played as children, or the way they turned the meadow into a shopping center. What wakes us up is love. We need to touch what we love. We need to act from love because greed, ill will, delusion, and ignorance have brought us to the edge of destruction.

Practice Suggestion

Recall the practice detailed in chapter 2. For a period of time, try "adopting" a life form—a tree, a plant, an animal, an insect, or a land formation. Observe it, study it, learn about it, meditate on it, send loving kindness to it, come to care for it. See what arises when you become intimate with it.

At each meal, I try to keep my awareness alive by reciting Five Contemplations before Eating from the Plum Village tradition, offered by Thich Nhat Hanh. I look at the plate of food before me and say:

> This food is a gift of the earth, the sky, numerous living beings, and much hard and loving work.
>
> May we eat with mindfulness and gratitude so as to be worthy to receive this food.
>
> May we recognize and transform unwholesome mental formations, especially our greed, and learn to eat with moderation.
>
> May we keep our compassion alive by eating in such a way that reduces the suffering of living beings, stops contributing to climate change, and heals and preserves our precious planet.
>
> We accept this food so that we may nurture our community, and nourish our ideal of serving all living beings.[19]

You have your own ways of feeling your love for nature and the Earth. Maybe it's bird-watching or stargazing or gardening or caring for a pet or resting in a field. The encouragement here is to go to your well, often and deeply. This is a crucial part of mindful social action because it helps ground us in love, connects us more with our natural world, and motivates us to act.

Facing the Immensity of Climate Suffering and Letting Our Hearts Break Open without Getting Overwhelmed

In Buddhism, there is a teaching that the ten thousand joys and ten thousand sorrows exist side by side. We can enter deeper dimensions of life through either portal. Sometimes when we are in the love-for-the-Earth mind state, we are overcome with great feelings of gratitude, of awe, of praise, of yes! Sometimes seeing the sunset, or looking deeply at a flower, or watching a butterfly, or smiling at a baby duck trailing after its mama makes our jaw drop open in awe or tears roll down our face.

Or the other door opens, and we contemplate the immensity of the catastrophe that climate change is bringing. The warning bells of climate disaster are sounding loudly. The number of animals has been reduced by half in the last forty years, and 50 percent of all species could be extinct in eighty years, according to the World Wildlife Fund? Half of the Arctic ice is gone now? Coastal cities around the world could be flooded in thirty years? There may be 1.2 billion refugees from climate change, conflict, and civil unrest by 2050?[20]

And things are likely to get worse: crop failures, food and water shortages, huge species die-offs, mass human migration, regional conflicts, tyranny, and failed states. And low-income communities and poorer nations suffer the most harm. One scientist says we are heading for inevitable social collapse, probable environmental catastrophe, and possible human extinction.[21]

Think about these warnings. If we are even halfway awake and don't turn away from this suffering, then we are going to feel heartbreak, deep grief, loads of anger and waves of despair, and probably bouts of confusion and doubt.

How do we allow ourselves to face and feel the enormity of what is upon us? If we don't allow those feelings to arise and heal, then we are in danger of shutting down, going numb, hardening our hearts, distracting ourselves, and playing small ball. We know deep in our hearts that something is fundamentally out of right alignment. Because everything is interconnected, we hurt inside even when we read about things far away, like refugees fleeing rising sea levels, or the loss of another beautiful species that is gone forever, or the explosion of an oil rig that coats the shoreline for hundreds of miles with sludge that kills the seabirds. Our hearts break. In the human realm too, we hurt when others are hurting.

Whether or not we allow space to express the feelings connected with climate suffering, those feelings are present in us. We need safe ways to let our hearts break open, to let the grief or fear or anger flow through us so we don't get emotionally constipated. We can deliberately find ways of getting close to suffering—watching a climate awareness video, reading dispatches from scientists, being with folks who had to flee a wildfire or flood—and allow ourselves to feel our emotions according to what we feel able to assimilate. We might read any number of excellent books about our situation. We also need to recognize and heal feelings of powerlessness that we have accumulated, which may make current issues loom larger in our minds than they would if we were clear of past emotions.

Feelings are only feelings. They are not the whole of reality, though persistent feelings can fool us into thinking, *That's how things are*, or *That's how I am*. Unwholesome negative feelings are waiting to be healed. For example, recall the stories in chapter 3 about the mafia hit man who transformed, and the boy who fell off his bike and poured his heart out to me. Such healing requires safety, courage, and intention. In my experience, being listened to respectfully and warmly allows old memories to surface. If a listener persists in offering me undivided attention, I find myself crying with grief, or shaking or shivering with fear, or trembling with anger, or expressing other signs of emotional release. I would like to reiterate that the co-counseling partnership I have maintained for over thirty-five years has provided a safe setting for me to release hurtful experiences and heal old habit energies, along with cultivating understanding and insight, which in turn has helped me bring more of myself to the issues I care about. I heartily recommend trying to develop a co-listening partnership for yourself.

Taking Full Responsibility for Protecting and Preserving Our Beloved Earth

Once we are in touch with our love for the Earth and all its amazing creations, and once we have let our hearts break open at the immensity of human-caused destruction, then we naturally want to do what we can to protect and preserve our beloved.

My hunch is that many people ask themselves repeatedly: what more can we do to help make things right? Actually, there's a huge menu of things we can do. I'd like to list a few interrelated elements.

Cultivate an empowering story about climate change. Returning to the notion of wise view, it is useful to ask from time to time: What is the story we are telling ourselves and others about the situation? Is it true? Ennobling? Uplifting? Does it communicate possibility and openness? Or might it be in the service of fear or discouragement?

Build community around us. We are better together. Maybe each of us can develop an Earth Buddy to think and act with. Maybe join or start a green committee in our church, synagogue, or local town sustainability commission. Maybe gather around us a Beloved Community Circle, a group of three to eight friends who agree to practice a shared set of spiritual teachings or rituals and commit to engaging in mindful action together.

Start where we are. We can see clearly how climate change highlights the interconnections among issues that were previously viewed as separate. The eco-crisis touches most every social issue.

This interconnection means we can start anywhere, especially with what touches our hearts most deeply.

Locate ourselves in a social change framework. There are millions of organizations around the globe focused on every aspect of planetary well-being. Any efforts of ours are embedded in this matrix. Knowing this helps contradict feelings of isolation and powerlessness. It also helps to have a framework to see how our work fits into the larger picture. I personally like Joanna Macy's framework for engaging in activities that stop the hurt, or build new models inside the collapsing society, or help change consciousness.

Add a framework for building Beloved Community to current activities. Each of us is part of a family, communities, and networks. We probably have more influence and more resources than we know. One strategy is to arrange a think-and-listen session with a friend or two about how to link our current projects to building the Beloved Community.

For those of us who like concrete actions, there is no lack of opportunities to contribute.

Refer back to "Discerning What to Do," earlier in this chapter, to review a sampling of action areas. Earth justice work requires the whole spectrum of engagement. What lights you up? Is it personal healing of your inner life? Is it adopting ways to reduce your personal carbon footprint? Do you want to preserve a local forest habitat? How about protecting an endangered species. Or are you focused on upending racism or combatting anti-Semitism? Maybe you want to join efforts at the state house to enact a carbon tax. Maybe you wish to support regenerative agriculture. Maybe you are a teacher and want to engage students in climate justice work. Go for it! It's all connected to realizing the Beloved Community.

Concretely, consider which of the activities below calls to your heart and appeals to your mind. The listed items are suggestive, not prescriptive.

○ **climate education and awareness:** Study; offer a citizens' course in climate change; educate others on the links between racial and ecological suffering; research best scientific summaries or solutions.

○ **healing:** Offer climate grief circles or listening groups for eco-anxiety; create ceremonies and rituals for feeling and healing, for visioning and empowering.

○ **regeneration:** Learn about and practice clean energy, eco-agriculture, green building, carbon capture, or a plant-based diet; engage in Project Drawdown.

○ **adaptation:** Dedicate time to flood control, firefighting, rescue missions, or relocation.

○ **resilience:** Work on migration assistance, poverty alleviation, family planning, food security, or girls' education in the developing world.

○ **electoral politics:** Run for office; support climate-friendly candidates; promote policies and ballot initiatives that highlight climate justice issues.

Innumerable organizations have been active in climate justice work for decades, and despite heroic outpourings of energy, money, and effort, why do we seem to be going nowhere fast? One reason is that we have not used our influence enough in a concerted and powerful way to elect local, state, and federal officials who support effective climate justice approaches, and who are willing to challenge the moneyed interests and corporations that benefit from the status quo.

The fossil fuel industry, for example, has powerfully organized to elect candidates who deny human-caused climate change, challenge overwhelming scientific consensus, roll back healthy climate laws and policies, and effectively legislate for continued fossil fuel subsidies.

Changing our personal habits is helpful but not sufficient. To have significant impact, many more of us will need to step into spaces of political power, where laws and policies are shaped and implemented. Specifically, without eliminating gerrymandered voting districts, without getting corporate money out of politics, without ensuring all people have an equal opportunity to vote, without electing climate-friendly candidates to office or running for office ourselves, we are ceding the future to those whose harmful patterns, wrong views, and power are hastening collapse of the ecosystems we all depend on. We need to give Mother Earth good partners in government.

We can do electoral work without demeaning or demonizing other candidates, without using divisive or disrespectful language. Instead, we can use kind speech, invite conversations about what kind of environment we want, skillfully link racial justice with climate justice with economic justice with immigrant justice and so on, without blaming or shaming.

Big things, yes! But surely worthy of the better angels of our nature. The Dalai Lama puts it squarely in our lap when he says, "Clearly, this is a pivotal generation."[22]

8

BELOVED COMMUNITY: A LONGING, A VISION, A CALL

A Longing for Beloved Community

> We shall not cease from exploration and the end
> of all our exploring will be to arrive where we
> started and know the place for the first time.

—T. S. Eliot, "Little Gidding"

This book began with the proposition that the Beloved Community already exists, in that it describes our inherent interconnectedness, and also that it is something to be cultivated, something waiting for us in the future. I experience how it already exists when I touch my deepest nature in the quiet of meditation, or in the vastness of natural beauty, or in the flowing connection with my love, or in other "blue sky" moments. And I experience it waiting for us in the future when I engage in efforts to usher in the full expression of what I carry deep in my heart.

The stories and teachings shared in this book are examples of ways I have consistently tried to cultivate Beloved Community—in my family, when I was a classroom teacher, in Children of War and YouthBuild, in the Buddhist community, and in the world at large. In the beginning, my social justice work was mostly motivated by a sense of the "wrongness" that I saw and wished to correct. I carried a strong stream of anger and disappointment that the world was messed up. I also felt deep betrayal as I learned about the human cruelty and systemic oppression that were contrary to beliefs I adopted as a child from Jesus' teachings and the ideals of the American dream.

As I matured emotionally and spiritually, I came to experience myself being supported by ancestors who carried forward efforts to build a more humane society. I came to feel more embedded in the natural world, not separate from it. In small steps, I began to let life move through me, guide me, make use of me. Through emotional healing, mindfulness, and a life of meaningful professional work in service to humanity, I have been able to reclaim much awareness of my inherent worth and sacred nature, to know I am not alone or separate, and to feel my intrinsic connection to all beings. This, in turn, generates compassion and efforts to help relieve suffering because I know I am helping myself as well.

In the Buddhist view, there are two dimensions of reality: the ultimate and the historical. In the ultimate dimension, all is well. We are invited to deeply relax into our true nature. We've all touched this dimension. We carry deep in our awareness the knowing beyond words that all is well; beyond the daily news, all is well; beyond the suffering of the world, all is well. There is a place we know where there is no worry, no fear, no hatred, and no loneliness; there is no oppression, no racism, no poverty, no suffering. Each one of us knows this at some level, maybe only in fleeting moments, maybe dimly glimpsed, but we have a knowing of this because it is our nature. I can't say this often enough or strongly enough—there is nothing wrong with you or me. You are amazing. You are radiant. You are whole. Me too.

But we forget that we dwell in the ultimate dimension. Or rather, we get crushed with deep conditioning to feel separate. Wrong views and hurts were imposed on us. We are so deep into the practice of separation most of the time that we don't notice we feel alone and scared. We might even think that's normal. I read about a little girl whose mother brought her to a chiropractor because she thought there might be something wrong with her daughter. She had never heard her daughter laugh and had only rarely seen her smile. The chiropractor examined the girl and discovered a spinal misalignment that she said could give the girl a terrible headache all the time, but it could be corrected. She made the adjustment, and the girl immediately broke into a big laugh. She had become so accustomed to her pain that it was normal for her.[1]

I think many of us are somewhat like that little girl—numb to much of the pain we carry around, oblivious to the ways we have accepted a half-life, thinking that a suffering world is just the way things are. Our practice invites us to explore all the seeds of separation in our consciousness. These are both individual and collective. As we practice, we become more adept at making conscious the individual seeds of what we label "our" suffering, which is never simply individual suffering but is deeply entwined with collective suffering and has infinite causes and conditions.

This is all to say that the Beloved Community is alive and well and already exists in our awareness at some level. It's largely what animates our desire to relieve suffering. As for myself, I can visualize the world I wish to see. I can almost taste it, touch it. I definitely long for it.

A Vision of Beloved Community

What follows is my vision of living in the Beloved Community. It is purely an exercise of my imagination. Admittedly, it is incomplete, inadequate, and temporary. It's short on detail and nuance and leaves out important pieces, like how we'll get there. Your vision would be different. In truth, we have little idea what living in the Beloved Community would be like, just as can't yet see what a world without patriarchy would be, or without racism, or without exploitation, because we are so soaked in the modern story of separation. So much will have changed in order to establish the

Beloved Community that the actual realization of it is beyond our conceptual ability.

However, trying to imagine what I want—rather than just what I'm against—frees up my thinking and fosters openness to new possibilities. As you read the vision below, you might notice your reactions. Maybe your heart resonates in longing and delight. Perhaps your eyes roll at how naive and impractical it seems. Maybe you dismiss it as a bridge too far. Then you might explore the roots of your reaction. Perhaps it touches some similar, deep knowing in your heart that a better world is possible. Or maybe it triggers old experiences of disappointment and hurt, so you doubt a better world is possible. Perhaps you think it is fruitless to dream. The invitation in reading the vision is not to embrace or take issue with my vision but to stimulate your imagination and sense of the possible.

O

Sometime in the future . . .

After edging close to the brink of ecological and societal collapse, and after enduring enormous suffering on our precious Earth, enough people of goodwill and skillfulness were able to do just enough to pull us back from that brink, so that complex life on Earth could continue. We now live in the Beloved Community. Along a twisted and lengthy journey, and with massive effort across the globe, we had to heal our individual and collective wounds and recover our love for ourselves, each other, and all beings. We slowly transformed our economy from one of exploitation and growth to one of cooperation, justice, and sustainability within Earth's limits. We eliminated racism and all oppression, which the old economy had used to cause so much damage. We helped restore health to the natural environment by reconnecting to our love for our Mother Earth and doing everything it took to reverse global warming and restore forests, habitats, soils, wetlands, and oceans. We built new culture and universal ethics aligned with love and opportunity, reverence for life, respect and generosity, right relationships, kind speech and harmonious action, and careful consumption based on our actual needs rather than our conditioned desires. We transformed a punitive justice system with restorative justice and nonviolent conflict resolution. We eventually abolished prisons, police, armies, and war. And as we addressed the real needs of people and all beings, step by step, there were fewer and fewer reasons for crime, violence, and retribution.

Now we live in small, close-knit communities embedded in healthy natural surroundings. We walk most places or enjoy comfortable public transportation. Huge cities have been bulldozed to the ground and replaced by human-size villages connected by bike paths, walking trails, and high-speed rail. Our neighbors and family members are a beautiful quilt of mixed racial and cultural backgrounds. Food is abundant, organic, and mostly plant-based, and it is grown locally using restorative agriculture that replenishes the soil and reduces the need for irrigation. We enjoy living simply and simply living because we have learned to transform greed into generosity, so we don't want unnecessary things. This means we no longer strain the capacity of Earth's resources, so we live within her limits.

Learning is prized and lifelong but is no longer tethered to school buildings and compulsory attendance. Young people are encouraged to follow their own ways of learning, to explore the world with all their senses, and to value their unique gifts and ways of being. We have no schools with grading and ranking and rigid curricula, but instead lots of learning environments and apprenticeship arrangements to deepen our interests and skills. This is true for people at all ages.

No one lives in poverty because we care for one another. "Love thy neighbor as thyself" is not just an empty religious platitude as it once was; now it's the way we organize society. No one worries about trying to get decent housing, enough food, quality health care, or economic security. These are all provided by our collective gift economy, our cooperative and sharing economy committed to the well-being of humans, animals, plants, and the Earth.

We once again do for ourselves what we used to pay others to do—we gather to make music, share stories, teach each other, care for each other's children as needed, create projects, play games and sports. Gone are big-budget movies, professional sports, the Olympics, and stadium concerts. We barter, share, and cooperate. No one owns separate tools, cars, equipment, or even land. We are shepherds of the land, not private owners.

Our intimate relationships are valued and protected by the collective. Sexuality is viewed as sacred energy that is enjoyed wholeheartedly in committed relationships. But pornography, sexual abuse, prostitution, and the hookup culture are gone. Young people learn about safe and respectful sexual activity early on. Unwanted pregnancies, abortion, and relinquishment (adoption) are rare. Children are wanted and cherished, and are raised in multigenerational communities. Young people are appropriately included in decisions that affect their lives, and adultist behavior is rare. Furthermore, our committed partnerships are more open and less possessive than traditional marriages were. Jealousy and infidelity don't get much play because we are secure in ourselves and not isolated. We know that one person cannot be the all and everything to us, so we have different kinds of intimacies with various partners—child-rearing partners, sexual partners, intellectual partners, spiritual partners, sports or exercise partners, work partners, and so on.

We have very little sickness because we've removed the many conditions that contributed to previous poor health—we eat nutritious whole food, not too much or too little; we have less stress and more happiness; we feel love and respect; we belong and are not isolated. We treat our bodies as precious temples of life and have learned to love our bodies completely, taking in only nutriments (food, sense impressions, images, notions, conversations) that protect and nourish our bodies. We have reclaimed and expanded the use of medicinal plants, alternative medicine, mind-body healing methods, and energy flows in the body, such as *chi*. Thus, traditional medicine and institutionalized care have a minimal role in our Beloved Community. The health insurance and pharmaceutical rackets are things of the past.

We govern ourselves by listening to the wisdom of our elders as it combines with an engaged population. There are no national borders or nation-states but rather local, regional, bioregional, and global councils that tend to their respective areas and are aligned with shared global goals, agreements, and aspirations. People can freely move anywhere they wish, but most like where they live, so migration is minimal. Conflicts that inevitably arise are solved peaceably with an eye to how decisions might affect all beings and future generations.

The world of work has been radically transformed. We no longer work because we have to, or only for a paycheck, or at meaningless or demeaning jobs. We stopped producing junk and unneeded things. We equalized compensation across occupations and offered more pay to those who choose to do society's nasty jobs, like garbage collection and sanitation and disaster recovery. With fairly equal compensation, people re-sorted themselves according to their interests and passions. For example, some doctors who never liked medicine became street musicians or carpenters, and factory workers became farmers or artisans. At workplaces, the workers make their own decisions, own and run the whole enterprise, take care of each other, and for the most part enjoy work as a meaningful contribution to the Beloved Community.

Technology has matured so it is a powerful tool for enhancing the Beloved Community. News media scour the globe looking for good news, human nobility, acts of kindness, and innovative solutions that water our positive inclinations and inform and inspire us. We now have universal access to tech programs that, for example, monitor our health, enhance our learning, assist in calming our minds, alert us to environmental imbalances, and connect us intimately with each other and other species.

Speaking of other species, we have reclaimed the capacities, long protected by Indigenous people, to "communicate" with animal and plant species for mutual benefit. We know we are on a wonderfully dynamic, living Earth, alive with information and energy available to us.

And since the sources of unhappiness and unnecessary suffering have been largely transformed, humans are exploring the vast inner dimensions of reality in ways only a few privileged people could do in the past. Through meditation, shamanic rituals, neuroscience, guided use of mind-altering substances, induced trances, and others, we are discovering our latent capacities for extrasensory perception, out-of-body experiences, altered states of consciousness, deep dream work, the power of collective energy, and mystical revelation. These enhanced heart-mind states generate ever more wonder, connection, and compassion.

For the most part, we live lightly on the Earth, in harmony with the natural environment, and with gratitude and contentment in the present moment.

A Call for Beloved Community

We need another dimension, the action dimension . . . the realm of the bodhisattva, the kind of energy that helps us bring the ultimate dimension into the historical so we can live our life of action in a relaxing and joyful way, free from fear, free from stress, free from despair.

—Thich Nhat Hanh,
Zen and the Art of Saving the Planet

What is *your* vision for the Beloved Community? How does it sit in your heart? What are you called to contribute to realizing it? This book explored six interrelated components of preparing for the Beloved Community; what might *your* components be? Where might you focus your energy and experience that would bring you even more alive?

There *is* a new world ahead of us. Will it be a hell realm or the Beloved Community or something else? We can't know, but we can choose a direction. I choose to put my faith in humankind's nobility, creativity, adaptability, and courage. I choose to hold fast to the idea that the Beloved Community already exists as our undeniable interconnectedness, and our task is to help it manifest in ordinary life.

I choose to believe that Life, in its mysterious ways, has put before humans the conditions that can help give rise to a higher level of human consciousness, a waking-up to our place in the family of beings, and an intimate sense of belonging. The long cherished idea of the Beloved Community is a North Star, guiding us, pulling us, inviting us to venture forth in this great unfolding.

Each of us has so much to contribute, in our unique way and time. There is no one way or right way or best way to contribute. There are no shoulds about what we do, but there are some encouragements: we have one another to turn to for support, learning, and love. We have ample evidence of human kindness, caring, and cooperation to reassure us that those capacities can be called on. We can be confident that everyone wants to be happy and no one wants to suffer—a tremendous and universal common ground. We have the wisdom of ancestors, spiritual teachers, and unseen forces to guide and support our efforts. Collectively, we have proven practices and means for healing: for transforming greed, hate, and delusion; for peaceful reconciliation of differences; for living in balance with nature. We are not alone.

As far as ancestors and unseen forces, two quotes come to mind:

> In Buddha fields around the universe, people are
> lining up to be born on earth right now, because
> this is a moment of exquisite realization.
>
> **—Joanna Macy**[2]

*I want you to close your eyes for a minute, and I want you
to think back through time of all the people who brought
you here, because I don't care what your ethnicity is or
where you're from, people died to get you here, people survived to get you here. I want you to think deeply, and I want
you to say the names of the people who brought you here
today. Call them here to you right now, call them into your
heart, call them into your voice, call them into your hands
because you do not walk this earth as one person. You walk
this earth as thousands and that Power is inside of you. All
that power is strength, and it will make you brave.*

—**Cherri Foytlin,** Afro-indigenous climate justice activist[3]

What's holding us back from wholeheartedly answering this call,
joining this great adventure to build the Beloved Community? Fear
or powerlessness? Lack of vision or trust? Busyness or exhaustion?
Illness or age? Loneliness or discouragement? A million and one
other reasons? These obstacles can be managed and healed in ways
we've touched on in this book. We can begin immediately. The
decision to do what we can to foster Beloved Community can itself
release new energy and power for this noble work. The invitation
is clear; the door is open.

The Beloved Community already exists in the spiritual dimension, so our work is to clear away the inner and outer obstacles to
realizing it more fully in the world. In the grip of fear or powerlessness, this work may feel daunting or even impossible. But as we
uncover the power of our true fullness and cultivate our inherent
capacities for love and mindful action, there emerges an increased
sense of agency, boldness, and confidence. Underneath the enormous grief we may feel about the way things are, there is an even
larger love we have for life and its beings. And we can learn to
do the work of personal and social transformation with a joyful
spirit, with spaciousness, with an inner calm, together on the path.

Day by day, we can nurture elements of the Beloved Community within ourselves until it radiates out in all directions and joins the ever-swelling human current of energy, insight, action, and love that eventually makes some beautiful version of the Beloved Community real. Then, indeed, as the old spiritual promises, "Deep in our hearts, we do believe, that we shall all be free someday."

ACKNOWLEDGMENTS

I am deeply grateful for the team at Parallax Press: Terry Barber, whose sharp first read helped reorient the focus of the book; Natascha Bruckner, whose wonderful sense of structure, order, and grace greatly improved the flow; and Hisae Matsuda, the publisher who believed in the project all along. Also special thanks to readers who gave me invaluable feedback—Valerie Brown, Melanie Gin, Dorothy Stoneman, Heather Mann, Andrew Rock, and Tom Roderick. And immense appreciation to those who read the manuscript and wrote stunning endorsements: Kaira Jewel Lingo, David Loy, Frances Moore Lappé, Valerie Brown, Jo Confino, and Lama John Negru.

The content of this book arises out of the flow of my entire life, so infinite acknowledgments are in order. A short poem from the thirteenth-century poet and mystic Rumi sums up the challenge:

> If God said, "Rumi, pay homage to everything that has helped you enter my arms," there would not be one experience of my life, not one thought, not one feeling, not any act I would not bow to.[1]

I bow . . .

To my blood family, my parents, Miriam and Jack Bell, who gave me life and enough early love and hardship to strengthen my resilience. To my wonderful younger brother, Mike, with whom I shared a tumultuous childhood.

To my lifelong partner, Dorothy Stoneman, for the immeasurable blessings of a life that has woven together the joys and worries of parenting, the shared decades of deeply satisfying social justice work, the wonderful opportunities for emotional healing and liberation. She has been my refuge, my rock, my inspiration, my teacher, my North Star, my love. Words don't come close.

To my adult children, Sierra and Taro, who taught me both patience and pride I hadn't known before, and whom I love to the moon and back. To Fernando Aguilera, my dear son-in-law, whose parenting of his son and my grandson, Antu, is stunning and unsurpassed. To young Antu, age eight now, for reminding me what living in the present really looks like! To Freddy Acosta, now in his fifties, who came to live with us as his second chosen family when he was fourteen years old, and continues to be a loving, resilient, and kind presence.

To my early friends: In high school, Cheryl Pickard, my first love, enjoying long slow evenings listening to Johnny Mathis. To Marty Hotvet, my first true friend and intellectual partner. In college, to my beloved roommate John Kavanaugh, who taught me to sing and showed me that a disability like sightlessness brings its own insights; and to Phil Starr, my renegade Latter-Day Saint friend who challenged my conventionality and introduced me to mescaline; and to Corb Smith, who introduced me to classical music with Beethoven's Fifth Symphony. To Lois and Wally Goldfrank, who housed my partner and me, fed us, and loved us year after year of a lifelong friendship.

To my early spiritual teachers, long gone—Jesus, Gandhi, and Martin Luther King Jr., spiritual revolutionaries who inspired my own revolutionary tendencies. These three men of color have been the well I have revisited all my life.

To the Black liberation thinkers who opened my eyes to racism, supremacy, and colonialism—but especially, early on, Ralph Ellison, James Baldwin, Martin Luther King Jr., Malcolm X, Frantz Fanon, Paulo Freire, bell hooks, Grace Lee Boggs, Alice Walker, and more recently, Ta-Nehisi Coates, Michelle Alexander, Heather McGhee, Ibram X. Kendi, and Bryan Stevenson.

To other thinkers along the way who expanded my awareness from narrow working-class beginnings to my current, fairly broad horizon. Among the hundreds, special thanks to Henry David Thoreau, Albert Camus, Fyodor Dostoevsky, Karl Marx, John Steinbeck, Abraham Heschel, A. S. Neill, Ram Dass, E. F. Schumacher, Wendell Berry, Ken Wilber, Robert Wright, Jared Diamond, Robin Wall Kimmerer, David Loy, Charles Eisenstein, Bessel van der Kolk, and Joanna Macy.

To my comrades in teaching who loved each other, talked deep into the nights, and lived together for years at 212 West 137th Street in Harlem in the 1970s—Tom Roderick, Tim Parsons, Ken Dawson, Fred Odell, Dorothy Stoneman, Esta Diamond Gutierrez, Tom Draeger.

To the parents and children of the East Harlem Block Schools, a storefront parent-controlled community school where I taught in the 1970s, who welcomed me into their lives and taught me the importance of ordinary people controlling their own organizations—Anna Rivera, Carmen Ward, Rosie Gueits, Victor and Albert Soler, and Chantay Henderson Jones.

To Harvey Jackins, the founding genius of Re-evaluation Counseling (RC), a peer counseling liberation tool that supported our marriage and helped liberate me from life-limiting emotional patterns. To Janet Pfunder, my early and longtime co-counselor in New York City, who helped me heal childhood hurts and shed layers of isolation. And to an impressive worldwide RC community of practitioners, steadfast in their intention to eliminate all oppression.

To Fred Small, my beloved co-counseling partner for over three decades, with whose safety and attention I have been able to heal from early and current emotional hurts and free myself to live more wholeheartedly and happily.

To my spiritual sister and wonderful friend, Judith Thompson, who was the guiding light of Children of War from 1984 to 1994, a profoundly impactful program from which I learned so much about the suffering and resilience of young people worldwide. Judith has offered me deep friendship and spiritual companionship for nearly forty years, a cherished blessing.

To the YouthBuild movement, that amazing cradle of leadership development and transformation of low-income young people that I was proud to help create and grow, alongside my partner Dorothy, for thirty-plus years. To my colleagues at YouthBuild USA whose skill and commitment to social justice nourished and buoyed me. To those special directors throughout eighteen years of the eight cohorts of YouthBuild Directors Fellows programs, whose hard work and commitment to the young people inspired me and whose friendship and closeness were and still are a treasure to me. And to the hundreds of YouthBuild young people and graduates who let me into their lives and whose intelligence, talent, resilience, and courage in the face of often unutterable hardship taught me about humility, determination, and keeping our eyes on the prize. There are far too many YouthBuild names to list, but special recognition to colleague Tanya Cruz Teller, Joel Miranda, and graduates Khepe-Ra Maat, Julian Ramirez, Noe Orgaz, Brandon Menjares, and Alexis Vasquez.

To the lifelong friends who became an extended family, sharing decades of sweet times in Great Barrington, Massachusetts, a family refuge and touchstone of love and blessings. Joan and John Kavanaugh, their daughter Lisa Kavanaugh, son-in-law Chauncey Wood, and their daughters, Carter and Isabelle. Ellen McTigue and Bob Harris, and their sons, Colin and Brian. Tom Roderick and Maxine Phillips, and their daughters, Emma Rose and Anne Marie. And our godchildren who spent many summers there— Paloma and Kwao Adams, Agape and Camlo Looper, and nephews Mark and Milo Shaffer. Friendly Pond lives in all our hearts, forever.

To newer friends who have offered me comfort, guidance, and companionship in recent years. I send my heartfelt thanks to

Michael Appel and Tamar Miller, Frances Moore Lappé and Richard Rowe, and Elaine Radiss and Rich Petrino.

To the poets and singers and dancers who have offered me portals to beauty and wisdom beyond measure over a lifetime. As poet William Carlos Williams wrote, "It is difficult to get the news from poems, yet men die miserably every day for lack of what is found there."[2]

To my Buddhist friends in the Dharma who have taught me so much and offered me their wisdom and kindness over the years. There are too many to name, but a few call out for specific mention. Lyn Fine, an early beloved co-counselor and then my steady, wise guide into the Plum Village tradition of Thich Nhat Hanh. My admiration and trust in her reach the stars. I have felt nurtured by others in this community: Aaron Solomon (Brother Fulfillment), Andre Vellino, Andrew Rock, Anh-Huong Nguyen, Anh Nguyen, Anne Woods, Brother Phap Linh, Brother Phap Dung, Chau Yoder, Elli Weisbaum, George Hoguet, Heather Lyn Mann, Ivan Trujillo-Priego, Jack Lawlor, Janey Gilman, Jeff Johnson, Jo-ann Rosen, Jo Confino, Kaira Jewel Lingo, Keith Miller, Kenley Neufeld, Marjorie Markus, Meena Srinivasan, Melanie Gin, Melina Bondy (Sister Ocean), Mihaela Andronic, Mitchell Ratner, Peggy Smith, Richard Brady, Simona Coayla-Duba, Sister Hien Nghiem (True Dedication), Sister The Nghiem (True Vow), Tree (Brother Phap Tri), Valerie Brown, Victoria Mausisa, Viviane Ephraimson-Abt, members of the Earth Holder Community Care Taking Council, the Earth Holder Regional Community Builders, the Healing White Racism Facilitators Sangha, and the members of my local Mountain Bell Sangha. Thank you all.

My deepest gratitude to Thich Nhat Hanh, my Buddhist teacher, for being a light in a dark world, a true teacher who wanted only liberation from suffering for his students, an example of socially engaged spiritual practice, and one who had quiet power to move millions of people toward greater happiness and harmony. The

Earth and its beings have benefitted enormously from his existence and deep practice.

Gratitude is due to an infinite number of causes and conditions that together gave rise to me as I am now. If your name does not appear above, please know that you are in me and I am in you, even unnamed, and I am grateful to you.

Finally, I bow to the ancestors in all dimensions, to the Earth elements, to the ocean of amazing human thought, to the miraculous beings of incredible variety, and to the great mystery that gives rise to it all—the Unbroken Wholeness.

NOTES

1. Beloved Community

1. Wikipedia, s.v. "We Shall Overcome," *https://en.wikipedia.org/wiki/We_Shall_Overcome*, last modified March 10, 2023.

2. The name "Beloved Community" is credited to a Christian theologian, Josiah Royce; in the early 1900s, he conceived of a unified global community based in love. This idea was carried forward by two directors of a venerable peace organization called the Fellowship of Reconciliation. A. J. Muste added nonviolence as essential. Howard Thurman added the need for racial reconciliation and community. Thurman, a mentor of Martin Luther King Jr., passed the idea to Dr. King, who embraced it and made it a cornerstone of the US Civil Rights Movement. In 1965, King introduced Vietnamese Zen master Thich Nhat Hanh to the term, although the Buddhist monk had reached his own interpretation of this aspiration long before he met Dr. King. Later, on hearing of King's death, Thich Nhat Hanh vowed to try his best to continue building the Beloved Community.

3. Charles Eisenstein, *The More Beautiful World Our Hearts Know Is Possible (Sacred Activism)* (Berkeley, CA: North Atlantic Books, 2013).

4. This framework was first described in John Bell, "Developing a Mindful Approach to Climate Justice Work," *Kosmos Journal*, Summer 2019, *www.kosmosjournal.org/kj_article/developing-a-mindful-approach-to-earth-justice-work*. Members of the Care Taking Council of the Plum Village Earth Holders Community helped refine the article.

5. David Bohm, *Wholeness and the Implicate Order* (London: Routledge, 1980), 218, *www.gci.org.uk/Documents/DavidBohm-WholenessAndTheImplicateOrder.pdf*.

6. Aldous Huxley, *The Doors of Perception* (New York: Harper & Row, 1954).

7. Attributed by Dorothy Day, *On Pilgrimage*, Ressourcement: Retrieval & Renewal in Catholic Thought (Grand Rapids, MI: Eerdmans, 1999), 80.

8. Mother Teresa, "National Prayer Breakfast Address," speech in Washington, DC, February 3, 1994, American Rhetoric, *www.americanrhetoric.com/speeches/motherteresanationalprayerbreakfast.htm*.

9. Martin Luther King Jr., "Christmas Sermon on Peace and Nonviolence, Massey Lecture No. 5," video, March 3, 2023, 7:10–7:40, YouTube, *https://youtu.be/1jeyIAH3bUI*.

10. Robert Aitken, attributed by Victor M. Parachin, "Robert Aitken: From POW to Zen Master," Buddhist Door Global, February 15, 2023, *www.buddhistdoor.net/features/robert-aitken-from-pow-to-zen-master*.

11. Bhikkhu Bodhi, "Appendix 3: Getting Real about Climate Change—Simple and Practical Steps," in *EcoDharma: Buddhist Teachings for the Ecological Crisis*, ed. David Loy (Somerville, MA: Wisdom Publications, 2018), 191–94.

12. Janell Ross and National Journal, "Epigenetics: The Controversial Science Behind Racial and Ethnic Health Disparities," *The Atlantic*, March 20, 2014, *www.theatlantic.com/politics/archive/2014/03/epigenetics-the-controversial-science-behind-racial-and-ethnic-health-disparities/430749*.

13. Hop Hopkins, "Racism Is Killing the Planet," *Sierra*, June 8, 2020, *www.sierraclub.org/sierra/racism-killing-planet*.

2. Cultivating Wise View

1. David Steinberg, "'Why Are You Bombing Where I'm Playing?': John McCutcheon Wrote a Collection of Songs for a Cellist in Bosnia," *Albuquerque Journal*, February 21, 2014, *www.abqjournal.com/356545/albuquerque-santa-fe-singersongwriter.html*.

2. Joanna Macy, "The Greening of the Self," in *Spiritual Ecology: The Cry of the Earth*, ed. Llewellyn Vaughan-Lee (Point Reyes Station, CA: Golden Sufi Center, 2013), 145, 147, 155–56.

3. Rumi, "Rumi, Pay Homage," in Daniel Ladinsky, trans., *Love Poems from God: Twelve Sacred Voices from the East and West* (New York: Penguin, 2002), p. 68.

4. Aubrey Marcus, "What?," AubreyMarcus.com, May 9, 2018, *www.aubreymarcus.com/blogs/poetry/what?*.

5. I experienced this chant personally many times, a kind of step-dance led by South African participants in the Children of War program that I helped facilitate from 1984 to 1992.

6. Thich Nhat Hanh, *The Art of Power* (San Francisco: HarperOne, 2007), 169.

7. Robin Wall Kimmerer, *Braiding Sweetgrass: Indigenous Wisdom, Scientific Knowledge, and the Teachings of Plants* (Minneapolis: Milkweed, 2015), 64.

8. Bhikkhu Bodhi, "A Buddhist Diagnosis of the Climate Crisis," 2015, *https://drive.google.com/file/d/0B9AtWA8ARopjR0NpMHI2d0JJbU0*.

3. Healing Hurt and Trauma

1. The two people's names have been changed to honor confidentiality and safety.

2. For a deeper dive into Buddhism, see Thich Nhat Hanh, *The Heart of the Buddha's Teachings* (Berkeley, CA: Parallax Press, 1998).

3. David Bohm, *Wholeness and the Implicate Order*, 218.

4. Thich Nhat Hanh named these italicized labels in "Taking the Hand of Suffering," *The Mindfulness Bell* 27 (Fall 2000), 1–3. The explanatory text is mine.

5. For a deeper explanation of this rich practice, please see Sister Chan Khong, *Beginning Anew: Four Steps to Restoring Communication* (Berkeley, CA: Parallax Press, 2014).

6. I owe much gratitude to the work of Bessel van der Kolk, Resmaa Menakem, Dan Siegel, David A. Treleaven, and Gabor Maté for my learning about trauma. Serious practitioners of healing would be well served by studying the work of these five authors and learning about sources of trauma, its impacts, and trauma-sensitive mindfulness. Another valuable resource is *Unshakeable: Trauma-Informed Mindfulness for Collective Awakening*, by Jo-ann Rosen.

7. Thich Nhat Hanh, *Zen and the Art of Saving the Planet* (New York: HarperCollins, 2021), 84.

8. Bill McKibben, "It's Not Entirely Up to School Students to Save the World," *The New Yorker*, May 24, 2019, *www.newyorker.com/news/daily-comment/its-not-entirely-up-to-school-students-to-save-the-world*.

9. Thich Nhat Hanh, *The Heart of the Buddha's Teachings: Transforming Suffering into Peace, Joy, and Liberation* (Berkeley, CA: Parallax Press, 1998), 80.

10. Claude Arpi, "The Precious Human Body," Claude Arpi's Blog, November 30, 2019, *https://claudearpi.blogspot.com/2019/11/the-precious-human-body.html*.

4. Transforming Racial and Social Oppression

1. For the wonderful story about the East Harlem Block Schools, see Tom Roderick, *A School of Our Own: Parents, Power, and Community at the East Harlem Block Schools* (New York: Teachers College Press, 2001).

2. See *www.youthbuild.org*.

3. For an animated adaptation of the Four I's of Oppression: Eliana Pipes, "Legos and the 4 I's of Oppression," YouTube video, July 29, 2016, *https://youtu.be/3WWyVRo4Uas*.

4. Vann R. Newkirk II, "Environmental Racism Is the New Jim Crow," *The Atlantic*, YouTube video, June 6, 2017, *https://youtu.be/nnF5I7lt6nQ*.

5. Alex Renton, "Suffering the Science: Climate Change, People, and Poverty," Oxfam International, July 6, 2009, i–ii, *https://oxfamlibrary .openrepository.com/bitstream/10546/114606/1/bp130-suffering-science -060709-en.pdf*.

6. Hop Hopkins, "Racism Is Killing the Planet," *Sierra*, June 8, 2020, *www.sierraclub.org/sierra/racism-killing-planet*.

7. I wrote about this in "What Went Wrong With Men That 12 Million Women Said #MeToo?," *Yes!*, December 15, 2017, *www.yesmagazine.org /social-justice/2017/12/15/what-went-wrong-with-men-that-12-million -women-said-me-too*.

8. The details of how this can be accomplished are beyond the scope of this book. Among the many resources available, United to End Racism (*www.unitedtoendracism.org*) is the racial justice initiative of Re-evaluation Counseling, and its approach is consistent with mindfulness and healing.

9. Greta Thunberg, "'Our House Is on Fire': Greta Thunberg, 16, Urges Leaders to Act on Climate," *The Guardian*, January 25, 2019, *www .theguardian.com/environment/2019/jan/25/our-house-is-on-fire-greta -thunberg16-urges-leaders-to-act-on-climate*.

10. National Center for Injury Prevention and Control, Division of Violence Prevention, "Fast Facts: Preventing Child Abuse & Neglect," US Centers for Disease Control and Prevention, April 6, 2022, *www.cdc .gov/violenceprevention/childabuseandneglect/fastfact.html*.

11. See Jacqueline Battalora, "Birth of a White Nation," YouTube video, July 10, 2014, *https://youtu.be/riVAuC0dnP4*.

12. A complete guide, "Listening Circles for Healing White Racism: A Brief Guide for Facilitators," is available at *https://drive.google.com /file/d/1PzVSVoO2VwuHeDp1NpnuU0PSm8kxow7Z/view*.

13. For more information about Beginning Anew practice, see Plum Village, "How to Begin Anew," *https://plumvillage.org/articles/begin-anew*.
14. Adapted from the United to End Racism website, *www.unitedtoend racism.org*.

5. Building Deep Local Community

1. Rebecca Solnit, "What is the best thing an individual can do for the climate?," Facebook post, April 17, 2016, *www.facebook.com/EarthShare /posts/10153727646598477*.
2. Joseph Ranseth, "Gandhi Didn't Actually Ever Say 'Be the Change You Want to See in the World.' Here's the Real Quote . . . ," JosephRanseth.com (blog), August 27, 2015, *https://josephranseth .com/gandhi-didnt-say-be-the-change-you-want-to-see-in-the-world*.

6. Living Ethically on a Daily Basis

1. Joseph Bruchac, *Entering Onodaga: Poems* (Austin, TX: Cold Mountain Press, 1978).
2. Van Jones, "Van Jones (CNN): Nelson Mandela Didn't Call His Enemies Out. He Called Them UP. He Called Them IN," YouTube video, June 18, 2022, *https://youtu.be/Pz5xYEpN9R4*.
3. Nelson Mandela, *Long Walk to Freedom: The Autobiography of Nelson Mandela* (London: Little, Brown, 1994), 568–69.
4. CBS/AP, "More Than 12M 'Me Too' Facebook Posts, Comments, Reactions in 24 Hours," CBS News, October 17, 2017, *www.cbsnews .com/news/metoo-more-than-12-million-facebook-posts-comments -reactions-24-hours*.
5. David Rosen, "Pornography and the Erotic Phantasmagoria," *Sexuality & Culture* 27:1 (February 2023), 242–65, *https://doi.org/10.1007 /s12119-022-10011-9*.
6. These statistics and more are compiled on a multisource website: Covenant Eyes, "Pornography Statistics," *www.covenanteyes.com /pornstats*.
7. Thich Nhat Hanh, "Thich Nhat Hanh's Statement on Climate Change for the United Nations: Falling in Love with the Earth," Plum Village, September 2015, *https://plumvillage.org/about/thich-nhat-hanh/letters /thich-nhat-hanhs-statement-on-climate-change-for-unfccc*.
8. In the early 1960s, fewer than 14 percent of individuals possessed a body mass index (BMI) of over 30, indicating obesity. The CDC National Health and Nutrition Examination Survey (NHANES)

reports that in 2017–2018, the age-adjusted prevalence of obesity in adults was 42.4 percent. Craig M. Hales, Margaret D. Carroll, Cheryl D. Fryar, and Cynthia L. Ogden, "Prevalence of Obesity and Severe Obesity among Adults: United States, 2017–2018," National Center for Health Statistics, Data Brief no. 360, February 27, 2020, *www.cdc .gov/nchs/products/databriefs/db360.htm*.

9. Thich Nhat Hanh, "Dharma Talk: Diet for a Mindful Society," *The Mindfulness Bell*, September 1991, *www.parallax.org/mindfulnessbell /article/dharma-talk-diet-for-a-mindful-society*.

10. Joseph Goldstein and Jack Kornfield, *Seeking the Heart of Wisdom: The Path of Insight Meditation* (Boston: Shambhala, 2001), 17, *https:// audiobuddha.org/wp-content/uploads/2021/07/Seeking-The-Heart-of -Wisdom-by-Joseph-Goldstein-Jack-Kornfield-1.pdf*.

7. Engaging in Mindful Social Action

1. Joanna Macy, "Three Stories of Our Time," Work That Reconnects Network, 2020, *https://workthatreconnects.org/spiral/the-great-turning /the-global-context*.

2. Stockholm Resilience Centre, "Planetary Boundaries," 2022, *www .stockholmresilience.org/research/planetary-boundaries.html*.

3. Acharya Buddharakkhita, trans., "Yamakavagga: Pairs" (Dhp I), Dhammapada, Access to Insight (BCBS Edition), November 30, 2013, *www.accesstoinsight.org/tipitaka/kn/dhp/dhp.01.budd.html*.

4. For an excellent book-length exploration of Gandhian nonviolence, I highly recommend Chris Moore-Backman, *The Gandhian Iceberg: A Nonviolence Manifesto for the Age of the Great Turning* (Reno, NV: Be the Change Project, 2016).

5. The King Center, "Dr. King's Fundamental Philosophy of Non-violence," *https://thekingcenter.org/about-tkc/the-king-philosophy*.

6. Ralph Ranalli, "Erica Chenoweth Illuminates the Value of Nonviolent Resistance in Societal Conflicts," Harvard Kennedy School, 2019, *www.hks.harvard.edu/faculty-research/policy-topics/advocacy-social -movements/paths-resistance-erica-chenoweths-research*.

7. A. J. Muste, quoted in "Debasing Dissent," *New York Times*, November 16, 1967, 46. See Wikiquote, s.v. "A. J. Muste," *https://en.wikiquote.org /wiki/A._J._Muste*.

8. Joanna Macy and Chris Johnstone, *Active Hope: How to Face the Mess We're in without Going Crazy* (Novato, CA: New World, 2012), 28–32.

9. Thich Nhat Hanh, "The World We Have," Lion's Roar, April 6, 2017, *www.lionsroar.com/the-world-we-have*. Adapted from *The World We Have: A Buddhist Approach to Peace and Ecology* (Berkeley, CA: Parallax Press, 2008).

10. Ayana Elizabeth Johnson, "How To Find Joy in Climate Action," TED, video, 2022, *www.ted.com/talks/ayana_elizabeth_johnson_how_to_find _joy_in_climate_action*.

11. Charles Eisenstein, *The More Beautiful World Our Hearts Know Is Possible (Sacred Activism)* (Berkeley, CA: North Atlantic Books, 2013).

12. Thich Nhat Hanh, *Being Peace* (Berkeley, CA: Parallax Press, 1996), 79–80.

13. Gratitude to writer and editor Natascha Bruckner for the essence of these suggested steps.

14. This name, Beloved Community Circles, was proposed by Episcopal Bishop Marc Andrus in his book, *Brothers in the Beloved Community: The Friendship of Thich Nhat Hanh and Martin Luther King Jr.* (Berkeley, CA: Parallax Press, 2021), and the name is used with the author's blessing.

15. Thich Nhat Hanh, *Peace Is Every Step: The Path of Mindfulness in Everyday Life* (Berkeley, CA: Parallax Press, 1992), 91.

16. For more information about gift economy, see *www.eastpointpeace .org/gifteconomics*.

17. Saint John of the Cross, "A Rabbit Noticed My Condition," in Ladinsky, *Love Poems from God*, 323.

18. Martin Luther King Jr., "Christmas Sermon on Peace and Nonviolence, Massey Lecture No. 5, Aired on December 24, 1967," YouTube, audio, December 3, 2014. *https://youtu.be/1jeyIAH3bUI*.

19. Blooming Heart Sangha, "Five Contemplations Before Eating," 2016, *www.bloomingheart.org/index.php?page=five-contemplations-before-eating*.

20. Jon Henley, "Climate Crisis Could Displace 1.2bn People by 2050, Report Warns," *The Guardian*, September 9, 2020, *www.theguardian .com/environment/2020/sep/09/climate-crisis-could-displace-12bn-people -by-2050-report-warns*.

21. Jem Bendell, "Deep Adaptation: A Map for Navigating Climate Tragedy," IFLAS Occasional Paper 2, 2nd edition, Initiative for Leadership and Sustainability, July 27, 2020, *www.lifeworth.com/deepadaptation.pdf*.

22. Dalai Lama, *My Tibet* (London: Thames and Hudson, 1990), 79–80.

8. Beloved Community

1. Charles Eisenstein, *The More Beautiful World Our Hearts Know Is Possible (Sacred Activism)* (Berkeley, CA: North Atlantic Books, 2013), 18.

2. Joanna Macy, "Deep Adaptation Q&A with Joanna Macy Hosted by Jem Bendell," interview by Jem Bendell, YouTube, audio, June 5, 2019, *https://youtu.be/k1wUY6945kY*.

3. Cherri Foytlin, speaking at "Fire Drill Fridays," Washington, D.C., January 3, 2020.

Acknowledgments

1. Rumi, "Rumi, Pay Homage," in Ladinsky, *Love Poems from God: Twelve Sacred Voices from the East and West*, 68.

2. William Carlos Williams, "Asphodel, That Greeny Flower," in *Journey to Love* (New York: Random House, 1955), 53.

BIBLIOGRAPHY

Acharya Buddharakkhita, translator. "Yamakavagga: Pairs" (Dhp I). Dhammapada. Access to Insight (BCBS Edition). November 30, 2013. *www.accesstoinsight.org/tipitaka/kn/dhp/dhp.01.budd.html*.

Andrus, Marc. *Brothers in the Beloved Community: The Friendship of Thich Nhat Hanh and Martin Luther King Jr.* Berkeley, CA: Parallax Press, 2021.

Arpi, Claude. "The Precious Human Body." Claude Arpi's Blog. November 30, 2019. *https://claudearpi.blogspot.com/2019/11/the-precious-human-body.html*.

Battalora, Jacqueline. "Birth of a White Nation." YouTube video. July 10, 2014. *https://youtu.be/riVAuC0dnP4*.

Bell, John. "Developing a Mindful Approach to Climate Justice Work." *Kosmos Journal*, Summer 2019. *www.kosmosjournal.org/kj_article/developing-a-mindful-approach-to-earth-justice-work*.

Bell, John. "Listening Circles for Healing White Racism: A Brief Guide for Facilitators." n.d. *https://drive.google.com/file/d/1PzVSVoO2VwuHeDpl NpnuU0PSm8kxow7Z/view*.

Bell, John. "What Went Wrong With Men That 12 Million Women Said #MeToo?" *Yes!*, December 15, 2017. *www.yesmagazine.org/social-justice/2017/12/15/what-went-wrong-with-men-that-12-million-women-said-me-too*.

Bell, John. *YouthBuild's North Star: A Vision of Greater Potential*. Somerville, MA: YouthBuild USA, 2014.

Bendell, Jem. "Deep Adaptation: A Map for Navigating Climate Tragedy." IFLAS Occasional Paper 2, 2nd edition, Initiative for Leadership and Sustainability. July 27, 2020. *www.lifeworth.com/deepadaptation.pdf*.

Blooming Heart Sangha. "Five Contemplations Before Eating." 2016. *www.bloomingheart.org/index.php?page=five-contemplations-before-eating*.

Bodhi, Bhikkhu. "Appendix 3: Getting Real about Climate Change—Simple and Practical Steps." In *EcoDharma: Buddhist Teachings for the Ecological Crisis*, edited by David Loy. Somerville, MA: Wisdom Publications, 2018.

Bodhi, Bhikkhu. "A Buddhist Diagnosis of the Climate Crisis." 2015. *https://drive.google.com/file/d/0B9AtWA8ARopjR0NpMHI2d0JJbU0*.

Bohm, David. *Wholeness and the Implicate Order*. London: Routledge, 1980. *www.gci.org.uk/Documents/DavidBohm-WholenessAndTheImplicate Order.pdf*.

Bruchac, Joseph. *Entering Onondaga: Poems*. Austin, TX: Cold Mountain Press, 1978.

CBS/AP. "More Than 12M 'Me Too' Facebook Posts, Comments, Reactions in 24 Hours." CBS News, October 17, 2017. *www.cbsnews.com /news/metoo-more-than-12-million-facebook-posts-comments-reactions -24-hours*.

Chan Khong, Sister. *Beginning Anew: Four Steps to Restoring Communication*. Berkeley, CA: Parallax Press, 2014.

Chenoweth, Erica, and Maria Stephan. *Why Civil Resistance Works: The Strategic Logic of Nonviolent Conflict*. New York: Columbia University Press, 2011.

Dalai Lama. *My Tibet*. London: Thames and Hudson, 1990.

Dass, Ram. *Be Here Now*. Harmony/Rodale, San Cristobal, NM: Lama Foundation, 1971.

Day, Dorothy. *On Pilgrimage*. Ressourcement: Retrieval & Renewal in Catholic Thought. Grand Rapids, MI: Eerdmans, 1999.

Eisenstein, Charles. *The More Beautiful World Our Hearts Know Is Possible (Sacred Activism)*. Berkeley, CA: North Atlantic Books, 2013.

Goldstein, Joseph, and Jack Kornfield. *Seeking the Heart of Wisdom: The Path of Insight Meditation*. Boston: Shambhala, 2001. *https://audiobuddha .org/wp-content/uploads/2021/07/Seeking-The-Heart-of-Wisdom-by -Joseph-Goldstein-Jack-Kornfield-1.pdf*.

Hales, Craig M., Margaret D. Carroll, Cheryl D. Fryar, and Cynthia L. Ogden. "Prevalence of Obesity and Severe Obesity among Adults: United States, 2017–2018." National Center for Health Statistics. Data Brief no. 360. February 27, 2020. *www.cdc.gov/nchs/products/databriefs /db360.htm*.

Henley, Jon. "Climate Crisis Could Displace 1.2bn People by 2050, Report Warns." *The Guardian*, September 9, 2020. *www.theguardian .com/environment/2020/sep/09/climate-crisis-could-displace-12bn -people-by-2050-report-warns*.

Hopkins, Hop. "Racism Is Killing the Planet." *Sierra*, June 8, 2020. *www.sierraclub.org/sierra/racism-killing-planet*.

Huxley, Aldous. *The Doors of Perception*. New York: Harper & Row, 1954.

John of the Cross, Saint. "A Rabbit Noticed My Condition." in Ladinsky, *Love Poems from God*, 323.

Johnson, Ayana Elizabeth. "How To Find Joy in Climate Action." TED. Video. 2022. *www.ted.com/talks/ayana_elizabeth_johnson_how_to_find_joy_in _climate_action*.

Jones, Van. "Van Jones (CNN): Nelson Mandela Didn't Call His Enemies Out. He Called Them UP. He Called Them IN." YouTube video. June 18, 2022. *https://youtu.be/Pz5xYEpN9R4*.

Kimmerer, Robin Wall. *Braiding Sweetgrass: Indigenous Wisdom, Scientific Knowledge, and the Teachings of Plants*. Minneapolis: Milkweed, 2015.

King, Martin Luther, Jr. "Christmas Sermon on Peace and Nonviolence, Massey Lecture No. 5, Aired on December 24, 1967." YouTube. Audio. December 3, 2014. *https://youtu.be/1jeyIAH3bUI*.

King, Ruth. *Mindful of Race: Transforming Racism from the Inside Out*. Boulder, CO: Sounds True, 2018.

Ladinsky, Daniel, trans. *Love Poems from God: Twelve Sacred Voices from the East and West*. New York: Penguin, 2002.

Lozoff, Bo. *We're All Doing Time: A Guide to Getting Free*. Durham, NC: Human Kindness Foundation, 1998.

Macy, Joanna. "Deep Adaptation Q&A with Joanna Macy Hosted by Jem Bendell." Interview by Jem Bendell. YouTube. Audio. June 5, 2019. *https://youtu.be/k1wUY6945kY*.

Macy, Joanna. "The Greening of the Self." In *Spiritual Ecology: The Cry of the Earth*, edited by Llewellyn Vaughan-Lee. Point Reyes Station, CA: Golden Sufi Center, 2013.

Macy, Joanna, and Chris Johnstone. *Active Hope: How to Face the Mess We're in without Going Crazy*. Novato, CA: New World, 2012.

Mandela, Nelson. *Long Walk to Freedom: The Autobiography of Nelson Mandela*. London: Little, Brown, 1994.

Marcus, Aubrey. "What?" AubreyMarcus.com. May 9, 2018. *www .aubreymarcus.com/blogs/poetry/what?*

Maté, Gabor, and Daniel Maté. *The Myth of Normal: Trauma, Illness, & Healing in a Toxic Culture*. New York: Avery, 2022.

McKibben, Bill. "It's Not Entirely Up to School Students to Save the World." *The New Yorker*. May 24, 2019. *www.newyorker.com/news /daily-comment/its-not-entirely-up-to-school-students-to-save-the-world*.

Menakem, Resmaa. *My Grandmother's Hands: Racialized Trauma and the Pathway to Mending Our Hearts and Bodies*. Las Vegas: Central Recovery Press, 2017.

Moore-Backman, Chris. *The Gandhian Iceberg: A Nonviolence Manifesto for the Age of the Great Turning*. Reno, NV: Be the Change Project, 2016.

National Center for Injury Prevention and Control, Division of Violence Prevention. "Fast Facts: Preventing Child Abuse & Neglect." US Centers for Disease Control and Prevention. April 6, 2022. *www.cdc.gov /violenceprevention/childabuseandneglect/fastfact.html*.

Newkirk, Vann R. II "Environmental Racism Is the New Jim Crow." *The Atlantic*. YouTube video. June 6, 2017. *https://youtu.be/nnF5I7lt6nQ*.

Nhat Hanh, Thich. *The Art of Power*. San Francisco: HarperOne, 2007.

Nhat Hanh, Thich. *At Home in the World: Stories and Essential Teachings from a Monk's Life*. Berkeley, CA: Parallax Press, 2016.

Nhat Hanh, Thich. *Being Peace*. Berkeley, CA: Parallax Press, 1996.

Nhat Hanh, Thich. *Call Me by My True Names: The Collected Poems of Thich Nhat Hanh*. Berkeley, CA: Parallax Press, 1999.

Nhat Hanh, Thich. "Dharma Talk: Diet for a Mindful Society." *The Mindfulness Bell*, September 1991. *www.parallax.org/mindfulnessbell/article /dharma-talk-diet-for-a-mindful-society*.

Nhat Hanh, Thich. *The Heart of the Buddha's Teachings: Transforming Suffering into Peace, Joy, and Liberation*. Berkeley, CA: Parallax Press, 1998.

Nhat Hanh, Thich. *Peace Is Every Step: The Path of Mindfulness in Everyday Life*. Berkeley, CA: Parallax Press, 1992.

Nhat Hanh, Thich. "Taking the Hand of Suffering," *The Mindfulness Bell* 27 (Fall 2000), 1–3.

Nhat Hanh, Thich. "Thich Nhat Hanh's Statement on Climate Change for the United Nations: Falling in Love with the Earth." Plum Village. September 2015. *https://plumvillage.org/about/thich-nhat-hanh/letters /thich-nhat-hanhs-statement-on-climate-change-for-unfccc*.

Nhat Hanh, Thich. *The World We Have: A Buddhist Approach to Peace and Ecology*. Berkeley, CA: Parallax Press, 2008.

Nhat Hanh, Thich. *Zen and the Art of Saving the Planet*. New York: HarperCollins, 2021.

Parachin, Victor M. "Robert Aitken: From POW to Zen Master." Buddhist Door Global. February 15, 2023. *www.buddhistdoor.net/features /robert-aitken-from-pow-to-zen-master*.

Pipes, Eliana. "Legos and the 4 I's of Oppression." YouTube video. July 29, 2016. *https://youtu.be/3WWyVRo4Uas*.

Plum Village. "How to Begin Anew." June 24, 2021. *https://plumvillage.org /articles/begin-anew*.

Pope Francis. Encyclical Letter "Laudato Si." May 24, 2015. *www.vatican .va/content/francesco/en/encyclicals/documents/papa-francesco_20150524 _enciclica-laudato-si.html.*

Ranalli, Ralph. "Erica Chenoweth Illuminates the Value of Nonviolent Resistance in Societal Conflicts." Harvard Kennedy School. 2019. *www.hks.harvard.edu/faculty-research/policy-topics/advocacy-social -movements/paths-resistance-erica-chenoweths-research.*

Ranseth, Joseph. "Gandhi Didn't Actually Ever Say 'Be the Change You Want to See in the World.' Here's the Real Quote . . . " JosephRanseth.com (blog). August 27, 2015. *https://josephranseth .com/gandhi-didnt-say-be-the-change-you-want-to-see-in-the-world.*

Roderick, Tom. *A School of Our Own: Parents, Power, and Community at the East Harlem Block Schools.* New York: Teachers College Press, 2001.

Rosen, David. "Pornography and the Erotic Phantasmagoria." *Sexuality & Culture* 27:1 (February 2023), 242–65. *https://doi.org/10.1007 /s12119-022-10011-9.*

Rosen, Jo-ann. *Unshakeable: Trauma-Informed Mindfulness for Collective Awakening.* Berkeley, CA: Parallax Press, 2023..

Ross, Janell, and National Journal. "Epigenetics: The Controversial Science Behind Racial and Ethnic Health Disparities." *The Atlantic,* March 20, 2014. *www.theatlantic.com/politics/archive/2014/03 /epigenetics-the-controversial-science-behind-racial-and-ethnic-health -disparities/430749.*

Rumi. "Rumi, Pay Homage." In Ladinsky, *Love Poems from God,* 68.

Siegel, Daniel J. *Mindsight: The New Science of Personal Transformation.* New York: Bantam, 2010.

Steinberg, David. "'Why Are You Bombing Where I'm Playing?': John McCutcheon Wrote a Collection of Songs for a Cellist in Bosnia." *Albuquerque Journal,* February 21, 2014. *www.abqjournal.com/356545 /albuquerque-santa-fe-singersongwriter.html.*

Suzuki, David. *The David Suzuki Reader: A Lifetime of Ideas from a Leading Activist and Thinker.* Vancouver, Canada: Greystone, 2014.

Teresa, Mother. "National Prayer Breakfast Address." Speech in Washington, DC, February 3, 1994. American Rhetoric. *www.americanrhetoric .com/speeches/motherteresanationalprayerbreakfast.htm.*

Thunberg, Greta. "'Our House Is on Fire': Greta Thunberg, 16, Urges Leaders to Act on Climate." *The Guardian,* January 25, 2019. *www .theguardian.com/environment/2019/jan/25/our-house-is-on-fire-greta -thunberg16-urges-leaders-to-act-on-climate.*

Treleaven, David A. *Trauma-Sensitive Mindfulness: Practices for Safe and Transformative Healing.* New York: W. W. Norton, 2018.

Van der Kolk, Bessel. *The Body Keeps the Score: Brain, Mind, and Body in Healing Trauma.* New York: Penguin, 2015.

Williams, William Carlos. *Journey to Love.* New York: Random House, 1955.

ILLUSTRATIONS

ABOUT THE AUTHOR

John Bell is an ordained Buddhist Dharma teacher in the tradition of Venerable Thich Nhat Hanh. He has been facilitating the Mountain Bell Sangha in the Boston area since 1997 and offers retreats around the country. He has served on the Care Taking Council (CTC) of the North American Dharma Teachers Sangha, on the core group of the racial justice initiative ARISE (Awakening through Race, Intersectionality, and Social Equity, *www.arisesangha.org*), and on the CTC of Earth Holder Community (*www.earthholder.org*), the earth justice initiative of Plum Village Community of Engaged Buddhism, as well as the CTC of the Beloved Community Circles project. In recent years, he has been arrested twice with a group of local faith leaders for protesting the installation of a fracked gas pipeline near Boston.

In his wider work life, John has forty years of experience in the youth field as a teacher, counselor, community organizer, leadership trainer, director, and father. He was a founding staff member of three youth leadership organizations: Youth Action Program in East Harlem (in 1978); Children of War, an international youth leadership organization (in 1984); and YouthBuild USA (in 1988). Until his recent retirement, John was the Vice President for Leadership Development at YouthBuild USA (*www.youthbuild.org*), an international nonprofit with 350 programs in fifteen countries that works with young people who have dropped out of school and provides them with further education, vocational training, building tangible community assets, personal counseling, and leadership skills. He is a nationally recognized trainer and consultant in the areas of youth leadership development, peer counseling and healing, and diversity. He has done training and consulting work for the Peace Corps in Africa and South America. He is an author of published handbooks, many articles, and the book *YouthBuild's North Star*. His blog is Begin Within, *www.beginwithin.info*.

Monastics and visitors practice the art of mindful living in the tradition of Thich Nhat Hanh at our mindfulness practice centers around the world. To reach any of these communities, or for information about how individuals, couples, and families can join in a retreat, please contact:

PLUM VILLAGE
33580 Dieulivol, France
plumvillage.org

LA MAISON DE L'INSPIR
77510 Villeneuve-sur-Bellot, France
maisondelinspir.org

HEALING SPRING
MONASTERY
77510 Verdelot, France
healingspringmonastery.org

MAGNOLIA GROVE
MONASTERY
Batesville, MS 38606, USA
magnoliagrovemonastery.org

BLUE CLIFF MONASTERY
Pine Bush, NY 12566, USA
bluecliffmonastery.org

DEER PARK MONASTERY
Escondido, CA 92026, USA
deerparkmonastery.org

EUROPEAN INSTITUTE OF
APPLIED BUDDHISM
D-51545 Waldbröl, Germany
eiab.eu

THAILAND PLUM VILLAGE
Nakhon Ratchasima
30130 Thailand
thaiplumvillage.org

ASIAN INSTITUTE OF
APPLIED BUDDHISM
Lantau Island, Hong Kong
pvfhk.org

STREAM ENTERING
MONASTERY
Beaufort, Victoria 3373
Australia
nhapluu.org

MOUNTAIN SPRING
MONASTERY
Bilpin, NSW 2758, Australia
mountainspringmonastery.org

For more information visit: *plumvillage.org*
To find an online sangha visit: *plumline.org*
For more resources, try the Plum Village app: *plumvillage.app*
Social media: *@thichnhathanh @plumvillagefrance*